KATHRY

author of *Die, My Love*

SCENT
HELL

THE TRUE STORY OF AN
ALTAR BOY,
A CHEERLEADER,
AND A
TWISTED
TEXAS MURDER

MORE SPELLBINDING TRUE STORIES
OF TEXAS MURDER FROM
KATHRYN CASEY

"One of the very best in the true crime genre."
ANN RULE

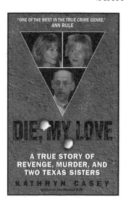

By Kathryn Casey

True Crime

A DESCENT INTO HELL
DIE, MY LOVE
SHE WANTED IT ALL
A WARRANT TO KILL

Coming Soon

EVIL BESIDE HER
(formerly *The Rapist's Wife*)

Fiction

SINGULARITY

KATHRYN CASEY

A DESCENT INTO HELL

THE TRUE STORY OF AN
ALTAR BOY,
A CHEERLEADER,
AND A
TWISTED
TEXAS MURDER

HARPER

An Imprint of HarperCollins*Publishers*

A Descent Into Hell is a journalistic account of the actual murder investigation of Colton Pitonyak for the 2005 killing of Jennifer Cave in Austin, Texas. The events recounted in this book are true, although some of the names have been changed and identifying characteristics altered to safeguard the privacy of these individuals. The personalities, events, actions, and conversations portrayed in this book have been constructed using court documents, including trial transcripts, extensive interviews, letters, personal papers, research, and press accounts. Quoted testimony has been taken verbatim from trial and pre-trial transcripts and other sworn statements.

HARPER

An Imprint of HarperCollins*Publishers*
10 East 53rd Street
New York, New York 10022-5299

First Harper paperback printing: July 2008

HarperCollins ® and Harper ® are registered trademarks of Harper-Collins Publishers.

Printed in the United States of America

Visit Harper paperbacks on the World Wide Web at
www.harpercollins.com

10 9 8 7 6

*In memory of Jennifer Cave,
the girl who dreamed of Oz.*

———————

"Abandon hope, all ye who enter here."

The inscription over the gate to hell,
DANTE ALIGHIERI's *Divine Comedy*

Preface

Some names and identifying features have been changed throughout this book. They include: Justin Walters, Eva Taylor, Brent, Frank, Tracey Ryan, Jared Smyth, Amy Pack, Michaela Sloan, Sammi Moore, Chris Collins, Louisa, Larry, and Nicole Ford.

A DESCENT
INTO HELL

One

The clock tower had placidly watched over Austin from 230 feet above since 1937. It was so loved that the sight of its vertical column soaring into a cloudless blue sky swelled alumni with pride. Few disputed that the imposing tower with its four twelve-foot faces rimmed in gold leaf was *the* symbol of the University of Texas, or that UT was *the* university Lone Star parents pushed their children to attend, the institution that inspired high schoolers to cram for exams and hoard birthday money in a college fund. For UT and its tower were much more than a university and a building; they were symbols of hope and the promise of a dream.

Yet the clock tower had another history as well, a much darker one.

On August 1, 1966, a twenty-five-year-old architecture student and ex-marine, Charles Joseph Whitman, climbed the UT clock tower stairs lugging a cache of weapons. The nightmare lasted eighty minutes. Before a police bullet found its mark and ended the carnage, Whitman murdered sixteen, including his wife and mother, and wounded thirty-one.

Fast-forward thirty-nine years to August 18, 2005. On this day, yet another shocking tragedy unfolded in the clock tower's shadow.

On the university's West Campus, a well-heeled neighborhood of sororities, frat houses, and expensive student housing, at 2529 Rio Grande, stood the Orange Tree, a block-long, three-story condominium project, one of the most prestigious on the campus. On the second floor, a locked red door with the number 88 marked the condo leased by Colton Pitonyak. A National Merit Scholar finalist who'd had the advantages of a prosperous upbringing, Pitonyak was a former Catholic school kid, an altar boy who spoke French and played the guitar and piano. When he left Little Rock, Arkansas, four years earlier with a full academic scholarship to study finance at UT's esteemed McCombs Business School, many believed he would one day make his name as a Wall Street whiz kid.

This night would prove them wrong. Instead, Colton Pitonyak's legacy would be markedly more sinister. But then, no one could have predicted the horror that waited behind the door marked 88.

The heat that August was nearly unbearable, well into the nineties. Summer in Austin could be blisteringly hot. Yet a breeze ruffled the trees, and no one in the small group gathered outside Colton Pitonyak's apartment noticed the sweltering weather.

They'd been there for hours: Sharon Cave; her tall, sandy-haired accountant boyfriend, Jim Sedwick; and Cave's oldest daughter, Vanessa.

A petite woman with thick, dark blond hair, Cave stared at the locked red door to unit 88. Her second child, twenty-one-year-old Jennifer, was missing. No one had seen her in nearly forty-eight hours, not since she had left a bar with Pitonyak. When Sharon called his cell phone from her Corpus Christi home, a surly Pitonyak refused to answer questions.

"Dude, I'm having pizza with my friend," he replied. "Don't bother me."

Worried, Cave and Sedwick rushed to Austin. Twenty-five-year-old Vanessa came, too, driving in from Dallas. They were all determined to find Jennifer, and their only clue was Pitonyak. But they'd pounded over and over again on his door, and no one answered. The afternoon wore on. Sunset passed, leaving the sky cloaked in darkness, as lights illuminated the somber tower. At the apartment marked 88, Sharon, Jim, and Vanessa stood vigil, for what they weren't sure. All Sharon knew for certain was that she had to get into Pitonyak's apartment. The answer to Jennifer's disappearance waited inside.

Like her mother, Vanessa, willowy with long, dark blond hair, understood things she couldn't explain. Sharon and all three of her daughters were like that, so connected it was a nearly psychic bond, an uncut spiritual umbilical cord that bound them together. Deep within them, Vanessa and Sharon unconsciously understood the importance of this day. Something grave had taken place, and they sensed the breaking of the tie that anchored them to Jennifer, the slipping away of her presence in their lives.

At 10 P.M. the University of Texas clock tower's carillon rang, marking the hour, and for Sharon, Jim, and Vanessa, time stood still. When it started again, Jim Sedwick crawled through a window into Colton Pitonyak's apartment, and their lives changed, forever.

Two

Bishop, Texas, lies thirty minutes by car south of Corpus Christi and inland from the Gulf of Mexico, but it's a world away from the hubbub of the city. Surrounded by fields of sorghum and cotton, the town grain elevator weighs the bounty from the fields, determining the financial health of the townsfolk. With a population that hovers just over three thousand, it's typical small-town America: a Dairy Queen and a truck stop, schools and churches that form the core of the community. The land is flat, the sky is big, and the horizon a full 360 degrees. Relentlessly straight roads appear to drop off the edge of the earth, and the local chemical plant is a city of pipe, its smokestacks burning off residue in a bright, hot, golden flame.

Jennifer Cave grew up in a quaint farmhouse, just outside town, on land that shares a fence line with the legendary King Ranch. Her parents, Charlie and Sharon, bought the place and its five accompanying acres in 1983, a year after they married. At the time, Charlie intended to fix it up, but, as is the way with old houses, it seemed there was always something left perpetually undone.

It was the second marriage for Sharon, a fun-loving woman with a broad, high-wattage smile. She'd grown up on a farm in nearby Alice, Texas, an oil town whose fortunes fluctuated with the price of a barrel of crude. During a teenage rebellious streak, she ran away at eighteen and married, giving birth to her oldest, Vanessa, in 1979. By then that marriage was troubled. They divorced, and then she met and married Charlie, a tall, handsome man who earned his living as a welder. He was a gregarious sort, the kind who'd never met a stranger, yet she'd later label him "mistake number two."

Sharon was a warm woman, the kind who greets friends with a hug and spends more time asking if others need anything or are comfortable than worrying about herself. She was that way with Charlie, believing she could somehow make him a better husband and a better father. "I always had a mission with Charlie," she says, sadly. "When he wasn't drinking, he was outstanding. Charming and fun. But I was always waiting for that other shoe to drop."

Vanessa was closing in on five when Jennifer was born on March 12, 1984. "She was a Gerber baby," Sharon says, with a chuckle. "Soft, and round, beautiful." Jennifer had red hair, her maternal grandfather's piercing blue eyes, and a generous helping of freckles. A year later, Lauren made her appearance, followed quickly by Clayton.

From the beginning, Sharon was fascinated by her children, in awe of them. "They were these perfect little creatures," she says, "and a constant source of amazement. I used to watch them, just to see what they would do."

Charlie named Jennifer his "Fuffa," and she became his sidekick. She was a tomboy, playing sports, fishing; an accomplished butterfly catcher, and a daddy's girl. One year when she was still quite young, Jen asked for a "pelican" gun for Christmas. She meant a pellet gun, and her mistake made Charlie laugh. "It was really like Sharon had two kids, Vanessa and Lauren, and Jennifer and Clayton were mine," says Charlie. "Those two were a lot alike. They loved the outdoors. Jennifer was my other boy."

"Jennifer used to say that she and I were alike because we both had really big hearts," says Clayton, a thin young man with shaggy brown hair and a thoughtful manner. "She said that was something we inherited from our mom."

Their parents were both musical. Charlie sang in a country-and-western band, and Sharon played piano and sang at church. Jennifer wasn't heir to those talents. "She couldn't carry a tune in a bucket," says Sharon, with a chuckle. "But even as a child, she loved music, and she loved to dance."

At times, Sharon told her girls that she was envious of their sisterhood. She'd had two brothers but no sisters. "I'm so jealous that you have each other growing up," she'd say. "You don't know how lucky you are."

The four children were a handful; that was true. At home, in an old shed behind the house, they raised pigs and participated in 4–H events. There were softball and soccer games, dance classes and spelling bees, county fair baking and sewing contests. "One minute they'd be ripping each other's hair out and the next they'd be hugging," Sharon says with a short laugh. Vanessa egged her siblings on, coaxing them to perform "all-star wrestling" on her bedroom floor. More often than not, the three girls and baby brother, as they called Clayton, played in the closet that connected Vanessa's bedroom with Jennifer and Lauren's room, dubbed "the little girls' room."

During the day, Sharon worked in the bookkeeping department at the Celanese plant just outside Bishop. When school wasn't in session, the children stayed with Sharon's parents on the farm in Alice. Their grandmother, Myrtle Custer, a woman with pin-straight bearing and cropped snow-white hair, sewed the girls wide-skirted and puff-sleeved dresses, and in pictures their cheeks were rosy and their smiles innocent. Jennifer and Lauren were so close, sharing the same bedroom, hugging and talking constantly, heads always together, that, although they were fourteen months apart, the whole family began to think of them as almost twins.

Yet the two youngest sisters were very different. Lauren was outgoing, afraid to talk to no one, quick to make friends. In contrast, Jennifer was a shy, quiet girl. While her sisters could form a head of steam and boil over, she rarely complained. Jennifer didn't cry when she needed stitches just above her eye at two. When she fractured her elbow, she said nothing. Sharon wouldn't have guessed if she hadn't heard Jennifer moaning in her sleep.

Even before Jennifer began school, Sharon understood that her second daughter was "scary smart." All the children attended Bishop's public schools; high school, middle school, and elementary strung side-by-side on a long block of beige brick buildings and playgrounds. Vanessa, Lauren, and Clayton had to study. Jennifer picked everything up easily. A voracious reader, she consumed the books in the school library and had a nearly photographic memory. Yet her intelligence never translated to self-confidence. By school age, she wore glasses, and later came braces. She hated her freckles. Sharon tried to reassure her. "I told Jennifer that she had them because she was so special. That her freckles were spots where the angels kissed her before she came down from heaven," she says.

Still, Jennifer grew up self-conscious and withdrawn. At school, she sat with Lauren and her circle of friends at lunch and sought them out on the playground during recess. "I made the friends, and Jennifer and I shared them," Lauren remembers. When Jennifer moved up with her class to middle school, she circulated back to the elementary school whenever possible to be with Lauren. After school, they walked home together, sometimes with Jennifer lagging behind Lauren and her friends, reading a book.

When they read the series *The Babysitters' Club*, Jennifer, Lauren, and Janna Thornberry, Lauren's best friend, tried to decide which of the characters in the book they most resembled. They all knew without discussion that Jennifer, or Jen as they sometimes called her by then, was their "Mary Anne," the shy, sweet bookworm. "Jen had this gentle sarcasm," says Janna. "She could be so funny, and she always got the joke. But when someone didn't understand, she never ridiculed them. Instead, she explained why the rest of us were laughing."

Life in small towns seems to move slower, and Bishop

was a safe place to grow up, comforting and friendly. "Everybody knows everybody," Sharon says. "And everybody's in bed by nine."

The summers were long and spent at the beach in Corpus or swimming in their grandparents' pool, and the pranks for the most part harmless, like toilet-papering houses and, in high school, sabotaging another class's homecoming float. Jennifer played volleyball, basketball, and tennis, and worked on student council. From elementary school on, both Lauren and Jennifer were cheerleaders.

At football games, they wore their green and gold uniforms with "Badgers" across the front, jumping high in the air, waving their pompoms and urging their school team to a win. With two girls on the squad, Sharon was the cheerleading mom who coordinated snacks and drinks. In church, she ran the kitchen. There, Jennifer learned the Lord's Prayer, and Psalm 23, her favorite, which begins, "The Lord is my shepherd."

In 1992, when she was eight, Jennifer's 222-pound black-and-white Poland hog, Spot, won reserve grand champion at the Nueces County livestock show. That year in Sunday school, Jennifer wrote down what she wanted God to do for her. She asked for a new job for her father, that her grandparents were kept safe on a trip, and wishes for everyone else in the family, but nothing for herself.

"That was just Jennifer," said Sharon. "She always thought first about others."

Despite appearances from the outside, in a community as small as Bishop, many understood that all wasn't idyllic at the Caves' charming farmhouse on the outskirts of town. "Everyone knew how Charlie was when he drank," says Sharon. Alcohol had the power to change her jovial husband. He stormed through the house, raging at Sharon, while the four children hid in their play closet, the one between the girls' bedrooms. At times, one or more of the children, especially Jennifer or Clayton, emerged to plead with their father to stop his rampage. "He'd shout at them and tell them to shut up," Sharon says. "And it would go on, sometimes all night."

Vanessa comforted her younger siblings, while they tried not to hear the turmoil that tore through their wood-frame house. "It was like clockwork, before, during, or after any holiday," says Sharon. "I was always a nervous wreck, waiting for it to happen."

The next morning, the old Charlie apologized, begging Sharon's forgiveness. For many years, she gave it. Too long, Vanessa thought. "Mom let it go on much longer than it should have," she says.

It was confusing for all the children. They loved the sober, happy Charlie. "My dad's a big man, and he always made us feel like little girls when we were with him," says Lauren. "He made us feel protected, even though he did some bad things."

With so much tension in the house, it's not surprising that Jennifer was fascinated by another little girl growing up in a farmhouse. She watched *The Wizard of Oz* so often, she wore out the tape. Perhaps she dreamed that she, too, could escape to a beautiful wonderland, one without her father's angry rages. Through it all, Jennifer and Clayton were the ones who stayed close to their father. While Vanessa and Lauren turned away from Charlie, Jennifer played peacemaker, attempting to calm his outbursts.

"Jennifer was never judgmental. She never wanted to make anyone feel bad or out of place," says Thornberry. "She was the type of person who never got into a lot of drama. She didn't see things as the end of the world."

For the most part, the Caves had a normal life, "except when Charlie was on a tear," Sharon would say years later. Despite all Sharon had been through, she stayed with Charlie. "I'd convinced myself I could save Charlie from himself. We went to counseling, and I thought inside there was a really good person worth saving. But I could see what it was doing to the kids. In the end, he came home drunk one time too often."

The afternoon the marriage ended, the Thursday before Easter vacation, Charlie arrived home late. Sharon watched the minutes tick off the clock, knowing that when her husband returned he would not be the easygoing Charlie she'd fallen in love with. She was right. He was in a foul mood. Drunk and angry, he threw everything from the refrigerator against the floor and walls, and the girls and Clayton again spent the night in the closet, banding together for support. "I wasn't an angel, either. I had a temper," Sharon said. "But this couldn't continue."

In the morning, the thirteenth Good Friday of their marriage, Sharon told Charlie, "I'm taking the children for their Easter photos and shopping. When I get back, I expect you to be gone."

"For how long?" Charlie asked.

"From now on," Sharon replied.

Charlie didn't argue. "I think he knew he'd kicked that dog one too many times," Sharon says. "By the time I got out of that marriage, it was a wonder I could walk upright, that I had any self-esteem left."

Looking back, Charlie wouldn't peg the demise of the marriage on his drinking. "We just couldn't get along," he says. "It didn't work, and we went our separate ways."

After the divorce, all the children except Vanessa, whose father was Sharon's first husband, were ordered to visit Charlie. Lauren didn't want to go. Throughout their young lives, Lauren had been the strong one, but it was Jennifer who took her sister under her wing. She led the way, putting her arm around her younger sister and saying, "It'll be okay, Lauren. We'll be all right."

Of the girls, only Jennifer made it a point to visit Charlie. She didn't hold a grudge for the turmoil and pain he'd caused in their family. "That just wasn't Jennifer," says Vanessa. "She never stayed angry at anyone. She never gave up on anyone. She absolutely refused to."

After the divorce, Sharon and her young brood moved into a small house in town, but life continued, at first, relatively unchanged. In junior high, Jennifer and Lauren begged Sharon for a dog, a dachshund like one of their friends had. When they found a small brown dachshund on the way home from school and no one came to claim it, Jennifer called it "a gift from God," and they named the little bundle Ginger. From that point on, Ginger went everywhere with Sharon and the children.

At times, Sharon loaded the four children and Ginger in the car, windows down, radio turned up, and barreled down the long, empty country roads, while they sang along to Aerosmith or Fleetwood Mac. "I had so much fun with them," Sharon says. "They were the center of my life."

In junior high, hiding behind her glasses, braces, and freckles, Jennifer still thought of herself as awkward and unattractive, even though her hair was a rich red and her eyes startling blue under thick lashes.

Despite her shyness, Jennifer had her place in the town. She loved children and became one of Bishop's most sought-after babysitters. One year, she read *The Diary of Anne Frank* over and over, studying the Holocaust, deeply touched by the suffering. At times, Sharon worried that her middle daughter cared too much about others. The friends Jen brought home from school were most often new kids or children like her, those who felt as if they didn't fit in. Sharon began to think of them as "Jennifer's strays."

Charlie was around, but not as much, and the children leaned on their mother. She cooked dinners for a houseful of kids before football games and took them to a friend's condominium in Corpus on the beach in the summers. Although growing up quickly, Jennifer must have felt caught between her two sisters, Vanessa the natural beauty and Lauren the cute, fun, outgoing one.

It was in junior high that Jennifer began to change. First, her owlish, big-framed glasses were replaced by contact lenses, showing off her extraordinary blue eyes. That year in her gold and forest-green cheerleading outfit, Jennifer jumped a little higher. She appeared to finally be opening up to the world. She still loved the outdoors, but the tomboy was giving way to an attractive young girl. A new Jennifer was emerging.

"I don't know if Jennifer ever really understood how pretty she was," says Sharon. "I think deep inside she was always that shy, freckle-faced kid, the one who just wanted everything to be all right and for people to get along. Maybe it was because she never really believed in herself that . . ."

Three

Parenthood is a dance of sorts. Mothers and fathers carry into their child-rearing years the baggage of their own up-bringings, their strengths and weaknesses, their biological and emotional temperaments. Children are mysteries, crea-tures to be nurtured, loved, worried and prayed over. Yet too often, for good reasons as well as bad, parents misstep. Try as they may, there are rarely easy answers. What works with one child, doesn't with another. And when lives spin out of control and collide, they can throw a family into turmoil.

"Mom always did everything she could for us to make things good," Lauren says. "But we were rambunctious kids."

The first to hit her difficult years was, not surprisingly, the oldest. Vanessa was beautiful and popular, and the entire family adored her. Perhaps especially Jennifer, who saw her older sister as what every girl coming of age strives to be: exciting and vibrant, independent and confident.

A stunning girl with the figure of a model, the kind who turns heads when she walks into a room, Vanessa was in high school the year Charlie and Sharon divorced. Her senior year, she was homecoming queen, and that year she had her first serious boyfriend, a teenager Sharon didn't care for. The tension in the house escalated, they argued, and Van-essa left home and moved in with her boyfriend's family. Sharon wanted her home. "Mom was up nearly every night, crying," says Lauren. "I'd never seen her so upset."

The other three children took to their mother's bed, hoping to comfort her. "Vanessa was a wild child at that point," says Sharon. "For a while, she put me through hell."

The crisis ended when, the teenage romance over, Vanessa crawled unannounced through the window one night and into her bedroom. In the morning, Sharon found her oldest daughter asleep in her own bed. For at least a little while, the family was whole again.

When Vanessa left Bishop for Blinn College, in College Station, Texas, the craziness escalated. Not unlike many college students, she focused not on her studies but on what made her feel good at the time, and Sharon responded with "tough love," coming down hard on her. "I told her she could do so much with her life," Sharon says. "She had to pull it together."

It would be a difficult few years, ones filled with sleepless nights and emotional arguments, but eventually Vanessa did just that. She moved to Dallas, where she finished college, earning a degree in communications and landing a job as a marketing coordinator. "I was so proud of her. We all were," Sharon says. "She's one tough little cookie. She hung in there and made it all work."

Meanwhile in Bishop, Jennifer remained a shy high school student. Her excitement revolved around basketball games, cheerleading, reading, and the outdoors, everything she'd grown up loving. She wasn't a child who adapted well to change, Sharon knew. But still, life isn't static, and lives rarely stay the same.

The year Vanessa left for college, when Jen was fourteen, Sharon began commuting to Corpus Christi, where she took a marketing job with the *Caller-Times* newspaper. Back and forth from Bishop, she commuted more than an hour a day. "It was hard," Lauren remembers. "All of a sudden, our mom wasn't with us. We were doing for ourselves, watching over Clayton after school."

Looking back, Clayton admits he was a challenge. "I was a real handful for my sisters," he says. "Lauren would get so mad. Jennifer was the one who was always there for me. She'd take me places, and we talked."

Still, Jen as well as Lauren resented the responsibility, wanting their mother home with them as she'd always been. They didn't understand why Sharon was gone so often. "We were angry, especially Jennifer," Lauren remembers. "Both of us felt it was unfair, when we were still just kids."

The following year, 1999, four years after her divorce, Sharon played matchmaker, trying to find a date for a girl-friend. Sharon's friend Harold Shockley, a Corpus Christi banker, recommended she set the woman up with a friend of his: Jim Sedwick, a lanky CPA with big blue eyes, a grav-elly voice, and a determined gait that telegraphed a take-charge attitude. Shockley thought Sharon's friend and Jim might hit it off. The two met, but neither Jim nor the woman expressed interest in a second date.

A partner in a well-established Corpus Christi accounting firm, Jim, like Sharon, had been born and raised in South Texas. Divorced, he had two teenage daughters, Whitney and Hailey, who fit in age between Sharon's three girls. Although Sharon liked Jim when Harold introduced them, "I wasn't looking for a man in my life. I had four kids to raise."

When Sharon and Jim went out to lunch a few weeks later, it was business. As part of his practice, Jim handled trusts and estates, and Sharon's father had recently died. But they had a great time together, talking and laughing, and they felt a strong attraction. Before long, Sharon and Jim were a couple.

On the one hand, life was looking up for her. When the marriage with Charlie ended, Sharon swore that if she ever fell in love again it would be with someone who respected her. "I wanted my kids to see a healthy relationship," she says. "And I had that with Jim."

Still, it was hard on the family. In addition to the long hours commuting to and from work, she now carved out what time she could to spend with Jim. There were crock-pot meals and casseroles made ahead. "But I always knew that the kids came first," Jim says. Their first date was spent in the bleachers watching Jennifer and Lauren cheerlead at a football game. Most nights, Sharon ran from work to see Jim, and then rushed home to Bishop to be with Jennifer, Lauren, and Clayton. In the end, Sharon would say she spent "most of 2000 exhausted."

That year Sharon turned forty, and the Cave sisters thought it was the most romantic thing they'd ever encountered when Jim took their mother to New Orleans to celebrate.

In fact, all Sharon's children grew to love Jim. A calm, solid presence, he moved easily into their lives, and he and Jennifer formed a special bond. Jim took the family deer hunting that fall. The furnace was out in the girls' cabin, and a blue norther blew in, an unusually chill wind coming in from the north. Jen was the only one awake and ready to go with Jim at five that morning. "I figure I might as well be cold out in the deer blind," she told him. They didn't see any deer, "but we had a great time," he remembers.

As she began high school, Jennifer came of age. She was still inordinately shy, but felt comfortable in Bishop, where most of the town had watched her grow up. But then, what must have felt like the inevitable happened. Sharon came home and announced that they were moving to Corpus Christi.

It was the logical thing to do. Living in Corpus, Sharon could jettison the hour commute, and she and Jim could live closer, to see where their relationship took them. "I was ready to leave Bishop. I couldn't wait," says Lauren. "But Jennifer didn't want to go. She was really mad at our mom."

Moving from a small town into a city where her high school had more than two thousand students terrified Jennifer. Sharon promised that if it didn't work out well, Jen could return to Bishop to live with a friend and graduate with her class. Only then did Jennifer agree. Sharon worried about Clayton more than the girls; he struggled with epilepsy, and there were all the temptations city life offered a young boy, so they made the difficult decision that he would move in with Charlie in Sinton, a small farming town just north of Corpus.

That summer, Sharon and the girls packed their possessions into the moving van. Corpus Christi awaited them, a warm and vibrant city. Yet for a young girl from a small town like Bishop, it offered an excess not just of possibilities, but also distractions. Before long, Jennifer would enter a world from which she would never successfully separate. "Vanessa never lured Jennifer into the drinking and partying," says Lauren. "It's more like Jennifer caught a glimpse, and it looked exciting. Jennifer wanted to be one of the cool kids, and this was a way to fit in."

On a bay off the Gulf of Mexico and at the mouth of the Nueces River, Corpus Christi, the largest coastal city in South Texas, lies two hundred miles south of Houston. The first Europeans to explore the area were the Spanish in the 1600s. An important center of Confederate commerce during the Civil War, the city in 1919 was devastated by a massive hurricane that killed nearly four hundred. By 2000, more than 277,000 residents dwelled in the sprawling, blue-collar city of palm trees, feathery pines, and one-story houses. The main highway ran along a coastline lined with refineries and into downtown Corpus, where high-rise condominiums hugged the bay. From there, expressways fanned out like fingers reaching into the suburbs. Jim lived south of downtown, in a newer part of the city, and Sharon rented a townhouse not far away.

Visitors to Corpus Christi's Mary Carroll High School were greeted by a fanciful mosaic of a pouncing tiger, the school mascot. The school colors were navy blue and white, and the motto was "We prepare our students for their futures." Built in the fifties, Carroll was a large, rambling place, busy with the confusion of thousands of teenagers rushing to classes. For Jennifer, "it felt overwhelming," says Sharon.

Lauren, a sophomore, integrated easily into the school, making new friends and continuing where her days in Bishop left off. But Jennifer's shyness made that impossible. One year ahead of Lauren, Jennifer, a junior, struggled with the lack of self-esteem that had plagued her from childhood. She remained that little girl in the closet, listening to her father's anger pulsate through the house, when all she wanted was for everyone to be happy. Yet she had Lauren, her little sister, her almost twin. Worried about how Jennifer would fare, Lauren changed her entire class schedule to sit with Jennifer at lunch.

Sharon, too, did what she could to ease the transition, throwing a party to introduce the girls when they moved in. She thought that perhaps all would go well, when on the first day of school Jennifer and Lauren were invited by a group of girls for breakfast tacos at Nano's Taqueria, a popular neighborhood spot. But whether or not the other teenagers were ready to accept Jennifer, her own self-doubt undermined her and kept her from seeing herself as others did.

There wasn't a single moment when Sharon realized her middle daughter had grown up. But by the time she entered Carroll, Jennifer had transformed into a striking young woman. At five-foot-five, she weighed perhaps 120 pounds. She still had her red hair and bright blue eyes, but she had more than her physical beauty. At times, it was as if a light shone inside Jennifer. "She had this amazing spirit," says her childhood friend Janna. "Jennifer could truly light up a room."

Heads began turning when the shy young girl from Bishop entered a room, the same way they did for Vanessa. "Jennifer had kind of grown into her face. We started looking a lot alike," says Vanessa. "She loved the attention, but deep down inside, she was still the little freckle-faced girl with big glasses."

That Christmas, Jim's daughters, Whitney and Hailey, came to visit, and they easily melded with Sharon's girls. Sharon and Jim called them "our babies," and loved the stir it caused when they walked into a restaurant with five attractive young women. "The waiters tripped over each other to take care of us," Jim laughs. Under the tree for Jennifer was her first cell phone, and she quickly became addicted to it. "Jennifer's just like you," Jim teased Sharon. "She gets in the car, starts the engine, and makes a call."

That invisible yet uncut cord that tied the Cave women together now included four or five cell phone calls a day. Sometimes, Jim joked that Sharon spent half the day talking to her girls about everything from what they wanted to wear to school the next day to where they were going after the dismissal bell.

When it came time for the holidays to end, Hailey decided not to return to Oklahoma, where she lived with her mom, Jim's ex-wife, Susie. "I saw this noisy, chaotic, open family, and I wanted to be part of it," she says.

"And we were off," Sharon says.

Although Sharon and the girls still lived in the rented town home, the Sedwicks and Caves had already begun thinking of themselves as a family. One friend compared them to the Brady Bunch, busy, boisterous, and fun, with a lot of strong personalities. They gave one another nicknames. Jim became Buffalo; Hailey was Goat; Whitney had the moniker Monkey; Sharon was Cat, because of her penchant for leopard-print clothes; Lauren was Turtle; and Vanessa was Deer for her big brown eyes. For his ability to "tear things up," Jim later said they should have renamed Clayton Bull in China Shop. Jennifer, who loved the little amphibians, was called Frog.

With her amazing memory, high school was easy for Jennifer, and she rarely studied. She picked up part-time jobs, her first at a small restaurant, and began mixing with a new group at school. Her braces came off, gifting her with a perfect, wide smile. Jennifer wore flirty dresses and strappy shoes, and her looks opened the door to the world of the cool kids, the kids who partied on weekends in whichever house was without parents. Still, she wasn't by nature a joiner.

Lauren would later believe that Jennifer started drinking to fit in. What began as a few drinks quickly escalated. "The drinks made Jennifer feel more at ease," says Lauren. "She could laugh and be fun, the life of the party."

Before long, Jennifer had a status in the new school, one that would, for the first time in their lives, split the younger sisters apart. Lauren stayed with her own group, kids involved in school projects, yearbook, and student council, while Jennifer joined the party crowd. "We'd been like the same person basically, we were so close," Lauren says. "But I was worried. I didn't want to have that kind of reputation. I had to separate from her, but that hurt. I think it hurt us both."

Always there was that connection between the mother and three daughters. When something bad happened, Sharon never really needed a telephone to know. Something else warned her, an inner voice that whispered all wasn't well. The night Vanessa had a car accident, Sharon knew before the phone rang. When Jennifer had her first auto accident, Sharon was already pacing the floor.

"Looking back, I didn't handle it well," says Sharon. "I wasn't a loving mother that day."

Jennifer didn't come home, instead going to Jim's. "Your mother didn't mean it," Jim told her about the argument they'd had.

"She hurt my feelings," Jennifer replied.

Feelings were being hurt on both sides, fueled by anger and resentment, and the tension in Sharon Cave's small townhouse built. By the spring of her senior year, Jennifer was tired of school, and she argued with Sharon, not wanting to go. To Sharon's chagrin, Jennifer had a new boyfriend, a dark-haired senior named Brent.

Once Brent brought Jen home after 2 A.M. Sharon waited at the curb, yelling when they pulled up, ordering him not to come back to the house again. The boy looked terrified, and Jennifer was mortified. At times, Sharon caught her middle daughter lying about where she'd been, which led to more screaming matches. Then there was the night Jennifer and a girlfriend were pulled over in a car. The police officer found pot, and arrested both the girls. Sharon was beside herself, until the friend admitted the drugs were hers, and the charges against Jennifer were dropped.

The mother and daughter argued yet again, and Jim chastised Sharon, telling her, "She's not going to listen to you when you're angry like that."

Yet by then he had his own concerns. His younger daughter, Hailey, had begun hanging out with Jennifer, going to the same parties. For Hailey, it would turn out to be a brief waylay, a little fun before she charted a straighter course. As Vanessa had before her, Hailey wouldn't need any help realigning her life.

In Sharon's darker moments, when she fretted over the turn Jennifer's life had taken, Vanessa's and Hailey's successes reassured her. If they came around, why wouldn't Jennifer? The party scene would grow old, Sharon told herself. Jennifer would move on. Yet as the months passed, Jen continued to flip-flop between the shy, smart, sweet girl she'd always been and the angry teenager who saw no reason to listen to her mother.

If the alcohol helped, the pot's fuzziness must have done even more to camouflage Jennifer's uncertainties. With friends, there were two Jennifers. The first was the one Sharon knew, the kind, intense, smart, and caring girl who'd do whatever she could to help a friend. When Leah Cook broke up with her boyfriend, Jennifer was the friend who drove her to the beach, where they sat and talked, Jennifer comforting Leah and reassuring her that life would go on.

Yet on the Carroll High School campus, Jennifer was known as a "party chick." After a spate of car accidents, Jennifer's friends began calling Lauren to pick up her sister at parties. When Lauren arrived, teenagers milled around outside the houses, smoking pot and talking. They were the "chill" crowd, the low-key kids. Inside the house were the partiers, throwing down shots and dancing. Jennifer was always among them, her hands up in the air, losing herself to the heavy beat of the music reverberating through the house.

The new Jennifer made Lauren uneasy, as if she instinctively sensed this change in her sister would not end well. On the nights Jennifer partied with friends, Lauren couldn't sleep. "I was always paranoid that something would happen to her. I didn't want to pick her up. I didn't want to see what she was doing. I didn't want to know," Lauren says. "People talk. I dissed her on the way she was living her life, so I knew others would gossip, too."

When Lauren complained to Jennifer about the company she kept, Jen snapped that it wasn't her little sister's business. And when Sharon expressed alarm, Jennifer waved it off, playing on the guilt her mother felt for uprooting her to Corpus. "You moved me here, and this is what the kids are like here," she'd say.

Throughout that year, Jim and Sharon talked of merging households, moving her possessions into his home, but they held off. Forming a new family was hard enough without an out-of-control teenager to contend with. "Jennifer wouldn't listen to me. She said she didn't have to," Sharon says. "We shouted and screamed at each other, but it didn't help. As bad as things got, though, we never stopped telling each other 'I love you.'"

Of them all, Jim was the one who seemed to understand Jen the best. They both smoked, and at family gatherings, they stood outside, enjoying a cigarette and dessert. Jim started calling Jen his "pie-eating buddy," after they once finished off an entire chocolate pie with their coffee. He talked with Jennifer about the course her life was taking, cajoling her to understand that there was a whole world ahead of her, and that she had everything she needed, including brains and good looks, to do whatever she wanted, but he never felt as if he got through. "Deep down Jennifer didn't believe she was capable of succeeding," Jim says. "She always felt like something held her back."

Despite her disinterest in school, when Jennifer graduated from Carroll High School in May 2002, she was in the top fifteen percent of her class. Jennifer's graduation came as a relief, and Sharon hoped the worst was over. Lauren wrote in her sister's yearbook, telling her "how important she was to me, and how much I loved her."

That summer, Jen worked for Sharon and Jim's old friend Harold Shockley, the tall, serious-looking banker who'd become such a beloved part of the family that the Cave and Sedwick kids referred to him as Uncle Harold. Jennifer delighted in dressing up every day and going into the office, circulating from department to department, working hard and doing whatever was needed. She always had a warm smile, and when Harold saw her, he didn't see self-doubt or pain. He thought Jennifer Cave's future couldn't look brighter.

There were big plans in the works that fall: college.

That August, Jennifer left for San Marcos, Texas, a small city on a river, halfway between Austin and San Antonio, to become one of Southwest Texas State University's more than twenty-seven thousand students. The school dated back to 1899, and changed names nearly as often as freshmen change majors, including the year after Jennifer arrived, when it became Texas State University. In its picturesque setting of green, rolling, tree-covered hills, the university's symbol was Old Main, a red-roofed, castlelike Victorian structure that housed the school of communication. The university's most prominent grad was President Lyndon Baines Johnson, who attended when it was still a small teachers' college.

On her application, Jennifer designated her major as finance, and Jim and Sharon urged her to pledge a sorority, to ensure she ran with a good group of friends. Sharon brought Jennifer along with an overflowing car full of her belongings to school that fall and moved her in, spending the night in nearby San Antonio. "We had a great time," Sharon says. "I just felt so good about it, so positive for Jennifer's future."

Although excited, Jennifer had mixed feelings. She had no real goals. Unlike Lauren, who'd known since childhood that she wanted to be a television news reporter, Jennifer wasn't sure where her future lay. She seemed to be floundering, wondering where she wanted life to take her. "She didn't want to go to college, because she didn't know what it would do to help her," says Lauren. "She just didn't have a goal."

Sharon tried to reassure Jennifer, to tell her that as a freshman she didn't need set plans. In fact, Jen had at least two years before declaring a firm major. But Jennifer's uncertainty was, as it had been throughout her young life, tempered with a pervasive self-doubt. She wanted to please her mother, her father, and Jim, but lurking behind her confident exterior and her wide smile was that nagging lack of self-confidence. Hailey, Jim's youngest daughter, saw it. "I think Jen was excited to get out of Corpus," she says. "But she was petrified out of her mind about college. She'd tell me, 'I can't do it. I can't make it work.'"

Jennifer Cave's stint at Southwest would be short. She dropped out of sorority rush after just a few days, telling Hailey, "It's just not my thing." Before long, Jen skipped classes, and her grades suffered. When Sharon asked why, her middle daughter always had an answer. "Your expectations are too high for me," Jennifer said. "I'm not smart enough. I'm trying but I don't get it."

Sharon felt her exasperation building. Jennifer was the brightest of her four children; how could she not realize that?

When things went wrong, Jennifer called Lauren, who acted as intermediary in the building war between Jennifer and their increasingly frustrated mother. It became Lauren's job to tell Sharon when Jennifer overdrew her bank account. "I told Mom and she started yelling at me," Lauren says. "I really started to resent Jennifer for putting me in the middle."

Then there was the day in late October when Lauren's cell phone rang and one of Jennifer's friends whispered more bad news: Jennifer was in jail. Again Lauren reluctantly delivered the message. Furious, Sharon called the jail, and one of the officers explained that Jennifer had been found in her dorm room with a boy who was smoking pot. The woman advised her to hurry and bail Jennifer out.

"She's just losing it in here," the officer said.

Worried and angry, Sharon put Jennifer's bond on her credit card, and she was released. The matter ended as Jennifer's high school escapade had when the boy said the pot was his, and the charges against Jennifer were dropped. When the mother and daughter finally talked, it didn't go well. Sharon was livid and told Jennifer as much. "Why do you keep picking up these strays?" she asked. "Why do you hang out with people who aren't good for you?"

Jennifer didn't have an answer.

Despite the boy's confession, the damage for Jennifer had been done. Her counselor informed her that she'd be allowed to finish the semester at Southwest, but having the pot in her room had broken a campus rule, and she wouldn't be allowed to return for the spring semester.

Sharon was upset, yet Jennifer didn't appear to be. "She never really wanted to be there in the first place," says Lauren. "She never felt like she fit in."

That December 2002, Jennifer packed her belongings for yet another move. She had a boyfriend, Mark, tall and blond, a good kid from a nice family, one Sharon thought well of. He was leaving Southwest and moving to Austin to continue his education at the University of Texas. Jennifer wanted to move to Austin to be near him, to get her own apartment, find a job, and attend Austin Community College.

Jim and Sharon were both in favor of the move, hopeful that Jennifer just needed time to maneuver through her problems and consider her future.

By then, Sharon had moved in with Jim and blended households, so they donated their excess furniture to Jen. Charlie loaded it into a trailer and hooked it up to his welding truck, then drove to San Marcos in January 2003. They packed Jennifer's few college possessions, mainly clothing, and with Jennifer in the lead in her rundown car, they caravanned on I–35 to Austin.

"Jennifer, slow down," Charlie said on his cell phone that day, as Jennifer wove in and out of traffic. The welding truck and trailer couldn't change lanes as easily as her little Dodge Intrepid. "You'll lose me, and I'll get lost."

"Just follow me," Jennifer said, with a laugh. "I'll get you there."

Despite all Jennifer put the family through, Charlie couldn't help but be proud. Sure, Jennifer had her ups and downs, but his little Fuffa had grown into a beautiful woman. On the outside, she looked confident and excited about her future, even if inside a shy little girl from Bishop worried about being alone in a bustling metropolitan area with a population of more than a million. The same girl who'd once resisted moving from Bishop to Corpus Christi now looked like she was ready to take on the world.

"It was just impossible not to love her," Charlie says. "Jennifer had a smile that could melt a heart."

After Charlie left, Sharon arrived to help Jennifer decorate her small apartment off Riverside Drive. It was just around the corner from Austin Community College, where Jen enrolled in classes for the spring semester. Jennifer was approaching nineteen years old and brimming with excitement. For the first time in her life, perhaps, she was in love. Mark, the young man she'd followed from San Marcos, lived nearby, and he'd already brought Jennifer home to meet his mother, who found her to be "a really lovely young girl."

As Sharon drove out of Austin a couple of days later, the Texas state capitol's graceful dome and the austere UT clock tower stood out in the postcard-blue sky from the city's forest of hotels and office buildings. Thick-leaved live oaks bordered downtown sidewalks in front of office buildings and old storefronts, some dating back more than a century. Any misgivings Sharon had as she settled Jennifer into her new home weren't enough to give her pause. "I thought Jennifer would find herself in Austin," Sharon says. "I hoped it was a good place for her. I wanted so much to see her grow into the woman I knew she had the potential to become."

There was, of course, much that Sharon couldn't yet know. She didn't understand the powerful lure of Austin's wild side, its vibrant nightlife with its deeply entrenched drug scene, and she hadn't yet heard the name of the young man who would fall in love with Jennifer and ensnare her in his dangerous, delusional world: Colton Pitonyak.

Four

Despite her hopes, Sharon moved Jennifer to Austin with some trepidation. She knew her middle daughter had dabbled in drugs, that Jen drank and had a history of befriending the wrong people. Yet she trusted in the other Jennifer, the happy, charming young woman with the wide smile and the big heart. Perhaps Sharon had no choice. Jennifer was legally an adult and claiming her independence. All Sharon could do was trust that the girl who tried so hard to please, to make everyone around her happy, would learn to trust in herself and find her way.

Eddie and Bridget Pitonyak, on the other hand, probably had no such qualms about how their younger son would tackle college and, following that, life. From his earliest days, Colton Pitonyak was an exceptional student, remarkably intelligent and focused on the future, bright-eyed and ready, the kind of young man any mother would want for a son, the type of young man any mother would want a daughter to date. But there were two sides to Colton Pitonyak. Perhaps his parents didn't know the other Colton, the one with the quick temper and the thirst that couldn't be quenched.

The Pitonyaks came from rural beginnings. Bridget, a slight woman with chin-length blond hair and an effervescent personality, grew up with the last name of Waddell in the small farming town of Carlisle, Arkansas. In her 1978 senior photo from Carlisle High School, she looked like the good girl next door, wearing a modest sweater, her long, silky brown hair held back in a barrette.

Four years older than Bridget, Eddie was a bit of a fire-plug, dark-haired, not tall in stature but well-built, with a determined, bulldog face. He'd been raised on the rich, fertile soil of a rice and soybean farm situated east of Little Rock between Hazen and Stuttgart. Like his father and grandfather before him, Eddie farmed in the early years of his marriage. But when the farming market took a downturn in 1984, he moved on. Those were hard years for America's farmers, and Eddie and Bridget had two young sons to build a future for. Their older son, Dustin, was then three, and Colton Aaron Pitonyak, just two, had been born on September 5, 1982.

"Farmers were going broke," Eddie has said. "We had to try something else."

The something else was a move into the farm machinery business. It would prove to be a good choice for Eddie, whom friends describe as an intense and quiet man. After leaving farming, Eddie started as a sales rep and manager for an equipment company. Eight years later, when Colton was ten, Eddie used his experience to start a wholesale farm parts distributorship. It was obvious that Eddie Pitonyak was a man on the move. After he sold the parts company to a Dutch concern, in 1995, he moved the family to Chesapeake, Virginia, peanut-farming country, to become president of EDCOR, Inc., a spare-parts company that supplied dealers. It was a short foray east, and a year later, the Pitonyaks were living back in Arkansas, where Eddie founded Pitonyak Machinery Company, PMC, geared toward buying and selling farm equipment. Eventually Eddie would expand, acquiring a company that had a good name, one that had been around since 1913: Brandt, a farm machinery company headquartered in Bridget's hometown of Carlisle.

Over the years, while Bridget sold real estate, Eddie nurtured the company. By 2006, he had twenty-five employees. At the PMC/Brandt plant surrounded by a chain-link fence, steel panels came in through a bay door and left as large-scale farm equipment, including grain carts that held one thousand bushels and levelers used to cultivate land for planting.

Though the plant was in Carlisle, the Pitonyaks lived thirty miles away in Little Rock, Arkansas' largest city and the state capital, situated on the banks of the Arkansas River. Named after a stone outcropping that marks where the Mississippi Delta merges with the foothills of the Ouachita Mountains, this part of Arkansas is a rugged land, one that offers spectacular scenery: the wide river, the rolling hills, the lush landscape that during fall deer-hunting season turns brilliant gold and red. In this southern city of more than six hundred thousand, locals enjoy their catfish fried, their breakfast sausage smothered in gravy, and pie à la mode.

"Little Rock is a big city with a small-town mentality," says someone who grew up there. "But it's a divided city. There's the poor, and there's the rich."

Judged by most standards, the Pitonyaks were well off. By the time the boys were teenagers, they lived in a large English Tudor with a wood-shingle roof on a quiet West Little Rock street. Named after the posh private country club it surrounded, their subdivision, Pleasant Valley, was considered one of the most affluent addresses in the city. Even within Pleasant Valley, the Pitonyak homestead on Valley Club Circle was impressive, a large, sprawling home on a hill across the street from a golf course, with a long driveway and an oversize lot covered with pines, magnolias, and a Bradford pear tree. It was a congenial setting, a neighborhood sightseers drive to ogle the houses. In Pleasant Valley, the neighbors were affluent professionals, including doctors, lawyers, and top executives. They lived well and could afford to give to their children the best America had to offer.

"We all had the same life," says a friend of Colton's. "We lived in nice big houses and never wanted for anything."

Among their Pleasant Valley neighbors, the Pitonyaks were well thought of. "We're talking about a wonderful family here," says one. "These are good people, who did their best for their children."

So much so that one young man who grew up with the Pitonyak boys would say, "If I could have picked different parents, I would have picked Bridget and Eddie. They were dedicated to Dustin and Colton. Especially Bridget's world revolved around the boys."

Physically, both boys resembled Eddie, dark-haired and medium height, compact but strong-looking. There was no question that Dustin was like his father. Quiet and reserved, they loved the outdoors, and Eddie and his oldest spent time fishing and hunting. Those were two things Colton didn't care about. From the beginning he had other interests, from skateboarding to playing the guitar. When Dustin and Eddie won a fishing contest in Virginia in 1996, Colton wasn't in the photo. And when they went hunting, he stayed home. "Colton told me he didn't like firing a gun. He didn't want to kill anything," says a grade school friend.

Once Colton went hunting with his father and brother, and when they killed a deer and began gutting it, Colton threw up. "Colton always had a weak stomach," Eddie would say.

"Bridget understood boys," says one neighbor. "She knew how to handle the boys." And while Dustin seemed to have more in common with his father, Colton was closer to his mother. "Colton thought the world of her," says a good friend. "He talked about her all the time, about how his mom had done this or that for him."

Looking back, Bridget would describe her younger son as an exception from the start. "He talked before he could walk," she said. By three, Colton was reading. When someone told him in second grade that Santa Claus didn't exist, Bridget asked, "What do you think?"

"There is no Santa," Colton replied. Then he presented her with a dictionary and pointed at the entry for Santa Claus, where it defined the jolly man in the red suit as "an imaginary figure."

The Pitonyaks were religious people. Eddie's father, Tommy, was a member of the Knights of Columbus in Slovak, the town where his family attended the local Catholic church. From the time Colton was in second grade, with the exception of their brief time in Virginia, Eddie and Bridget enrolled them in Catholic schools. In Little Rock, they attended Christ the King Catholic school and church, an imposing structure built in 1967 to serve the city's affluent western suburbs.

"People assume that if you go to Christ the King, you're rich," says one former student. "It's the rich folks' parish."

At Christ the King, students attended morning Masses and, along with math and English, memorized the Ten Commandments and read the Bible. According to the school's Web site, "the purpose of Christ the King Catholic School is to instill the spirit of the living Christ in all students so that they may develop spiritually, physically, academically, and socially into responsible, strong Christians."

At least to outsiders, the Pitonyaks appeared to be a special family. For the annual Medieval Festival at the school, Bridget sewed a purple and green jester costume, first worn by Dustin, then Colton. She paid attention to the details, sewing bells on the hat and stuffing the curled toes of the shoes. "That's the kind of mom Bridget was," says a mother of one of the boys' classmates. "She went the extra mile and made sure her boys had one of the best costumes."

At Christ the King, both of the Pitonyak boys made good grades, but Colton was brilliant. He habitually made the all-A honor roll. But he wasn't what the other kids would label "a nerd." He played sports, including football and basketball, and acted as a guard on safety patrol. "He was smart but really outgoing," says one of his classmates. "A lot of fun to be around."

In the classroom, Colton was a force to be reckoned with. "He overwhelmed teachers at times. He had a strong personality, and he was hyper, incredibly smart," says one friend. "Colton seemed bored at school. You'd think he wasn't paying attention, but he'd be the one who always had the A on his tests."

As an altar boy, dressed in a pure white robe, Colton assisted the priests during Mass and helped serve Communion. Standing before the altar, lighting the candles, Colton appeared virtuous. His dark hair carefully combed to the side, he'd meticulously memorized every step. But then Colton was that way with everything, focused and not afraid to study hard to make sure he had it right. Bridget would one day say that her younger son enjoyed serving at the priest's side so much that when others didn't show up, Colton volunteered.

"Colton excelled at everything he did," says a childhood friend. "He seemed to be able to do absolutely anything he wanted and do it well."

Yet even at such a young age, there were indications that Colton Pitonyak had another side.

Tim Lim, a year older than Colton, would long remember the day he first met Colton Pitonyak in piano class. The piano instructor brought Colton into the room to introduce him to Lim. "This boy's from your school," she said. In front of their teacher, Colton was always on best behavior, polite and calm. He practiced and advanced quickly, becoming quite good on the piano. But Lim saw something else in him.

One day Lim remarked to Colton, "You're a good piano player."

"I know I am," Colton snapped back.

If his classmate's ego seemed inflated, something else bothered Lim more: He grew to believe that Colton Pitonyak was a racist. Christ the King was a nearly all-white school, and Lim and his brother were the only Asian-American students. "I was older than Colton, and usually there's a pecking order. The underclassmen in a private school don't hassle the older kids," he says. "But Colton didn't have any respect for that."

Instead, Colton poked fun at Lim, making derogatory remarks about his Asian heritage. Frequently when Lim drank out of a water fountain, Colton came up from behind and pushed his face into the water, while he mimicked a Chinese accent. When Lim looked up, Colton Pitonyak was walking away laughing. "He was this punk kid," says Lim, "But in front of the teachers he put on this angelic show."

Still, those close to him didn't see anything particularly duplicitous about young Colton. Was it more a case of a boy just being a boy? "Colton was a nice funny kid. By the time he'd grown up he seemed like any normal teenage boy allowed to get just a little wild," says a relative. "I never thought of it as being too excessive."

Along with the piano, Colton played guitar, and he loved music. In eighth grade, he performed with two friends in the school talent show, playing the guitar while they sang Deep Purple's "Smoke on the Water." "They were really good," says a childhood friend. "He seemed really passionate about music."

From Christ the King, the Pitonyak brothers moved on to Little Rock's Catholic High School for Boys, one of the city's more prestigious institutions. Nearby was Mount St. Mary Academy, a private all-girls school. Both were conservative, disciplined, and focused on academics. Catholic High reserved the right to turn down applicants not up to its high standards. "We're a college-preparatory school," says the school's guidance counselor, Brother Richard Sanker, a scholarly man with gentle sags under his eyes. "Nearly all our boys go on to college, many top schools not just in Arkansas and the Southwest, but the nation."

The school, founded in the thirties, is far from impressive on the outside, a low-slung building on a hill, hidden by trees. Catholic High's colors are purple and gold, and the 640 boys who attend are expected to present the right image: khakis, button-down shirts with ties, clean-cut with no facial hair. The school boasted an exceptional curriculum including classes in Latin, British literature, anatomy, and physiology. It abstained from labeling any classes as honors level, reluctant to foster an "intellectual elitism." It's a school where an A requires at least a 93, and a B an 85.

Outside the main building, the United States, Arkansas, and Catholic diocese flags fly over the school. Inside, visitors are greeted by a statue of Christ with his arms extended in welcome. Two days a week students attend Mass in the school chapel, a solemn place with stained glass windows. Each time he walked into the chapel during the four years he attended classes at Catholic High, Colton Pitonyak passed a plaque of the Ten Commandments that included "Thou Shall Not Kill."

"We're not immune from the problems other schools have," says Brother Sanker. "But we try hard to instill Christian values, and we rarely have any kind of a problem at the school. We can't control what happens after the students leave, however."

For students who break the rules, the price is high: expulsion. "We don't tolerate drugs or alcohol on the campus," says Sanker. "Rarely do we have a student who comes to the school drunk or high."

A gregarious teenager, Colton arrived at Catholic High School a straight-A student, one year behind his brother. Tommy Coy, a math teacher who would have both the Pitonyak boys, found they were both good students, but Colton was special. "Dustin wanted to go to the University of Arkansas and have a good time. He wasn't a troublemaker, he just seemed comfortable with himself," says Coy. But Colton "was brilliant and driven."

At Catholic High, Colton signed up for and made the football team. He took a class in moral theology and ran with a crowd of mostly other Catholic High and Mount St. Mary kids. He studied and made exceptional grades. "Colton had this incredible ability to focus," says a fellow student. "He was whip-smart. We all copied from his chemistry homework. He was just outstanding at everything he did."

But Colton's dark side arrived at Catholic High as well.

Tim Lim wasn't happy to see his fellow pianist walk

through the high school's doors. "It started all over again, the name calling, the harassment," says Lim. "I watched Colton put on a façade in front of the teachers, and then mock me. I grew to expect some kind of a slur from him." That Colton was bright "made it seem worse that he could be filled with so much hatred."

After school, the Pitonyak house was a busy place, the boys' friends coming and going, sometimes sitting on the white brick wall that bordered the driveway, smoking and talking. "Even though he was in prep school, Colton was kind of a skater type . . . wearing baggy jeans and shorts," remembers a friend. "He would skateboard, and was good at that, too."

Bridget would later say that Colton had as many friends who were girls as guys. One of them was Tracey Ryan, a cute girl one year younger, who went to Mount St. Mary. Years later, Tracey would describe Colton as a boy who'd take his shirt off in the rain to give it to a girl without an umbrella. On the weekends, sometimes Ryan's girlfriends slept over at her house, and boys from Catholic High knocked on the window. Tracey let them in, and when it got loud, her parents came to investigate. If Colton was among the interlopers, Tracey's mom never minded. "My mom always loved Colton," she says. "So long as he was there, I was not in trouble. He was the responsible one.

"Colton was like a brother to a lot of people," says Tracey. "He always checked in with his parents when he was out late, and if he had too much to drink, he walked home instead of drove." Sometimes the parties were at the Pitonyaks' house. On one such night a friend sat talking to Colton, a junior that year. They drank beer and discussed the normal things teenage boys are interested in: girls, school, and sports. "Everyone drank," remembers one girl. "Even the smart kids."

Looking back, the teenagers coming of age in Pleasant Valley would see their upbringing as privileged. "There was this thing about the rich kids. We all hung out together, kind of a rich-kids' cult, a bunch of rich kids who would do anything to cover up their mistakes," says one of Colton's friends. "We had lots of money, and we thought we had impunity, we could do whatever we wanted and no one could touch us."

There was an undercurrent in Little Rock, a need for boys to be tough, to stand by their word, and to grow into men's men. "There was a lot of testosterone floating around, and on weekends, especially Friday nights after football games, the kids wandered off into the woods. There were lots of places to get lost with friends," says a friend of Colton's. "The guys would find reasons to fight. Colton was kind of a wimpy kid in some ways. He got in lots of fights, but he never won. When he was drinking, he had a short temper. And Colton drank a lot."

Another of Colton's classmates would later agree: "We didn't have anything to do but drink, do drugs, have sex, or go to church. Colton wasn't into hunting and such like most Southern boys, but he did love to drink."

There was little doubt that Colton Pitonyak had multiple sides: the scholar and gentleman his teachers and Tracey knew, the racist Tim Lim met, and the insolent drunk many saw emerging. By his junior year, boys from Catholic High, not unlike those across the nation, experimented with not only drinking but drugs, mainly pot. Colton was among them. "I saw him smoking pot a lot," says one friend. "But then, lots of kids did." With Colton, however, it seemed to have more than the usual effects. Mixed with alcohol, pot made him mean.

One night at a party, high and drunk, Colton screamed without reason at one of the Mount St. Mary girls, calling her a slut and a whore. "My brother and my boyfriend were there," she remembers. "They beat him up, pretty bad. I never liked talking to Colton after that, and he avoided talking to me, probably afraid of my brother."

Colton's fights became a regular occurrence. "If someone called you out to fight and you didn't, the others ganged up on you and beat your ass," says a friend of Colton's. "You had to stand up and defend yourself. We were a bunch of rich kids with too much time on our hands and a fascination with being hard-core tough."

One day relatives visited the Pitonyaks and noticed a car with a window smashed. Bridget said they thought some of the boys' friends might be responsible. Whether or not his parents were aware of it, Colton was building a reputation as someone who got into brawls. "Colton wanted to be tough, because that was a way to be popular," says a friend. "And Colton cared about being popular."

Louis Petit began at Catholic High in his sophomore year and was seated alphabetically near Colton. They became fast friends, hanging out together, going on summer and spring break trips. Petit, tall and thin, is the son of a family that owns a Little Rock restaurant, and in the summer of 2000, he and Colton worked out together, lifting weights at Powerhouse Gym. Perhaps Colton thought bulking up would help him win a few of those fights in the woods, or perhaps he was just trying to fulfill the expectation that the kids in Arkansas had, that to be a real man he had to be strong.

Colton and Petit spent months learning poses and stances, building muscle. One night at a party at the Pitonyaks' house, no one could find Colton until a group discovered him in his bedroom, putting on artificial tanner for a body-building competition the next day. Colton and Petit tried out for the Mr. Teen Arkansas title, but didn't win. "It was really funny," says a friend of Colton's. "He worked at the body-building like he did everything else, really focused. Colton never did anything halfway."

By the fall of 2000, Dustin had graduated from Catholic High and gone off to the University of Arkansas. That year, Colton was a senior at Catholic High, wearing his class ring and the purple, green, and gold school tie. His parents sold the big house on Valley Club Circle and bought a smaller house in the nearby St. Charles subdivision. At the end of a cul-de-sac, with a lot and a price tag one-third smaller than the old house, the new house, at least as neighbors saw it, was an indication that Eddie and Bridget were scaling back, downsizing now that Dustin was gone and Colton was getting ready to leave.

On September 19 of that year, the *Arkansas Democrat-Gazette* ran a list of the 166 seniors in the state who were National Merit Scholar finalists. There were seven at Catholic High, including Colton Aaron Pitonyak.

Tommy Coy, Colton's math teacher, had continued to be awed by his brilliant young student, not only by Colton's intellectual capabilities but also by his determination. That year, Colton presented a class project on the stock market. Coy was so impressed that he asked the young man who'd helped him.

"No one," Colton said, and Coy didn't doubt it.

"It was mind-boggling how much he knew about the stock market," says Coy. "Absolutely amazing."

In Coy's grade book, Colton scored nothing below a 98 in calculus and ranked among the top five students in the class, this at a school where many were high achievers. Coy never saw a wrinkle in Colton Pitonyak's demeanor. "I never even saw him get angry," the teacher says. When Colton asked, Coy happily wrote letters to universities, urging them to accept Colton.

His senior year, Colton had one goal in his sights: the University of Texas in Austin's blue-chip McCombs Business School. It was difficult to get in, highly competitive, even more so for out-of-state students, but Colton was determined. To Coy and others, Colton talked like a young Donald Trump or Dale Carnegie, a budding tycoon destined to conquer the business world.

Catholic High legend would later have it that when Colton showed up to take the ACT, the American College Testing Program exam that universities use to judge whom they admit, he was hung over from a party the night before. If so, it didn't hurt him. Colton scored a 32 on the exam, only four points below a perfect score.

At graduation that spring, 2001, Colton was sixth in his class and had a perfect 4.0 grade point. To do that he'd averaged 93 or above in every class he'd taken in his four years at Catholic High. His stellar grades attracted $150,000 in scholarship money. Colton had also applied to the University of Pennsylvania and New York University, but his parents would later say they were pleased when he chose UT because it was closer to home. Along with the acceptance came a full academic scholarship.

There must have been celebrating in the Pitonyak house the day Colton's acceptance letter arrived from McCombs. It was yet another honor in Colton's fast-growing list of accomplishments. His teachers, family, and friends alike had reason to believe there were more conquests ahead for the young man, who in his high school graduation photo looked like a perfect son, snappily dressed in a coat and tie, his dark hair carefully trimmed and combed. Colton's Catholic High yearbook carried a testament from his family: "Colton, you have made us very proud," from Eddie, Bridget, and Dustin.

In July, Bridget took her son to UT's orientation. Once there, she was even more impressed. It turned out that Colton was one of only twelve admitted from out of state to McCombs that fall. At UT, he bought his grandmother a present, a bumper sticker for her car. Beside the "My Grandson Goes to the University of Arkansas" banner for Dustin, she now had one in honor of Colton that read, "My Grandson Goes to the University of Texas."

In the fall of 2001, Colton Pitonyak had the world spread out before him like a sumptuous buffet. He had the advantages many crave but so few have: a family who loved him, loyal friends who supported him, and the money, credentials, and intellect to aim as high as his imagination could take him. He brought three of his favorite books to Austin with him: *The Three Musketeers*, *Robinson Crusoe*, and *The Power of Positive Thinking*. Tommy Coy expected to one day see his former star pupil make his mark as a sage venture capitalist or Wall Street mogul.

"We all expected truly great things of Colton," Coy says. "He was that outstanding."

Just four years later, Colton would be in headlines across the country, his face splashed on national television. But the context would be very different from anything Tommy Coy ever imagined. Instead of making his name as a financial tycoon, Colton Pitonyak would be forever linked to the most gruesome murder in the history of the University of Texas, and family and friends in Arkansas would be left to wonder how it happened, and why.

Five

On April 6, 2001, the spring Colton Pitonyak graduated from Catholic High, *Blow* premiered, a movie starring Johnny Depp as George Jung, who in the seventies partnered with the Medellín drug cartel to powder the noses of Hollywood and then America. In real life, Jung made tens of millions escalating U.S. drug habits, introducing first celebrities and later the general populace to cocaine. In the movie, the young drug king lived the dream, even pairing up with a woman portrayed by the stunning Penelope Cruz. The movie was dark and moody, and in the end Jung lost his money and his freedom.

In August when classes commenced at the University of Texas in Austin, more than fifty-two thousand students flooded the local shops and bookstores, where everything possible was covered in UT burnt orange displaying the university's longhorn logo. But alongside the UT notebooks, T-shirts, sweatpants, and key rings were *Blow* posters sold to decorate apartments and dorm rooms. If *Blow* didn't suit, the bookstores stocked posters from HBO's *The Sopranos* and gangster and drug movies, including *Goodfellas*, *The Godfather*, and the brutal *Scarface*.

The stores stocked the posters for a simple reason: They sold.

"*Scarface* was our generation's movie," says one of Colton's friends, with a shrug. "We listened to gangster rap and saw the rappers' mansions on MTV. They showed off their home theaters with their DVD collections. *Scarface* was always there. It's all about the image. You may be a white suburban kid, but you've gotta be tough."

In Austin, the University of Texas comprises a city within the city, covering 350 acres with 156 buildings, organized into eighteen separate colleges. At Jester Hall, UT's largest dorm, so enormous that its thirty-three hundred residents have their own zip code, kids from small towns and big cities unpacked their computers and their clothes, perused their class schedules to buy their books, and a healthy percentage of the young men hung a gangster poster on the wall. For most of them, it would be a brief fascination, an imaginary armor perhaps to toughen them up for their first experience away from home. The first time out from under parental supervision, freshmen spread their metaphoric wings, setting their own limits, and many paid as much attention to fitting in as to classes and grades. Once settled and accepted, most moved on, abandoning the need or the desire for a tough-guy image: But not all.

While the masses moved into dorm rooms, Colton Pitonyak took the path of the privileged. He pledged a fraternity and moved into the Delta Tau Delta house, at Twenty-eighth and San Jacinto, on the north side of campus, a rambling stone building with the fraternity's symbol proudly displayed. Windows overlooked the street, and inside leather couches and an Oriental rug formed a sitting area under soaring ceilings, while the walls were lined with photo montages of members dating back to when the chapter, Gamma Iota, began in 1904. Residents' rooms fanned out from the lobby, past the cafeteria. Late-model sedans, SUVs, and pickup trucks filled the parking lot, and the basketball courts off to the side had a homemade wooden bar for parties.

On campus, jeans and UT shirts were ubiquitous attire, proper for nearly any and all occasions. Colton arrived on the campus looking much as he had in Little Rock, wearing polo shirts, jeans, shorts, and tennis shoes. As the son of well-to-do-parents, much of what he owned was marked with the Polo logo, the designer Ralph Lauren's pony-riding polo player. Yet one frat brother remembered Colton's expensive shirts, jeans, and shorts all seemed oversize, and that he wore his baseball cap backward, which seemed odd for a prep school grad.

At the University of Texas, the Greek scene, a.k.a. fraternity and sorority life, was flourishing, one of the most active in the nation. The Delts were known as an old-line, big-name fraternity, with a comfortable house, overseen by the stereotypical frat mom, a rather crusty, fiftyish woman who looked out for her boys. "The fraternities talk about raising money for charity, but it's all about the parties, and the Delts had amazing parties," says a student. Because the Delt house is on the North Campus, not the West Campus where most of the frats and sororities have impressive houses, it tends to "fly under the radar," another says. "They seem to be able to get away with more." One of UT's most famous Delts was the hard-partying actor Matthew McConaughey.

Some UT students would look at frats as a good place to network, while one Delt would later look back and say it felt more like "paying for friends." Within the fraternity, Colton quickly stood out as someone who was "different," says a frat brother. At the parties, Colton flirted with the young sorority women. He could be charming and fun, at times the life of the party, and they seemed drawn to him, and he to them.

One evening, a frat member named Frank talked to two young women he found rather pedestrian conversationalists and decided to exercise the tactic known as "the classic hand-off," calling over an underclassman, introducing the girls, and then excusing himself and walking away. The pledge he called over was Colton, but before Frank could extricate himself, Colton made an excuse and left. Frank was dumbfounded, thinking this was a pledge who didn't understand the customary order of frat life. But then something else happened.

"I can't believe Colton didn't even remember my name," one of the girls said.

"Well, there are thousands of people at UT. It's hard to remember everyone you meet," Frank said. "Don't take it personally."

"You don't understand," she said, still peeved. "I slept with him last week."

That same Colton Pitonyak hosted his old friend from Little Rock, Tracey Ryan, and her friend, inviting them to stay with him in his room at the Delt house. When they did, he was the perfect gentleman, including giving the two girls his bed and sleeping on the floor.

In so many ways, Colton seemed such a contradiction. Some of his new brothers noticed an apparent disconnect in the new member, as the brilliant Catholic school kid from suburban Little Rock slowly took on the mannerisms of the inner-city kids in the rap videos. "He was always about acting tough," says one. "Colton talked about doing drugs, bragging that in high school he went into the bad sections in Little Rock to buy cocaine. We didn't know whether to believe him or not."

For most, it didn't matter. The drug scene was flourishing in Austin, a laid-back city with a serious sense of funk, which prides itself on being on the liberal edge. "This is Austin," says one Delt, as if the name of the city alone explained. "Even the studious kids smoke pot. It's expected."

Drugs, of course, weren't unusual anywhere in America. Cities from the Midwest to the East Coast to the West Coast struggled with drugs smuggled in daily from across the borders. And partying was an obsession at most of the big college campuses. In Austin, however, it had been elevated to nearly an art.

Evenings, students flocked en masse to "the drag," seven blocks on East Sixth Street, bordered by I–35 on the east and Congress Avenue on the west, a slice of hotels and restaurants, trendy nightclubs, and seedy neon-lit bars, taverns, T-shirt and souvenir stores, tattoo and massage parlors, many in rambling storefronts that date back to the 1800s or early 1900s. On weekends, rock, hip-hop, rap, country-

and-western, and jazz reverberated through open doors, and the street was barricaded off, to protect the overflowing crowds.

Rough-edged, with strippers in netting and feathers, disheveled homeless men, even the occasional transvestite in furs and paste jewels circulating among the crowds of students, the drag offered an eclectic charm with a vaguely dangerous undercurrent. As nights on the drag passed, clutches of twentysomethings, many tripping-over-their-own-feet drunk and/or high, spilled out onto the street, where they congregated in small groups that ebbed and flowed, forming and re-forming as they scattered from one circle to another, from one bar to the next, hoping for a good time. Colton Pitonyak was front and center. "He took to Sixth Street like a convert to Communion," says one friend. "On Sixth Street, Pitonyak was in his element."

On Sixth Street, Colton was as disorderly and abrasive as he'd been in Little Rock. "He kept trying to get into fights," says the friend. "If he couldn't get into one with a stranger in a bar, he'd pick on a friend."

Despite the distractions Austin offered, Colton initially focused on why he was there, his drive to be a major force in business. That first year, he earned As and Bs, a feat in the highly competitive McCombs School. All seemed to be going well, even if there were subtle changes in the way he dressed and acted. After years of having his attire dictated by parochial school dress codes, as the months passed at UT, Colton's polo shirts looked baggier, his beard and hair scruffier. A few of his frat brothers began to wonder about him. A rumor circulated that he tortured a cat in the frat parking lot, and then there was the morning Colton was found asleep in the alley behind the Delt house, passed out on garbage bags filled with debris from the party the night before.

In Little Rock that year, Eddie Pitonyak expanded PMC, Pitonyak Machinery Company, by putting together the deal to buy the Brandt farm machinery company. In an industry newsletter, Eddie cautioned Arkansas delta farmers, his main customers, about buying from companies without their interests at heart, those headquartered in states where congressmen weren't pushing for farm subsidies. "If enough people say something, these companies will call their congressmen," he said.

The following August 2002, his second in Austin, Colton moved from the frat house to an apartment in a converted house on Elmwood Place, across the street from the Delt house's parking lot. He hung with a group that included Roel Escobar, a slightly built young man from Houston, and Juan Montero, a bulkily built UT student Colton met during freshman orientation. Montero and Pitonyak were kindred souls, since the former also had as one of his goals "making that all mighty dollar." One of Montero's favorite sayings was Machiavelli's "The end justifies the means."

Like other UT students, Colton and his pals went to football and basketball games, where they held down their middle two fingers with their thumbs and flashed the school's hook-'em-horns sign, in support of Texas Longhorn sports and the school mascot, Bevo, a longhorn steer. At night, they migrated with thousands of other students to Sixth Street and the bars.

Jared Smyth pledged the Delts that fall and met a chain-smoking Colton sitting outside the frat house. A sophomore finance major, Colton was still doing well in classes, and he told Jared about his $150,000 in scholarship money. UT's business school was tough, and Jared was impressed, plus Colton seemed like a good guy. Jared wondered why Colton was such an outsider at the frat house.

When Smyth asked around, he heard the stories about Pitonyak. Brother Pitonyak, he heard, often looked glassy-eyed and high. When Colton showed up at parties, he stayed until the empty beer keg floated in the barrel of ice water, and the alcohol and drugs made him aggressive. At the Delt house, Colton Pitonyak's bad-boy act started to worry the other members; some wondered if it had become more than an act.

When Colton went home to Little Rock, he and Tracey Ryan again spent time together. To her, Colton was the same great guy she'd grown up with. Still, one night when she was supposed to see Colton, she ditched him in favor of a night with her old girlfriends. That didn't stop Colton, however, from consoling Tracey after another group of friends didn't show up to go out with her as they'd said they would. Tracey called Colton crying, then picked him up and brought him to her house, where they spent the night watching movies and talking. A gentlemanly Colton didn't rebuke Tracey for standing him up; he never even mentioned it.

Spring semester 2003, Colton earned an impressive 3.5 grade point average. That summer, he stayed in Austin, picking up part-time jobs and taking classes. After his first two years, Colton was on track to become yet another triumph for McCombs, a school that educated more CEOs of S&P 500 companies than any other. UT business grads ran major companies across the nation, from ConocoPhillips and American Airlines, to H. J. Heinz. Colton often talked in more esoteric terms, expressing pure moneymaking goals like becoming a venture capitalist. At other times, he bragged about his future, saying that one day he'd eclipse even billionaire Donald Trump, whose television show, *The Apprentice*, was high in the ratings.

Yet that summer, Colton rarely made it to class and barely squeaked through. By then another kind of talk surrounded Colton; some suspected the drugs had become more than a pastime. Word around the Delt house was that Pitonyak was hooked on the drugs he'd been toying with ever since he arrived in Austin. Some sized up the new Colton Pitonyak and didn't like what they saw.

More and more his frat brothers pulled away, and Colton spent less and less time at the Delt house, rarely even showing up for parties. Before long, Colton left North Campus and moved into a rundown apartment complex on UT's West Campus, a long, narrow, Moorish-looking building called the Camino Real apartments, constructed around an interior corridor with a swimming pool. When his old friends from the frat ran into him, Colton laughed too loud, got too close when he talked, smelled of alcohol, and cursed like a rapper on steroids. And he talked about drugs. To close friends, Colton bragged that he'd hooked up with a prime source, one he called "the Asians," a Vietnamese-American gang with a connection for top-grade ecstasy, a club drug that heightened sexual pleasure. The "Asians" sold to Pitonyak at $3 a pill, and he bragged that because of their purity, he could trade the pills at $10 apiece to other dealers for marijuana, cocaine, methamphetamines, heroin, and Xanax. On the street, he sold the ecstasy pills for up to $15 each.

"I can get you anything you want. Absolutely, fucking anything," he told a frat brother one night. "If it's a drug, I've got a supplier."

Cocaine was big on campus, along with pot and ecstasy. Meth or methamphetamine was popular with the girls. Cheaper than cocaine, it jazzed up their metabolisms, made sleeping and eating inconsequential, and the weight dropped off. In a society intent on body image, where magazines like *People* and *Us* displayed emaciated starlets and pseudo celebrities on their covers, thin was the rage, and meth made it easy. Never mind that melting the crystals, called "ice" or "shards," and inhaling the fumes burned up bodies and minds so fast that at thirty, users looked fifty. Twentysomethings considered themselves bulletproof, rarely worrying about what might or might not happen decades in the future.

Some of his college friends began buying from Colton Pitonyak. It seemed safer than circulating through Sixth Street looking for pot or coke or risking a trip into Austin's shadows to meet a dealer. Before long, he was approaching students on the street, asking if they were in the market for drugs.

If nothing else, Colton was a capitalist at heart. He had a product with a high profit margin and in ready supply: drugs. And he had buyers: his fellow students. What could have been easier? After all, he'd come to UT to make his fortune, and selling drugs was a quick means to that end. Word got out that Colton Pitonyak was dealing, and students lined up to buy.

At times, friends would later say, Colton tried to quit using and selling. "But once the word gets out on campus that you've got a pipeline, your phone rings," says one of Colton's friends. "He'd quit for a few days, and then he'd be high again, and off to deliver more drugs. He was caught up in it, the whole lifestyle."

One of his old frat brothers, Smyth, had stayed in touch and went out a few nights with Colton, but the drugs flowed and the crowd Pitonyak hung with dressed like rappers. To Smyth, his old frat brother seemed to be walking a tightrope. Smyth guessed that it had to be coke that made Pitonyak so tense. After a couple of parties, Smyth stopped returning Colton's phone calls and deleted his number from his cell, in college life a symbol of excommunication. "I knew no good was going to come from hanging out with Colton Pitonyak," says Smyth.

When Colton talked to another friend that fall, he admitted his grades had dropped. High much of the time, he stayed in his apartment, rarely going to class. "But I'm going to pull it together," he told him. "I've got to get my grades up or my parents will pull me out of here, and I'll end up back in fucking Little Rock."

As he had been with his friends in Little Rock, Colton was dedicated to his tight group that included Montero, Escobar, and Jason Mack, a muscular kid with arms covered by tattoos who'd been in and out of trouble since his teenage years. "Bros before hos," Colton said, expressing his loyalty, raising his fist in the air.

At his one-bedroom apartment on Salado Street, Colton lived a quiet life. It wasn't good to attract attention, not when the business transacted behind closed doors was illegal. At night, he circulated to friends' apartments. High on drugs and drunk, he laughed, full of fun, the life of the party. One night he tore off his clothes and ran full speed into an outdoor pool at a friend's apartment. A student who lived there would later remember, "The pool was so small that no one ever swam in it. We used it to throw our empty beer bottles in, and the homeless people bathed in it."

Later Colton would admit that by winter 2003, he was high and drunk nearly every day. He rarely went to class and was on a collision course with failure. Then, in December, the brilliant honor student from Little Rock was jailed for driving while under the influence. Bridget came to see her younger son and realized that he had a problem. She packed him up and took him home.

In Little Rock, Colton worked out and went to the gym again, as he had with Louis Petit in high school. When his old friends saw him, they barely recognized him. "He looked like a drug addict," says someone who ran into him at a store. "I almost walked past him. When I turned around, realized it was him, and said hello, but he looked at me and didn't have a clue who I was. He looked high, really out of it."

Another old friend who ran into him looked at Colton and wondered if his behavior could be explained by rebellion against a lifetime of straitlaced schools. "I figured he was finally free and decided to do it his way," says the kid.

In January, Colton returned to Austin to start the spring semester. There a frat brother ran into Colton at a party. High, drunk, or both, Colton came up to him, got within inches of his face, and said, "You ever been to County, dog?"

The college kid realized Colton was talking about the Travis County jail, not somewhere he particularly wanted to spend a night. "No, all I've ever gotten is a speeding ticket," he said. Pitonyak laughed, as if that somehow defined the other kid as not in his league. That night Colton seemed to revel in his first experience on the wrong side of the law.

In the end, it wouldn't be about guilt or innocence; it would be about finding a way to make it all go away. Colton Pitonyak had grown up believing that he was special. His boyhood circle of friends felt they had a right to do as they wanted, without fearing the consequences. "We felt like we had impunity," says a Little Rock native, who grew up in Colton's circle. "We were rich kids, and when we got in trouble, we covered it up." Sometimes their parents helped.

This time, Colton's offense would be negotiated down, plea-bargained. He pleaded guilty to a misdemeanor: obstructing a highway passageway. The DUI charge disappeared, and all Colton had to do was pay a fine and go in for counseling. The only serious repercussion: UT suspended him.

In the spring, Colton, the former UT whiz kid and would-be tycoon, signed up for classes at the same school Jennifer Cave enrolled in when she arrived in the capital city: Austin Community College. At least for now, he wasn't welcome at UT. A few months later, Colton met Jen, and events were set in motion that led to the terrible night Sharon Cave stood outside Colton Pitonyak's condo, pounding on the door and calling out her daughter's name, praying she'd find her alive.

Six

Jennifer had been in Austin for nearly a year in December 2003, the month Colton was arrested for the first time. She was thin and had no real goals, and Sharon worried that her middle daughter was taking drugs. She asked her, but Jennifer insisted, "I'm okay."

Mostly, Jennifer was Jennifer, flinty and shy, worldly and innocent, self-assured and unsure. She'd become increasingly comfortable with her good looks, wearing flirty little dresses, and Sharon loved to take her shopping; what fun to hit a sale at Dillard's or Ann Taylor, combing through the racks, looking for just the right dress to go with Jen's beautiful long red hair, something to bring out those remarkable blue eyes.

That spring semester, school didn't go well. Jennifer talked as if she intended to study, but within weeks she lost interest, rarely going to class, and eventually dropped most of the classes. Still, she seemed happy. Jennifer was in love with Mark; that Sharon was certain of. Jennifer talked of him constantly, Mark this, Mark that. For Sharon, it was fun to see Jennifer in the throes of her first real love.

Mark, blond and six feet tall, handsome, had grown up in another small Texas town, and Sharon liked him. He studied hard at UT and was doing well. Mark's parents had taken to Jennifer just as quickly. "Every time she visited, she was good to have around," said his mom with a soft chuckle. "She was so intent on helping, not being a burden, that she'd pull out the vacuum and start cleaning. We laughed and had fun, and I thought Sharon had raised her well."

Along with her boyfriend, Jennifer had fallen in love with Austin. She lived in her little apartment off Riverside, with a black cat with green eyes she rescued off the street. In the mornings, she frequented Little City, a bohemian coffee shop on Congress Street, in view of the state capitol. Evenings, she worked as a hostess at Sullivan's, a posh steakhouse with a 1940s boxing motif, in Austin's trendy Warehouse District. The place had a jazz and cigar bar and catered to an upscale clientele. Jennifer loved dressing up and going to work. Once there, she worked hard, always smiling and happy to pitch in. One night when Jim and Sharon had dinner at the restaurant, one of the managers mentioned, "We all love Jennifer here. She's doing a great job."

If Sharon was disappointed about Jennifer's lack of drive when it came to college, she was mollified by the fact that her middle daughter appeared to be prospering. Jim felt Jennifer was faring well. "If she wants to work, let her work," he advised Sharon. "College will be there when she's ready."

Their lives were all going on, and they didn't see a reason to worry.

In Corpus, Jim bought and gutted a house three doors away from his house. The new place, a single-story house that wrapped around a courtyard and a swimming pool, looked dark at first, but he and Sharon hired a contractor who knocked down walls, opening it up. Along with the new house, Sharon had started a new business, her own company, selling promotional items, everything from bill caps and shirts with embroidered company logos to pens and awards. It was exciting having something of her own, and all the children were proud of her. "The kids knew Sharon had rough times and she'd come through them," says Jim.

That uncut Cave umbilical cord connected them all: Sharon in Corpus; Vanessa in Dallas; Jennifer in Austin; Lauren, who'd graduated from high school and moved to Denton, Texas, to attend the University of North Texas; and Clayton in Sinton. Their cell phones rang throughout the day. Lauren and Jennifer, the almost twins, remained mildly estranged but dependent on each other. When Lauren considered Jennifer's thinness, she worried. "She looked like she was taking drugs," says Lauren. "I asked her about it, but she told me to live my own life."

Still, when Jennifer drove to Denton that fall to see Lauren's school, the younger sister was glad to see her. "I was so proud that she'd come all that way to be with me," she says. "It just meant the world."

Two years after leaving Corpus, Jen still had that calm shyness she'd had since childhood and a need to smooth over the rough times for others. When a high school friend moved to Austin, Jennifer took her on a tour of the city. When the girl called again months later, crying because she feared she was pregnant, Jennifer invited her over and suggested she bring a pregnancy test. Then Jennifer stayed with the girl, talking her through it while she took the test. "She made me feel like everything would be okay," says the girl, whose test was negative. "She acted like it wasn't a big deal."

Despite the ups and downs of her own life, Jennifer worried about her family. When Hailey told Jim and Sharon one weekend that she was staying at Jennifer's apartment in Austin when she was really with friends, Sharon ordered Jennifer to pick Jim's youngest up. In the car, Jennifer chastised Hailey, demanding, "What do you think you're doing?"

"What do I think I'm doing?" Hailey charged back. "What are you doing, taking classes you never finish?"

"I'm excited about my job," Jennifer said, dismissing Hailey's accusations.

Although Jennifer hadn't done well in the spring semester, Sharon had great hope for that fall. One class in particular grabbed Jennifer's interest, a political science course. Intrigued with the ideas, Jennifer called Sharon off and on throughout the week, saying, "We had this conversation in class today . . ." Before long, Sharon began to hope that maybe, just maybe, Jennifer had found her niche.

But then the bad news came: Charlie was in San Antonio

working when a friend rushed him to the emergency room. Jennifer's father had suffered a series of strokes that left him disabled. Worried about him, Jennifer rushed home. While her classes continued on through the fall in Austin, Jennifer commuted back and forth to Sinton, trying to help care for her father. She became his rock, supervising his medical care. "When she went back to Austin, she called," says Charlie. "Jennifer was a good daughter."

Sharon was pleased that Jennifer wanted to help her father, but that semester, again, she fell behind and pulled out of her courses, leaving her credits paid for but unearned. "What happened with Charlie just seemed to derail Jennifer again," says Sharon.

When Jennifer came home for Christmas that year, 2003, Sharon urged her to focus her life, go to class, and earn a degree. It bothered her that a girl with Jennifer's potential wasn't using it. But Jennifer insisted that college wasn't important. "I'm fine and I'm happy," she said. "I'm living the way I want to."

To get her point across that Jennifer was on the family payroll only if she was moving ahead with her studies, Sharon told her that from there on out, she was on her own. She'd need to pay her own bills, including her rent, until she proved that she was serious about school. It was time for Jennifer to understand, Sharon decided, how hard it was to make ends meet and how much a college degree could help.

After dinner, as always, Jim and Jennifer took plates of pie and their cigarettes outside. They stood on the patio, eating and talking, Jim trying to explain why Sharon pushed so hard, that she wanted her children to be independent, to live good, prosperous lives. Jennifer was angry and hurt.

"You have the desire and the ability to do well," Jim said. "You have all the ingredients. You just need to apply yourself."

"I do know what I want to do," Jennifer said.

"What is it?" Jim asked.

"I want to go back to school. I want to get a degree."

"Then do it, Jennifer," he urged. "You're the only one standing in your way."

"I will," she said.

Jim knew that Jennifer craved their approval, and he wanted to believe her, but he couldn't. He'd seen her make plans too many times and then not follow through. He wondered if this time Jennifer meant it or if she was just "blowing smoke up my ass."

Off and on, Clayton and Jennifer had some alone time to talk. The brother and sister had always been close, and he confided in her that he'd been to a high school party where kids pushed him to drink and take drugs. "Don't let anyone talk you into anything. If you don't want to, don't do it," she said. Then she got quiet and intensely serious. "Once you start, you may not be able to stop."

With no money coming in from Sharon, Jennifer had only a small monthly stipend from her grandparents' trust fund, which was supposed to pay for college. Worried about money, Jennifer gave up her apartment and moved with a friend, Kristina, into a less expensive one in Austin. Lauren came to visit one weekend, and the two sisters stayed up all night, sharing stories as they had when they were children. "I always thought that if Jennifer knew I was there for her, she'd clean up her act," Lauren says. "But in the end, I guess it wasn't enough."

The arrangement with Kristina lasted for a few months. When Jennifer couldn't pay her share of the bills, Kristina kicked her out, keeping some of Jennifer's possessions to sell to pay the electric bill. Jennifer's world was shaky, but she hadn't hit bottom. Soon something would happen that would throw her life into chaos, and Sharon's deepest fears would come true, as Jennifer's life spun further out of control.

In the Cave family, 2004 would forever be known as Jennifer's "dark year."

Seven

In Little Rock, the Pitonyaks moved that spring. They sold the house on a cul-de-sac they'd purchased when Colton was a senior and bought a more expensive home in their old neighborhood, Pleasant Valley. It wasn't as grand as the house across from the golf course they'd sold three years earlier, but it was a charming English Tudor with a wood shingle roof.

In Corpus Christi, Jim and Sharon made changes as well, finally selling Jim's old house and moving into the remodeled home. Sharon had done an amazing job, and the thirty-year-old house looked modern. The fireplace area in the bedroom was perfect for a small sitting space, and nearly every room had a view of the pool. The kitchen was bright and airy, and the living room warm and cozy. Sharon decorated the two extra bedrooms, one for her girls and one for Jim's. She hung a collage for each of the girls, filled with photos and mementos, and in the Cave sisters' bedroom, she included a print of three women under hairdryers and one Jen found of three stylish women wearing floppy hats. Sharon was happy. She had a lot going right in her life, but she worried about Jennifer.

It would turn out that Sharon had reason to be apprehensive.

That spring in Austin, Mark ended his relationship with Jennifer. Distraught, she didn't show up for work at Sullivan's, and then walked into the restaurant to report for duty high on drugs. They fired her. "The breakup with Mark really hit Jennifer hard. She went off the deep end, on a binge that lasted for days," says Sharon. "We didn't know what to do. We were worried. I wanted her to go to a rehab."

Sharon insisted that Jen needed help, in the form of an inpatient rehab program. Jennifer claimed as staunchly that she wasn't an addict. Yes, she used drugs, she admitted, but not a lot. The breakup hurt her, and she'd made bad decisions. She understood that. But she wasn't a drug addict.

"I'm not there, Mom," she said. "That's not who I am. I'm not that person."

"You're giving me every sign that you are, Jennifer," Sharon said. She could see that her middle daughter's life was in chaos. Jennifer wasn't going to school, and now she had no job and no money coming in. Still, Jennifer didn't look like a drug addict. She had the same bright-faced, wholesome appearance she'd always had. Her daughter just needed some tough love, Sharon decided, hard lessons to convince her to straighten up. That was the approach she'd taken with Vanessa, and it had worked. It would for Jennifer, in time.

"Tell me why I shouldn't send you to a hospital?" Sharon demanded.

"You don't need to," Jennifer said, sobbing. "I'm not there yet."

"If this keeps up, I will," Sharon warned.

"Don't do that," Jennifer pleaded. "Please, those places are bad. One of those places could really screw me up."

Later Sharon would realize that something else happened about that time. Jennifer met Colton Pitonyak.

By then, Colton was back at UT, taking classes, doing well. He had all As going into spring break, but he gorged on booze, cocaine, and Xanax over the vacation and never went back. Colton found the classes easy but staying off the drugs hard. At the end of the semester, he'd earned three Fs and one C. Later, he'd say that wasn't a report card he phoned home to brag about.

If Sharon thought counseling could help Jennifer, Colton had already gone through his first round, an alcohol program required as part of the plea bargain that wiped away his DUI, and come away with an even bigger problem than before. "It didn't do any good," he'd later say. "I just wanted to get it over with."

At any one time, Jennifer Cave had four or five friends who thought of her as their best friend. Something about her appealed to people. Few could verbalize exactly what it was, other than her broad smile and her way of making them feel accepted. "She never judged anyone," says Thornberry, her old friend from Bishop. "In small towns, you grow up accepting everyone. Jennifer was that way to the extreme. She never wanted anyone to feel bad, so she went out of her way to make everyone comfortable."

Perhaps that's why Jennifer kept that tie with Charlie, unlike Lauren, who had little use for their father after the pain he'd caused in her childhood. Something else seemed to come from those years with her father. "I think Jennifer felt like she didn't have to be afraid of people, that no one would ever really hurt her," says Lauren. "I think that came from living with our dad. He'd yell and scream and threaten, but he never physically hurt us. And Jennifer always felt like she could handle our dad, and if she could handle our dad, she could handle anyone. "

Throughout her coming of age, Jennifer made it a habit to pick the wrong friends. At times, that had gotten her in trouble. Now, as she neared adulthood, she had another new friend, Colton Pitonyak. Perhaps Jennifer didn't see who he really was. Or perhaps she thought she saw more in him than others did. "Jennifer looked for the good in people," says a friend. "She was just that way. And on one side, Colton was this tortured genius, this brilliant but troubled guy."

Caring about Colton Pitonyak wouldn't turn out to be a good thing for most young women. No matter where their lives were when they met, if they got too close, he pulled them into his world, the seedy underside of Austin, a netherworld fueled by drugs.

So it would be for Jennifer, beginning that spring 2004, when they met at a party. "There was an immediate attraction," a friend of Colton's would say. "He was drawn to her."

Justin Walters met Colton that same spring. He was introduced to him by a friend, as a potential connection for drugs. Justin, an affable, bright, scrub-faced, preppy UT student, looked like a someday lawyer, but he was hooked on cocaine. He'd tried repeatedly to quit, but couldn't. "The drugs get in your soul. The first time I used cocaine, I went on a three-day binge," he says. "It grabs you and won't let you go."

When he met with Colton at his apartment, the place was in disarray, and Pitonyak was disheveled and dressed like a rapper. He'd heard about the brilliant scholarship student, but saw little of that in the kid with the ready supply of drugs. "The National Merit Scholar ship had sailed," says Walters. "At that point, Colton Pitonyak was a thug."

Still, Colton was funny and bright, and he and Walters hit it off. From that point on, Walters sometimes hung with Colton's circle of friends. At times they talked, and Walters saw a glint in Colton's eye, an understanding about what the drugs could do for him. "Colton had a real entrepreneurial side," says Walters. "The profit margin selling drugs was ridiculously high. By the time I knew him, Colton realized how much money he could make and how it could pay for things he wanted. Colton was in."

That spring, Jennifer and Sharon talked two to three times a day, as they always did. Sharon was still paying for Jennifer's cell phone and car, but not her apartment or expenses. At first, Sharon thought little of the Colton references Jen made. But then, one day, something caught her off guard. "What did you say?"

"Colton went through one of those alcohol programs, Mom," Jennifer said. "It didn't work for him. He just came out worse than before."

"Who's this Colton?"

"He's a friend," Jennifer replied. "He goes to UT."

Sharon accepted Jennifer's explanation, and thought little more of it.

Amy Pack liked Colton, too. They met when she began dating one of his friends, and Amy, reed-thin with long blond hair, thought Colton was a rare kind of guy, the type who could be friends with a girl and not want anything from her. He let her borrow his car when hers was in repair. When she didn't want to go out, she called him and ended up at his apartment, watching television and smoking pot. "Chilling," she says. "He was my boy."

On those nights, Amy, who'd spent all twelve years through high school in parochial schools, swapped stories and laughed with Colton about the priests and teachers. Some nights, they headed to Sixth Street. The music in the clubs had a heavy hip-hop beat, and Colton loved to dance.

But there was that special thing about Colton, the thing so many young women seemed to latch on to. "He listened to me," Amy says. "He didn't turn me off."

When she was stressed, Amy found she could go to Colton to explain what was bothering her. "He didn't just say, 'I don't care,' and turn on a sports game," she says. "He talked to me, told me not to worry, that it would be all right. He was reassuring."

It was Colton who, at times, became the voice of reason in the group, like the night Amy fell asleep in a bedroom during a house party. A boy wandered in, didn't know she was there, and also fell asleep on the pile of coats. When they woke up and realized they were in the bedroom together, they laughed, but Amy's boyfriend was furious. He wanted to beat the kid up, and enlisted his bros to help. "Colton was the one who talked him out of it," says Amy.

Another night, one of the group contemplated suicide. It was Colton who talked him into living. "He stayed with me," says the guy. "He was a friend."

Amy met Jennifer at Colton's apartment, hanging out, "talking bullshit, like we did all the time," Amy says. At first, she didn't like Colton's friend Jen. The girl with the long red hair seemed almost too friendly. "I'd met girls like that, fake," says Amy. "But then I started to realize that Jennifer was just being herself. She really was that nice."

Sometimes Amy wondered about Colton, thinking about how he wasn't really the way he appeared, a thuggish drug dealer. Part of Colton was still the Ralph Lauren–dressed kid from a well-to-do family with Wall Street dreams. He had a gentle smile and a soft laugh, and "he was into being true to his friends, not being stupid."

One night, when they were "chilling," Colton pulled out an old VHS tape, from his bodybuilding days. He popped it into the player, and Amy saw him pose in a competition, muscles bulging, his body tanned and shaved. Bodybuilding wasn't something Amy thought particularly well of. It seemed a bit smarmy to her, but Colton was so proud of the way he looked, she started to think of it more in terms of his dedication, the work it had taken to get in shape to compete.

Of course, the Colton Amy knew looked markedly different. On the drugs, he'd become increasingly thin, his face strained, anxious. It wasn't just his looks that had changed from the fresh-faced kid from Little Rock. High and drunk, he screamed at others, even his friends, getting in their faces, threatening. At times Pitonyak and a friend ended up wrestling until the others pulled them apart. There were nights on Sixth Street when Colton's temper flared and he picked a fight with anyone available. "When he was messed up, Colton could be really aggressive. He gave people things, and wouldn't remember. Then he'd accuse them of stealing. Someone would have to hold him down," says a friend.

To Amy, a UT student majoring in communications, Pitonyak's demeanor wasn't unusual. "It was the typical post-adolescence thing," she says with a sardonic smile. "Sure Colton got angry, but the other guys acted the same way. None of it was a surprise. Mostly what they did was just walk around talking bullshit."

The one part of Colton that remained a mystery to Amy was Jennifer.

"I knew he adored her," says Amy. "But I didn't know if she was his girlfriend or what. I couldn't define their relationship. When I asked him, he didn't want to talk about it. All I knew was that he was crazy about her."

Eight

"Tell me about your friend, Colton," Sharon asked Jennifer one day on the telephone, when her middle daughter was in a particularly talkative mood.

"Well, he's from Arkansas," Jennifer said. "And he goes to UT."

"Is he a boyfriend?" Sharon asked.

"He'd like to be, but he's not," Jennifer said. "I don't think of him that way."

In hindsight, if Sharon had known what was truly going on with Jennifer that summer 2004, she would have gotten in the car, picked her up, and taken her somewhere to get help. But living 217 miles away in Corpus Christi, she had no way of judging for herself. Jennifer had all new friends, most people Sharon hadn't met, and a life separate from Sharon and Jim. If Sharon had interceded, would it have made a difference? Therapists and counselors say unless a patient wants help, there's little they can do. Jennifer was twenty years old, and Sharon was in a quandary familiar to tens of thousands of parents across America and the world every year, powerless to make an adult child do what she should.

On the phone, Jennifer sounded well, and when Sharon saw her, except for being thin, Jen looked the same, a beautiful, young girl without a care in the world. Sharon didn't know how the drugs were eating away at Jennifer, taking over her life, and making things she never would have done in the past seem all right.

That summer, Jennifer worked at Nordstrom's junior department as a clerk. She lived with Michaela Sloan, a friend who worked in the misses dress department. Like so many others, Michaela was drawn to Jennifer, and they quickly became close friends.

Much of the time, Jennifer went to Colton's apartment. For most drug users, money controls how much they can consume. Once Jennifer hooked up with Colton, she no longer had that cap on her desires. "Jennifer would disappear for days, over at Colton's," says Michaela. "I knew Colton was using and selling. He was heavily into the drugs. Once Jennifer got involved with him, he took her down with him."

Financed by his drug sales, Colton flashed a bankroll and gave Jennifer all the drugs she wanted, bought her food, took her out. They meshed well together. They both hungered after good times, never missing the opportunity to party. Jennifer enjoyed the frenzied and exciting Sixth Street scene and Fourth Street, where Austin had a burgeoning, more sophisticated bar scene. The Light Bar was one of her favorites. At the trendy, minimalist bar with a wall-size waterfall, the DJs played fusion or techno club music, layering recordings on top of each other, matching beats, for a heavy, hypnotic sound. She liked the lyrics strong, soulful, evoking emotions. As she had in high school, Jennifer spent the nights on the dance floor, her hands in the air, swaying her body, losing herself to the music, her enjoyment fueled, at least in part, by the drugs. Colton appeared to enjoy the club scene as much as she did, and they danced, drank, and indulged in his bounty of drugs. He took cocaine, Xanax, and a variety of drugs, while Jennifer took ecstasy and meth.

More than a decade earlier, Jennifer had been a little girl in love with *The Wizard of Oz*. Perhaps the drugs transported her to an Oz of sorts, much as the tornado had Dorothy. With the drugs, her nagging self-doubts were calmed, the world was more beautiful, there was nothing to fear, no one to disappoint, no future to fret over, only the immediate moment to enjoy.

Yet all wasn't well. Jennifer and Michaela once went to a house with Colton for a party. Drugs were scattered throughout, and people sat all over shooting up and snorting coke. "It was the scariest place. We couldn't believe we were there," says Michaela. "When we went out with him, Colton was touchy-feely with Jennifer. He rubbed her back and they talked. They were close. At times, he seemed possessive of her."

If Jennifer left, Colton got angry. He wanted to be with her. "But she didn't want to be with him, not that way," says Michaela. "If we went out together and didn't include him, he got upset because she was doing things with someone else."

"I don't believe Colton," Jennifer complained at such times. Even when Colton grew petulant, Jennifer never looked overly concerned, certainly not fearful.

"Jennifer was the type of girl who tried to look like she could take on the world. She never let on if she was worried or afraid," says Michaela. "And she had this really big heart. We'd fight, and she'd say, 'You're right. I'm sorry.' She couldn't tolerate it when people argued. She just couldn't fight or have anyone mad at her."

When Jennifer came home to Corpus, she appeared to be relatively well. She liked her job at Nordstrom's, and she talked about enrolling at the community college again in the fall and getting back on track. She earned extra money helping Sharon, and by the time Jennifer left, she'd worked around the house, organizing Sharon's closet, grouping the clothing by season and color, and lining up all Sharon's shoes in boxes marked on the outside. Sharon worried about Jen, but didn't know what to do. She didn't give her money for rent, but Jen's car was failing, with one breakdown after another. Not knowing about the drugs and the parties, Sharon thought Jennifer seemed to be doing better. So Sharon and Jim arranged for Jennifer to buy a new car, a 2003 black Saturn Ion. It was her first car in her name, her first car loan, and Jennifer was proud.

When Sharon took her shopping for clothes, Jen appeared grateful and happy, and Sharon hoped yet again that perhaps her middle daughter was finding her way. "Now, leave here with that new car and your new clothes and do something," Sharon told her. "Prove to me that you're serious, and I'll send you to any school you want to go to."

"I will, Mom," Jennifer said hugging her. "I love you. I'll make you proud."

"I love you, too," Sharon said. "And I am proud of you, Jennifer. I always have been."

Jennifer drove off in her new car bound for Austin, and Sharon hoped her daughter meant it, that she'd refocus her life. Sadly, as they had so many times before, Jennifer's good intentions evaporated in her self-doubts and now her growing reliance on drugs. Before long, she'd lost the Nordstrom's job, and Sharon ended up making the payments on the black Saturn Ion.

Along with Michaela, there were other like-minded girls Jennifer met at parties and at clubs. Friends introduced them, or they simply started talking and never stopped. Eva Taylor spent much of the summer with Jennifer, doing drugs, mainly meth, pot, ecstasy, coke, or mushrooms. They wore little dresses with straps or T-shirts, shorts, and platform sandals, all the rage, and went to the bars, where middle-aged men bought them drinks and they danced long into the night.

"Everyone was doing meth that summer," says another of the girls Jen hung with. "It was like the drug of choice. Smart people with good jobs were doing it. It didn't seem like a dirty drug. So many people were doing it that meth felt like drinking a cup of coffee."

Within days of hooking up with a new friend, Jennifer introduced her to Colton. "She didn't like going to his apartment alone, because he'd try to keep her there. It made her uneasy," says Eva.

Before they arrived, Jennifer explained to her friends that they couldn't get drugs unless they stayed and used them with Colton. He was more than willing to supply whatever they wanted, but his recompense was time with Jennifer. It would have been easy to believe that Jennifer used Colton simply for free drugs, but it wasn't true. Eva and others noticed that Jennifer and Colton had a special connection. They laughed and talked, finishing each other's sentences. "They were cute together, silly, giggling and stuff," says Eva. "They were rolling around on the floor, hysterical, telling jokes only the other one got. Jennifer liked going there, being with Colton."

The drapes pulled in the apartment, Colton sat in the dark, more often than not already high when they arrived. One night, Eva watched as Jennifer and Colton were on the floor together, Jennifer acting like her family nickname, Frog, leaping about on all fours, and Colton roaring and acting like a lion.

The apartment in disarray, Colton turned on the dishwasher. Out of dishwasher detergent, he squirted liquid dish detergent inside. It overflowed into the kitchen, bubbles everywhere, and Jennifer and Colton giggled like grade school kids. After a while, Jennifer spent more and more time at Colton's. "It got to the point where she couldn't get friends to go with her, and she went alone," says Eva. "She didn't like doing that, but she never seemed to be afraid of him."

One day, Eva and Jennifer went driving with Colton, and police pulled them over and searched his 1994 white Toyota Avalon. Nothing was found, and Colton snickered all the way home, saying the police were "too stupid" to know where to look. Back at the apartment, Colton showed Jen and Eva his bodybuilding video, and Eva glanced from the muscular, fit, bright-eyed teenager on the screen to the drawn young man with the glazed and sagging eyes sitting on the couch. On other days, heavy rap music with gritty talk of sex and guns filled the apartment or a gangster movie flickered on the television. "Did you see the scene in *The Godfather* when . . ." Colton said, eager to talk about gory scenes.

On another night, Jennifer went to a meth house with Nicole Ford, a friend she'd met at one of the clubs. It was on such nights that the reality of what she'd become involved in hit Jennifer. The two pretty young women looked around the room at the shrunken faces of the other drug users as the lighted rose pipe, a glass cylinder containing the melting crystal meth heated by a lighter or a flame, was passed from one to the other, each sucking in the fumes. Afterward, they talked. "We were worried about each other," says Nicole. "Jen would say, 'Do we look like they do? Is that who we are?'"

At times, Jennifer told Nicole that she felt as if she were being chased by a devil, a demon. The need for drugs stalked her and wouldn't let her go. "In the beginning, meth doesn't seem like a dirty drug. It's fun, gives you energy, and you lose weight. But the withdrawal is awful," says Nicole. "You feel like your skin is on fire. A meth house is like walking through the gates of hell."

"What are we doing?" Jennifer asked.

"I don't know," Nicole replied.

"This drug is like Satan," Jen said. "It won't let us go."

Later, Nicole looked back on those months she spent with Jennifer. "We'd try to quit, and we would for a while," she says, her eyes serious and sad. "But then one of us started using again and pretty soon we were both doing it. There were months where we planned our days around getting high. I felt like I'd lost my soul."

Meanwhile, Colton's behavior was growing increasingly odd. When Justin went to see him that summer, Colton stared out the apartment window, as if obsessed that someone was after him. "He hung out with a lot of unsavory types," says Justin. "Scary people, the ones he bought the drugs from, some of the people he sold to. And he thought the police were watching the apartment. He was paranoid."

When someone knocked on the door, Colton checked through the peephole before letting him in. "Colton looked worse and worse. He kept losing weight, and he was thin and covered with sweat," says another friend. "Colton had changed."

Large amounts of cash funneled into Colton's small apartment. One night, a UT student, a sophomore named Larry, called to say he and his friends wanted cocaine. Colton had started selling to him six months earlier, after he'd approached Larry and a group of his friends outside a UT apartment building. Over that time, Larry paid Colton thousands to feed his growing habit. Without Larry asking, Colton fronted him the coke, and then showed up unannounced, threatening and demanding payment, sending Larry scrambling for the funds. This night, Larry was already $300 in arrears, but Colton sounded friendly on the telephone, so Larry wasn't worried.

"Sure, come over," Colton said.

When Larry arrived, he walked past a cluster of Colton's friends in the living room, bunched around a coffee table covered in money. Colton invited Larry to the kitchen to do a line of coke. When Larry bent down, without warning, Colton clubbed him in the face. Blood streamed from Larry's broken nose, but Colton's friends watched and did nothing.

"He said he was going to do that when you called," one kid said.

Larry went outside and peeled off his shirt to mop up the blood, as Colton followed. He didn't apologize but talked calmly, as if nothing unusual had just happened. "You need to pay me, dude," he said.

Violence was becoming a growing part of Colton Pitonyak's life.

One night, Colton crashed at Justin's apartment. When he got up the next morning, Justin walked into the living room and found Colton asleep on the couch. On the floor beside him lay a gun. Justin did a double take. At Colton's apartment, he had paintball guns that looked like assault weapons. They acted like kids at times, chasing each other around and shooting the guns. But when Justin inspected this gun more closely, he realized it was real, "a revolver like the kind cops use."

Months earlier, Justin had talked with Colton after he'd come to the apartment with a knife. "I instituted a no-weapons policy. I didn't want him bringing that kind of stuff to my place," says Justin. Obviously, Colton wasn't concerned about violating Justin's rules. Not knowing what to do, Justin decided to say nothing: "This time I just told myself, I'm going to get my books and leave."

Colton signed up for two classes in summer school 2004. He finished one and dropped the other. Later, even he would say that "my paranoia was out of control." He was on co-caine, booze, Xanax, and Ambien.

On July 4, 2004, around nine that morning, Dustin Do-bervich, a UT math major, sat in his first-floor apartment, number 104, at the computer, next to the living room window that looked out on an open passageway. He'd lived next to Colton Pitonyak for months and heard little from him. Around the complex, he'd seen Pitonyak coming and going, sometimes saying, "Hey," and nodding as he walked past. He'd never had a conversation with him, and Colton, by college standards, was a relatively quiet neighbor. Lots of people came and went, music played, but nothing excessive, and Dobervich thought little about him.

That day through the slats in the blinds, Dobervich saw someone standing in the passageway outside his window, men wearing tennis shoes and blue jeans. He heard arguing. "I figured it was a bunch of guys wrestling around, joking," he says. "I didn't think anything of it."

Voices rose, and suddenly someone pushed someone else into Dobervich's window. It crashed, shattering into shards of glass that showered down, some into the apartment. Do-bervich jumped back, and outside the figures scattered. By the time Dobervich rushed outside, everyone was gone.

Angry about the mess and the lack of a living room window, Dobervich called the building manager. He wasn't in, and Dobervich left a message and decided to start cleaning up. He'd just begun when someone knocked on his door. He opened it and found Austin PD officers K. Covington and Corporal K. Yates.

"I was just about to call you guys," Dobervich said.

"So, you didn't call? Who did?" one of the officers asked.

"I have no idea," Dobervich said.

Yates and Covington looked surprised. Someone had called 911 asking for help and whispering the address to apartment 105, next door to Dobervich. Covington had already knocked on 105 without an answer, and the dispatcher had called the telephone number back, but no one answered. When they saw the broken glass, the officers assumed dispatch had gotten the number wrong, and it was 104. They'd also noticed that the fire extinguisher between 104 and 105 was broken and hanging from the box. Now Dobervich was telling them that he hadn't placed the 911 call.

Dobervich watched as the officers again knocked on the door to apartment 105. Again: no answer. With that, Covington and Yates turned and left, intending to write a report and head to the next call.

A brief time later, Covington heard Yates called back to 2810 Salado, the Camino Real apartments, where Dobervich and Pitonyak lived. Another whispered 911 call from apartment 105. When Covington arrived, Yates was already there. He knocked and no one responded, and the officers wondered if someone hurt or injured could be inside, unable to get to the door. When Sergeant R. Pulliam arrived on the scene, he decided the 911 calls gave them probable cause to go in through the window.

Yates worked at prying the window open, as Covington knocked again, shouting, "Police. Open up."

Suddenly, the deadbolt lock slid back, and the door eased open. Colton Pitonyak stood inside holding his cell phone in his hand, his eyes bloodshot and glassy and his speech slurred. The officers smelled booze.

"Did you call 911?" Covington asked.

"No," he said.

Covington looked inside and saw white powder on a glass mirror on the coffee table.

"Do you live here alone?" Covington asked.

"Yeah," Pitonyak said.

With that, they asked if they could walk inside. Pitonyak motioned, and they entered. One of the officers found a green baggie on the table with more of the white powder.

"I had friends over last night," Colton said. "It must belong to one of them."

The officers searched the apartment and found more baggies, these containing Xanax and 10 mg Ambien pills.

"Have you got a prescription for these?" Covington asked.

"No," Pitonyak replied.

"How'd that window get broken in the apartment next door?" Covington asked.

Launching into an explanation, Colton said two young white guys were "messing around" outside, and when he walked outside to leave his apartment, they started a fight. "But I don't know how the window was broken," he said.

Curious, Covington asked dispatch to call the phone number that called 911, the one that had requested help at Colton's address. Pitonyak's cell phone rang, Covington answered, and it was the dispatch operator. "Why didn't you answer your cell phone?"

Pitonyak shrugged.

"Why did you call the police?"

"Someone was knocking on my door trying to get in," he said.

"Well, you're under arrest," Covington said. With that, the officer turned Colton around, handcuffed him, and walked him from the apartment. Dobervich was outside as they walked by, sweeping up glass. A short time later, two men in their twenties arrived, looking for Colton.

"What happened?" one asked Dobervich, looking at the broken window.

"Someone broke it," Dobervich said, as the other man knocked on the door to Colton's apartment. "He's not there. The police handcuffed him and took him way."

Three days later, on the seventh, Colton was arraigned in the Travis County Courthouse on a felony charge, possession of a controlled substance, with a potential punishment of up to two years in prison. By then the white powdery substance confiscated from his apartment had tested positive for cocaine. Later, he'd say that he didn't initially call to tell his parents in Little Rock. The DUI had been seven months earlier. Perhaps he feared upsetting them more, or thought that if they knew, they'd take away his financial support. Whatever the reason, he made bail himself and hired a lawyer, David Hughes.

Colton's case was assigned to the 147th District Court, presided over by Judge Wilford Flowers, who had a reputation in Travis County for being fair but tough. A courtroom veteran, Flowers is a dignified man who'd been one of the first African-American judges in the county, and he ran his courtroom with a sense of decorum.

From that point on, Colton's favorite topic of conversation with his "bros" was legal strategy, specifically, how Hughes would get the charges either dismissed or dropped down to a misdemeanor. Pitonyak's friends got a blow-by-blow account as the lawyer filed a motion to suppress the evidence found in Colton's apartment that day, claiming it was an illegal search. If Hughes succeeded, none of the drugs found could be used against Pitonyak.

Meanwhile, Colton seemed anything but repentant.

Sometime later, a UT student was at a party when Colton showed up looking disheveled and high. Something happened that night that the UT student never forgot. He stood near Colton and heard him bragging about how his lawyer was going to get him off, and then expounding on what kinds of guns were the most accurate and which bullets the most deadly. Suddenly, without warning, Colton hurled a knife across the room. The blade cut into the wall with a loud thunk, and the party grew instantly quiet.

With the startled eyes of everyone in the room on him, Colton Pitonyak, the erstwhile scholarship student and once eager altar boy, now turned drug-dealing gangster wannabe, smiled.

Nine

Weeks after his arrest, Colton moved into a rented second-floor unit at the Orange Tree, a condominium project in the heart of UT's West Campus, surrounded by imposing frat and sorority houses, including gracious old colonials with manicured yards. The priciest addresses in the university area, West Campus had panache among UT students. While a one-bedroom could be found for $600 a month or less on other parts of the campus, on West Campus most went for more than a thousand.

The Orange Tree, too, was of note. A quality development, it was a good investment, and some parents bought the units, then sold them when their sons or daughters graduated, often making enough appreciation in the four or five years to recoup all or much of the money they'd laid out for their children's educations. The parking garage took up most of the first floor of the complex, with the majority of the condos built above it on the second and third floors. An open second-floor courtyard ran nearly the length of the complex, with a swimming pool in the center, the scene of all-night weekend parties.

From the Orange Tree, the campus was a brisk five-minute walk, and a sign posted on the garage barred interlopers. Near-campus parking spaces were at a premium, and less fortunate students fought the daily annoyance of finding a close-in spot. The Orange Tree, with its parking lot, was a rarefied setting by UT student housing standards.

That August, as every August for decades before it, freshmen arrived at the university, both apprehensive and excited about their futures. Some pledged at the houses surrounding the Orange Tree, and the sound of young women leading sorority cheers and chants filled the streets, while at the frat houses, young men milled about discussing plans for the fall and what houses they would pledge. Just three years earlier, Colton Pitonyak had been such a bright-eyed student.

That summer, with classes starting at the end of the month, the glassy-eyed, unkempt Colton moved his belongings into Orange Tree unit number 88, a small studio. It should have been his senior year, but he'd earned only enough credits to be a sophomore.

Unit number 88 had little room to spare. Colton tucked a bed into the alcove to the left of the door, between a glass block divider and a hallway that led to the vanity and the bathroom areas. To the right, just inside the red door marked with gold numbers, was a small living room area. Colton positioned his television next to the fireplace and across from a dark cloth couch and a coffee table. Through a doorway to the left of the television was the kitchen, dark wood cabinets lining the walls and the dishwasher visible from the living room. To keep out prying eyes, he hung heavy curtains over the three living room windows, which looked out onto the courtyard.

Outside, the staircase to the apartment above formed a roof over his front door, shading it from the often blistering Texas sun. From the closest stairway, the UT campus was easily visible and, surging above a lush green carpet formed by the leafy crowns of gnarled live oaks, the school's famous clock tower. When the carillon rang, it echoed through the Orange Tree's courtyard.

That month, Jim and Sharon drove to Austin to see Jennifer. Sharon was apprehensive about the meeting. She was disappointed in the way Jennifer was living her life and intended to tell her. It was frustrating talking to Jennifer and getting promises that never materialized.

"Well, I didn't find a job," Jennifer said, when they sat down at a Fuddruckers hamburger restaurant.

Jim had stopped on the way and picked up a copy of the *Austin American Statesman* and two free newspapers with employment ads. "If you're not going to go to school, get a good full-time job with benefits, Jennifer," he said. "Look at all these jobs."

They went through ones he'd circled, but Jennifer had reasons that none of them would work: They were too far or didn't interest her. She wanted something with more pay or better benefits.

In the past, Jim had always been the one reassuring Sharon, cautioning her not to get upset; Jennifer was just going through a stage. This time, even he was angry. "You know, Jennifer, this is bullshit," he said, and he got up and left, going outside to smoke.

"Well, great. He's mad at me," Jen said, cocky.

Sharon tried to talk to her, but Jennifer was evasive and revealed little about what was going on in her life. They argued and Jennifer cried, and the emotional distance between them loomed so vast, it saddened Sharon. "Forget school," she advised. "Get a job until you figure out what you want to do. Don't even waste any more money registering for classes."

"Well, I can't do anything to make you happy, Mother," Jennifer said.

"Yes you can, but that's not what's important here. It's about you building a good future," Sharon said, meaning it. "I love you, Jennifer. I just want you to do well in life."

Angry, Jennifer stormed off, and when she drove from the parking lot, she was still sobbing.

All the way home to Corpus, Jim and Sharon cried. "The drugs were ruining Jennifer's life," Sharon says. "We knew it, but we felt helpless. We tried, but she just wasn't listening."

From Corpus Christi, Sharon continued to call Jennifer daily. At times, Sharon knew Jennifer was upset with herself, like the day she recounted running into a high school friend who was graduating from college in a year.

"When are you graduating?" the girl asked Jennifer.

"I'm not," she replied.

"I felt like a dummy," Jennifer told Sharon.

"Well, Jennifer, you should feel like a dummy," Sharon said. "You're screwing this all up. But the good news is that you can turn it around anytime you want."

Always her daughter's loyal supporter, Sharon urged Jennifer to make changes. As she'd done so many times before, Jennifer insisted she would but then did nothing. As always, before Sharon hung up, she said, "I love you."

"Colton got arrested," Jennifer said on the telephone to Sharon, one day. Then she told her about the possession charge. "His attorney wants him to go into rehab."

Hughes was trying to negotiate a deal for Pitonyak, the same type of plea bargain that had dropped his DUI down to a misdemeanor. So far, the prosecutor resisted. That fall, Colton talked constantly about his drug case, analyzing his attorney's strategy and bantering about what Judge Flowers might rule.

Meanwhile, Jennifer continued to be at loose ends. She didn't have a job and partied so often that Michaela kicked her out, and before long, Amy realized that Jennifer was living in Colton's apartment. Amy thought that, too, was odd. She couldn't understand their relationship, except that she sensed Colton wanted more from Jennifer than just friendship.

That fall, Jennifer stayed at Colton's for little more than a month. Why she left was something she never truly explained, except to say that something had frightened her. One night after she moved out, she was at a friend's apartment listening to music and talking to Justin Walters. When he asked why she'd left Colton's, she said only, "I didn't feel safe there."

Taking it at face value, Justin assumed Jennifer didn't like all the students dropping in to buy drugs or the suppliers Colton dealt with, underworld types. "Colton complained that his parents weren't sending him the money they used to, and he'd started doing bigger deals. He wasn't nickel-and-diming it anymore. The higher-ups in the drug chain are not nice people," says Justin. "The higher up, the more unsavory."

That night when Justin and Jennifer talked, Colton showed up, looking for Jennifer. "I want to talk in private," Colton said to her. To Justin, Pitonyak looked strung out.

"No, no, no," Jennifer said, visibly frightened.

"What if Justin is in the room with us?" Colton asked.

Jennifer thought about that for a while, and then agreed.

Later Justin realized the conversation lasted only twenty minutes or so, but it felt like he, Colton, and Jennifer were in the bedroom together for more than an hour. Over and over, Colton told Jennifer, "I love you. We belong together."

"I don't feel that way about you, Colton," she said.

As he watched, Justin sensed that Colton had thought long and hard about what he would say to Jennifer, planning how he would convince her to be with him. Colton looked surprised at first and then angry that his profession of love didn't propel Jennifer into his arms with a breathless "I love you, too."

As he continued to plead, Colton grew progressively angrier, his voice louder, his face flushed, and his words more insistent. "I love you," he said. "Why shouldn't we be together?"

"No," she said. "It's not going to happen. I don't love you that way. We're friends and that's all."

"I love you, and I want to be with you," he pleaded. "Please, let's . . ."

"You scare me, Colton," Jennifer said with an air of finality. "I can't be with you."

"You're scared I might have a knife?" he said. With that, Colton pulled out a knife, a black-handled folding knife, the type used in hunting. He popped the blade open and locked it in place.

"Oh, my God," Jennifer screamed, running into the nearby closet.

Colton rushed toward her, but Justin, taller and heavier, held him back, inserting his bulk between Colton and the open closet. All the while, Justin talked calmly, trying to cool the situation down. Since they'd met, Justin had often been able to placate Colton when their other friends couldn't, on nights when Colton seemed intent on starting brawls.

"Put the knife away, Colton," he ordered. "We talked about this before. I don't want weapons around. It's dangerous."

At first Colton pushed harder toward Jennifer, and Justin thought that his friend intended to enter the closet and loom over her, frightening her. Justin never considered that Colton could actually hurt Jennifer. Colton was threatening at times, out of control, but Justin had never seen him hit a woman. Despite Colton's gangster demeanor, Justin believed that on some level his friend was still the funny, bright college kid. The old Colton just didn't emerge as often as he used to, now that the drug-dealing Colton was in control.

Finally, Colton put the knife away, and, while Jennifer hid, Justin talked him out the door. Once Colton was gone, Justin consoled a frightened Jennifer. Perhaps, if she'd been thinking clearly, Jennifer would have ended the relationship then, excising Colton Pitonyak from her life. But the tie that bound them was strong.

"Jennifer never stayed mad at anyone," says Justin. "I don't think she ever believed in her heart that Colton could hurt her."

Not long after, Jennifer began telling friends that she and Colton had talked, and that while he wanted more from her, he agreed they would only be friends. Perhaps she truly believed that he was able to turn off his deep feelings for her, bury them and go on.

That October, Eddie Pitonyak was in Austin, and Colton introduced him to Jennifer. Later Bridget would say that she and Eddie heard Jennifer's name often from Colton that year. In fact, she was the only girl he'd mentioned to them since moving to Austin. Eddie gave Colton his credit card that night to take Jennifer out for dinner. By then, Eddie and Bridget knew about Colton's arrest and the charges pending against him. They must have felt much like Sharon Cave: that they had little control over their son and feared where his life was taking him. How they must have agonized over what was happening to him. Colton had been a star, a son to be proud of, but now they faced a battle to simply keep him out of prison.

On his attorney's advice, that November, Colton committed himself to La Hacienda, a posh drug and alcohol treatment center in Hunt, Texas, not far from Austin in the bucolic landscape of rolling and jagged hills called the Texas Hill Country. The thirty-two-acre campus on the Guadalupe River had walking paths and a waterfall. The facility offered a full medical and counseling staff for individual and group therapy, and prayer and meditation sessions in an open-air, A-frame chapel on the river, called Serenity Hill.

The Pitonyaks undoubtedly hoped the facility and its well-trained staff would repair the damage the drugs and alcohol had done to their son. Certainly, La Hacienda had everything Colton needed if he were so inclined. Later Colton would say, however, that his stay there was a performance, put on for the benefit of Judge Flowers and the prosecutor, to convince them to lower the charges; Colton Pitonyak had no desire to change.

With his superior intellect, Colton had no problem saying what he needed to in order to successfully complete the rehab program. Once released and back in Austin, Colton drank and used drugs with all the determination he had before the weeks of therapy. La Hacienda hadn't even slowed him down. "His schedule and his consumption would have exhausted most mortal beings," says a friend.

Meanwhile, Jennifer was still floating around, staying with one friend, then another. Just before the holidays, she met Katrina deVilleneuve, a pretty, compact young woman, with smoky dark eyes and a strong, supple body, who worked as a dancer at an Austin topless bar. A few years older than Jennifer, Katrina came from a tumultuous childhood. Her mother died young of cirrhosis of the liver, after years of alcohol and drug abuse. Her only brother died in a car accident when Katrina was sixteen, and her father of a brain aneurysm when she was twenty-one.

A friend brought Jennifer to a party at Katrina's house, and introduced the two women. When Katrina learned Jen had nowhere to stay, Katrina invited her to move into her two-bedroom duplex, a cluttered, funky place with a pink living room and electric-blue bedroom. Katrina had a spare bedroom, and Jennifer quickly agreed.

The duplex was filled with the trappings of Katrina's trade, filmy lingerie and stiletto heels, wigs, and makeup. She'd started dancing two years earlier, when a friend told her she could make $100 a night. She didn't believe her, but tried and it was true. Early on, her father objected and she quit, but he died not long after, and she went back to the clubs. She'd worked at most of the topless venues in Austin: Joy, Sugars, and Maximus. The money wasn't the only attraction, although it was more than Katrina could make anywhere else. "I like the attention," she says. "I like being told I'm pretty. I get to dress up and flirt. It's like you're getting dressed up to go out, but you get paid for it."

When she met Jen, Katrina danced five nights a week at Ecstasy, a club off Springdale, and was considering massage school, although she hadn't yet applied. "I'm not going to do this forever," she said. "I'm not going to be a forty-year-old dancer."

While Katrina went to work, Jennifer watched television, listened to music, and cleaned the duplex, organizing Katrina's closet, as she'd done for Sharon the year before, putting Katrina's costumes in order and boxing up and color-coding her shoes. In the wee hours of the morning, Katrina made her way home. At times, they stayed up and talked, took ecstasy or smoked pot. Jennifer told her about Charlie and his drinking. "I wish you could have had my dad," Katrina told her. She adored her father and kept a framed photo of him on top of the television. "He was a great guy."

At times, Jennifer cried. There was something wrong, an emptiness that Katrina believed Jennifer couldn't find a way to fill. Jennifer talked of disappointing her family, and Katrina held her to comfort her. "I think she was trying to pull it together," says Katrina. "She talked so much about wanting to make her family proud."

Off and on, Jennifer circulated over to Colton's. She told Katrina about the night with the knife, and Katrina warned Jennifer never to see him again. "Colton's okay if he's not high," Jen said. "I just make sure I'm not alone with him."

Yet more often that not, she voiced a growing frustration with him. One night in particular, Jennifer returned from Colton's upset. "I can't fix him," she said, crying. "I try, but I can't."

"Jennifer, you can't fix anyone but yourself," Katrina, older than her years, replied. "Just concentrate on you."

If she tried, Jennifer never found a way to turn her concern for Colton off.

One evening, she stopped at Colton's with a foil-covered plate of food she'd made for him, on her way to listen to music with friends on Sixth Street. Off and on, she cut hair for people, a knack she'd developed in high school. Whenever Colton asked her to, Jennifer stopped at the Orange Tree with her scissors and a comb, to cut his.

That winter 2004 was unusually cold, and one night during Christmas break, Amy, Jennifer, and Colton were at his apartment in the Orange Tree, snorting cocaine and smoking pot, watching television and talking. Temperatures had been near freezing at night for weeks. "It's fucking cold out," Colton said, looking out the windows. "Come on. Let's jump in the pool."

Colton tore his clothes off and sprinted naked through the door into the frigid courtyard toward the swimming pool. Laughing hysterically, the others followed, discarding their clothes on the way, jumping into the icy water. "It was wild," Amy says. "A supreme college moment."

When he went home to Little Rock, Colton ran into his old high school friends, Ben Smith and Louis Petit. "He was out of it," Ben would say later. "It didn't matter if it was ten in the morning, Colton was high."

"He wasn't the Colton I knew," says Petit. "Colton had definitely changed."

The hearing that would determine if the evidence found in Colton's apartment could be used against him in court came up that December. As important as it was, he didn't show up. Colton's attorney, David Hughes, went to the Orange Tree, but Colton didn't answer the door to unit 88. The Pitonyaks instructed Hughes to go in through a window, if necessary, to get their son and take him to court. As instructed, Hughes pried open the unlocked window and began to climb in, just as Colton, asleep on the couch directly below the window, woke up and rolled onto the floor.

On the trip to the courthouse, Colton had little to say.

Before Judge Flowers that day, Hughes argued that the evidence, namely the drugs found in Colton's apartment, should not be admissible. The drugs, the pills, and the statements Colton made should all be excluded because it was the poisoned product of an illegal search. Police had no right to enter unit 88, Hughes argued, and their actions violated the Fourth, Fifth, Ninth, and Fourteenth Amendments.

Judge Flowers denied the motion, and Colton Pitonyak faced a trial and, if he lost, up to two years in prison.

When she drove to Corpus that Christmas, Jennifer dropped in at the high school in Sinton to see Clayton. She arrived during his journalism class. Afterward, all his friends asked about her, calling her pretty and smart. Clayton was filled with pride.

Yet that winter, the entire Cave-Sedwick family had exhausted all patience with Jennifer. None of them knew what to do. Hailey wondered if Jennifer was pulling away from the family simply to continue partying. But when Hailey talked to Jennifer, she came away with the opinion that Jennifer's troubles ran deeper. "Jennifer didn't think she had what it took to make something of herself," says Hailey. "She kept saying, 'I can't do it. I can't do it.' Failure was a self-fulfilling prophecy."

"You can do it, Jennifer," Hailey argued. "We all know you can."

There were few illusions when it came to Jennifer and drugs. The whole family knew she was using them, something she admitted but couldn't seem to fix. "Don't do it, Clayton," she warned when her brother said someone had given him pot. "It was a bad choice I made, and now I don't know how to stop."

The holidays were emotional and difficult. At one point, Jennifer said to Sharon, "It's hard, Mom."

"What's hard?"

"Being with all of you, because you're just condemning me," she said.

Sharon took her middle daughter by the arm and escorted her into the bathroom, then stood with her in front of the mirror. "Look at yourself, Jennifer. Really take a good look," Sharon said. "This is what the world sees. This is who you are. You're pretty and you're smart. You're kind and good inside. You have so much potential."

"I don't feel like I can. It's just too hard," Jennifer said.

"You have to pull your life together. That's where it's at, kiddo," Sharon said. "And you're the only one who can do it. It's only going to get harder if you don't turn yourself around."

Sharon again brought up a drug rehab program.

"Colton went to rehab. It didn't do him any good," Jennifer said. "He's using more drugs than when he went in. I don't know why he went in the first place."

That winter, Sharon considered keeping Jennifer at home in Corpus, but decided it wouldn't help unless she committed to change. Of them all, Lauren said little. Jennifer was important to her, an almost twin, and she wanted her back in her life, even if to do that, "I had to erase what I thought she was doing."

With all the strife over that Christmas break, there were the happy times. Jennifer played with her eight-year-old cousin, Hannah, and Sharon loved to watch. Jennifer had always been so good with children, and the little girl loved her. Jennifer connected easily with the little girl and had endless patience, pulling out crayons and paper and glue and scissors, sleeping together on an air mattress.

Snow fell on Corpus Christi that Christmas Eve, a minor miracle since snow so rarely falls in South Texas. Afterward, the family gathered outside the house, and Jim used a timer to snap a photo. In it, Jennifer had a wide smile on her face, and no one looking at the photo who didn't know better could have imagined the uproar in her young life.

Outside on the patio, eating pie and smoking after Christmas dinner, Jim and Jennifer talked. "I'm going to do better, Jim," Jennifer said. "I really am."

"Jen, don't do this to me," he told her, hurt by all the frustration he and Sharon both felt with her. "Don't lie to me. Don't tell me you're going to go to school when you're not. Be straight with me. You need to be careful about the path you're on. It's not good for you."

"I'll straighten out," she said. "You'll see."

A week or so later, after New Year's, Jennifer called Sharon. Jennifer had lost her cell phone, and Sharon, still determined to do the tough love approach, refused to replace it.

"Where are you calling from?" Sharon asked.

"Scott's apartment," Jennifer said. "I've moved in."

Sharon had never heard Scott's name before. She wasn't sure who he was. "Who's Scott?" she asked.

"A guy I met. I really like him," Jennifer answered.

"Is that a good idea?" Sharon asked. "Should you be moving in with him so quickly?"

"I think it is," Jennifer said. "I really do."

This time, Jennifer was right. Scott Engle gave her an opportunity to become the person she said she wanted to be, one her family could be proud of. For the brief time they were together, Jennifer had a family of her own, experiencing the joy of raising a child and the devotion of a man she loved.

Ten

Their paths had crossed the previous November at a party. Scott Engle met Jennifer at a mutual friend's apartment. That afternoon, Jennifer was on a casual date with Scott's friend Shaggy, nicknamed after the *Scooby Doo* character. Shaggy hid Jen's car keys to prevent her from leaving, and she needed a ride. Scott offered her one, but instead they spent the evening talking. The Christmas holidays were busy, Scott traveling to Kansas to see family, and somehow he didn't see her again. But he didn't stop thinking about her. He told Katrina about the pretty redhead he'd met. Then, in January, Scott went to Katrina's duplex for a party, looked across the room, and Jennifer smiled back at him.

"That's the girl. That's Jennifer," Scott told Katrina. "The one I told you about."

"That's *your* Jennifer?" Katrina said. "She's my friend. She's been staying with me."

From that moment on, Scott and Jennifer were inseparable. "We just had that fire between us," he says.

In ways Scott, four years older than Jennifer, looked a little like Colton, dark-haired and not overly tall, yet Colton was drug-thin and scruffy. Scott was muscular, strong, with playful brown eyes under bushy dark brows. He had the body and the puffy face of a fighter, but a warm manner. "Scott likes people. Really likes them," says Katrina. "That's one of the first things you notice about him, that he's genuine and that he cares."

"I'm the person my friends call to talk to when they have a problem," says Scott. "I've been there."

In her own way, Jennifer was like that, too. On the outside, she was flinty and determined, if underneath the self-doubts gnawed at her. She gave advice to others, and then didn't follow it herself. Perhaps she saw in Scott someone who could help her become the woman she wanted to be, independent and strong.

A single dad raising a four-year-old, Madyson, Scott worked evenings as a waiter in an upscale, downtown Austin restaurant, but dreamed of playing a synthesizer in a band. Instead, he sang karaoke at a bar not far from his north Austin apartment, his favorite song: Johnny Cash's "Walk the Line." On his arms were tattoos representing the Chinese symbols for father, love, eternity, and daughter, along with a celestial cross.

Born in Wichita, Kansas, Scott migrated to Texas along with his parents when he was nineteen. Madyson was born the following year to a girlfriend. Since he was the solid one with a job, he took the baby to care for. His biological father had never been part of his life, and he wanted to be there for his little girl. At twenty-five, Scott Engle was a combination of rebel and concerned father, party boy and dedicated dad.

It wasn't a fluke that he dropped in at Katrina's party that night. They'd been close friends for more than a year. At one time, their relationship had been intimate, but they'd moved beyond that, building a bond that Katrina describes as more like "a brother and sister." When Scott and Jennifer got together, she pulled away from Katrina. "It was awkward. I think Jen wanted Scott to herself. That Scott and I were close bothered her," says Katrina. "Jennifer was crazy about Scott. They drew each other in like magnets."

"I want you to meet Scott," Jennifer told a friend in early 2005. "He's amazing, and we're really kindred spirits."

It was clear to see that for the first time since her split with Mark, Jennifer was truly in love. The same week their paths crossed at Katrina's party, Jennifer began staying at Scott's two-bedroom apartment, and soon she moved in her clothes and few possessions from Katrina's. During the day,

Jennifer cooked and cleaned and played with the little girl, caring for her while Scott worked, teaching her the alphabet and her numbers, how to write her name. Jennifer read to Madyson, a brown-haired sprite with enormous round eyes. Before long, Jennifer and Scott talked about building a life together, one where Jennifer would raise Madyson as her own, and the cute little girl with the turned-up nose began calling Jennifer Mom.

The apartment, in a large complex called Brook Meadow Village, in north Austin, was far from the university. Working people, including young families and empty nesters, lived in the gray cedar and tan brick three-story complex, with its open stairways. The developer built around the trees, and old oaks and pines graced the well-kept grounds, where Scott, Jennifer, and Madyson shared their second-floor apartment, number 633, with a mother cat and her five kittens.

"With her red hair, Jennifer stood out in a crowd. But her blue eyes really caught my attention," Scott says. "She was all girl, feminine, and beautiful. And when she smiled, it just felt like sunshine. Once people met her, they felt like they'd known her forever."

Scott knew about Jennifer's drug use, and he understood. As a teenager, he'd had experiences of his own, an LSD and cocaine habit that escalated shortly after he got to Austin. One night, he'd snorted so many lines of coke on top of LSD that when he came down off the high, he realized he could have died. That night, he'd had an out-of-body experience, and saw himself lying in a coffin. "Wild stuff," Scott says, shaking his head. "After that, I was more careful."

From that day forward, Scott eased off the drugs, using only rarely and then small amounts, but he believed the acid had changed him, expanded his mind. He studied sixties' guru Timothy Leary and his turn-on, tune-in, drop-out theories on LSD and expanding consciousness, and believed that he, too, had connected with the universe.

Drugs had made Scott Engle a spiritual man.

Scott talked to Jennifer about being herself, not the

person others wanted her to be, and about the importance of living her life doing what she said she would do, not making promises and then backing away. "Scott was a dad, and he acted more like one to Jen," says a friend. "He was steady, and he was there for her."

With Scott, Jennifer changed. With his encouragement and support, she eased off the drugs, including the meth. "I didn't want drugs in the house, around Madyson," Scott says. For someone who'd professed the inability to quit in the past, Jennifer appeared to let go rather easily. She told friends one way she stopped was to cool her close ties with Colton. "Our relationship was all about drugs," she said. "It's all I do with him, so I have to be careful."

Living with Scott, Jennifer gained fifteen pounds, filling out and looking healthy for the first time in more than a year. And she seemed content. "She was a different person. She hung out with Madyson all the time, and she had better things to do than party," says Michaela. "With Scott and Madyson, Jennifer was settled. I think that maybe for the first time, she felt safe."

Jennifer called Sharon and talked about going back to school. She wanted to go into advertising, like her mother, and Scott was encouraging her to do that, looking for ways he could help her. "Sharon was understandably dubious," says Scott. "She needed Jennifer to show her she was pulling herself out of it. That put pressure on Jennifer, and they argued."

That spring, Lauren wrote Jennifer a letter, telling her that she wanted a relationship with her, that she missed having her in her life. "I just want you to be honest with me. I want you to call me if you have a problem," she wrote. "I just want you to be my sister again."

"I was done with criticizing Jennifer," Lauren says. "It came between us."

Off and on, Jen began calling her younger sister to share the good things that were unfolding and the joy of raising little Madyson. To Lauren and to her friends, Jennifer recounted stories about her day-to-day life, telling them about the funny things Madyson said. Jennifer giggled explaining how, on a picnic at a lake, a minnow swam up the little one's swimsuit, sending her into a screaming, arm-flailing run from the water. There were stories about her attempts at disciplining the little girl. "What do you do when a little girl says 'butt'?" she asked one day.

"I don't know," a friend answered. "What did you do?"

"I wasn't sure. We do time-outs, but this time I put a drop of hot sauce on her tongue," Jen said, laughing. "But Madyson liked it."

On Sundays, Scott, Jennifer, and Madyson went to church together, sometimes with Katrina and Laura Ingles, a friend of Scott's majoring in music at a nearby college. During the week, Ingles, pretty with dark brown hair and eyes that matched, hung out with Jen and Madyson. Laura didn't do drugs, and was solidly against them, but she sympathized when Jen talked about how they'd taken over her life and how glad she was that she'd put them behind her. Jennifer confided that more than anything, she thought she'd like to be a good mother for Madyson, and Laura, who loved the little girl, believed Jennifer would be.

In March, Jennifer met Denise Winterbottom around the pool. Denise, tall with long, light brown hair, was a decade older and had a bachelor's in psychology from a Maryland college. She lived with her boyfriend, Scott Wilson, the apartment complex's manager and handyman, a building away, in an apartment that came with Scott's job. Denise, who suffered from CRPS, Complex Regional Pain Syndrome, a rare, painful disorder, babysat for a four-year-old named Gracie for another single dad in the complex.

It was at the pool one day that Jennifer approached Denise and introduced herself and Madyson. "I thought maybe we could hang out and let the girls play," Jennifer said.

Denise and Jennifer, it would turn out, had a lot in common. Like Jennifer, Denise started using drugs in high school, "to be rebellious." She'd tried heroin at seventeen, but got hooked on Xanax and pot, and finally ended up at Narcotics Anonymous. Denise had been in recovery for eleven years when she and Jennifer met, but did have occasional setbacks. "Nothing serious," she says. "I never got heavy into it again."

It didn't take long before Denise and Jennifer spent nearly every day together with Gracie and Madyson. They took the girls on outings, including to McDonald's for lunch and the park and playground. Once the weather warmed up, they spent mornings at the pool, Jennifer teaching Madyson to swim. Madyson was fairylike, tiny, smart, and wiser than her years, while Gracie was a sturdily built tomboy. The girls loved playing together, "And I was enthralled to have an adult to talk to," says Denise, in her throaty, raspy, cigarette voice.

At times, Jennifer talked to Denise about moving back to Corpus Christi, but said she couldn't. "All my friends are in Austin, and I have Scott and Madyson," she said. "I have a life here, now."

In the evenings, Jennifer and Denise walked her dog, Speedy, a Lab-chow mix, while they smoked. Before long, Jennifer left the cigarettes home and pulled out a joint, and their evening walks became a quiet, laid-back time when they smoked pot and talked. "I knew I shouldn't. Neither one of us really should have," says Denise. "But it wasn't much. Just one joint, and we shared it. It took the edge off."

Soon, in the afternoons while the girls napped, they began sharing a second joint.

Early on, Jennifer told Scott about Colton. In fact, he'd been something of a presence in their relationship. Before Jen weaned off the heavier drugs, they'd stopped at his apartment one night so she could get cocaine. Then, as they grew closer, she confided in him, telling Scott about the incident with the knife. "Jennifer didn't seem frightened. It wasn't like she thought he'd really hurt her," he says.

Another night, Jen took Scott to a party, and Colton was there. At first, it bothered Scott just looking at Colton, remembering what Jennifer had said about him. But as Scott watched, Jen and Colton acted like old friends, telling stories and laughing at inside jokes. "Colton was talking one hundred miles per hour about nothing," says Scott. "And he was wrapped up in himself. He didn't have a clue of what life was like without drugs."

At one point, Colton leaned over and said to Scott, "If you ever need anyone taken care of, I've done that before."

Scott didn't believe him, but he wondered why Colton thought that sounded cool. To Scott, Colton seemed out of touch with reality.

As the night went on, the two young men talked, and Colton mentioned that he wanted to get off the drugs, to stop dealing and regain his life. Scott wondered if he could help him, even if they could be friends. Jennifer cared about Colton. Scott understood that.

At the apartment, the phone rang at odd hours, especially at night, and Jennifer rushed out, saying Colton needed her help. At times, she stayed out all night, but Scott didn't worry. "I knew it wasn't like that with them. It wasn't sexual," he says. "I could tell that Jennifer thought of him as a friend, and that she worried about him."

That February, Colton's parents came to Austin for a farm equipment trade show, and Colton invited Jennifer and Scott to go out to dinner with them and with Said Aziz, a friend of Jennifer's and Colton's who was set to graduate in a year from UT; and Colton's longtime pal Juan Montero. Aziz had spent the summer working in Washington, D.C., as a legislative aide, and Scott thought when they all gathered that night at Sullivan's, the steakhouse where Jennifer had once worked, that Colton was showing off for his parents, inviting his more presentable friends.

It would turn out to be a pleasant dinner. Eddie mainly talked to Colton, Said, Juan, and Scott, while Bridget and Jennifer conversed. Throughout the evening, Colton's parents appeared anxious about their son, peppering the conversation with questions about his activities. Smiling and acting nonchalant, Colton claimed his classes were going well, and that he'd been putting in a lot of time studying. But when Scott looked at Colton, he could tell Colton was "all coked up."

Later, Eddie would say that when he and Bridget later asked about Jennifer, "Colton became very defensive."

That month, Colton stopped at Justin's apartment and handed him a box. "Will you keep this for me?" he asked. Reluctantly, Justin agreed, afraid to ask what was inside. At times, he wondered about Colton and what he was becoming. At that point, Colton spent much of the time shooting morphine, using cocaine, popping pills, and drinking; partying on Sixth Street; and hanging out with drug dealers. "There must have been times when he sobered up enough to take a good long look at himself and felt stone-cold disgusted," says Justin.

Once when Justin met Colton for lunch, he insisted he was going to turn his life around. "Yeah, I'm going to get back in the gym and become a trainer, then get back to school and pull it together," Colton said.

"Colton had plans. He wanted to stop selling the drugs," says Justin, who'd gotten himself clean about eight months earlier. "Colton didn't like the way his life was going. But day turned to evening, and evening turned to night, and people called wanting drugs, and it was impossible for Colton, the entrepreneur, to resist meeting that demand."

That March 12, 2005, was Jennifer's twenty-first birthday. Sharon and Jim had given the other girls trips for their big birthday, but, with Jennifer's progress still so uncertain, Sharon drove to Austin and took her out instead. Sharon booked a room at a La Quinta hotel, and they went to Sullivan's for dinner, and then to a cozy wine bar. Afterward, they lounged together on the hotel bed watching a movie and talking. The following weekend, Vanessa, too, drove in to celebrate. The sisters spent a night on Sixth Street, partying and dancing. Two beautiful women, they garnered a lot of attention.

For their celebration, Scott brought home "magic" mushrooms from a friend, mild hallucinogens. After cooking dinner, when Madyson was asleep, they ate the mushrooms, and Scott gave Jennifer a massage. Soon, he visualized black clouds rising up around her, and he started pulling at them, tearing them out. As he worked on her shoulders and her back, untangling the stress points of her muscles, he continued to see dark clouds materialize and then evaporate in his grasp. Before long, Jennifer sobbed. Crying hysterically, she lay on the bed for more than an hour, while Scott kneaded her back.

Afterward, Jennifer lay in Scott's arms. They talked, and Jennifer confided that before that evening she'd felt something dark and frightening hanging over her. At least temporarily, it was gone. "You saved my life," she said, and, for the first time, Jennifer told Scott, "I love you."

"From that point on, we were even closer," Scott says. "It was like we were at a deeper level of intimacy."

One of the things Jennifer called out that night while Scott kneaded her back and visualized the black clouds gathering around them was a name, "Colton."

Not long after, a friend of Scott's painted a portrait of Jennifer, strong lines in grays and blues. The painting was of Jen's nude torso, and it would later seem eerily prophetic.

Eleven

While Jennifer was busy setting up housekeeping with Scott and Madyson in early 2005, Colton continued to redefine his image, leaving ever further behind the former altar boy and scholarship student and cultivating the gangster persona he'd worked on since arriving at UT nearly four years earlier. If Scott was Jennifer's "kindred spirit," as she'd told friends, Colton had found his own counterpart, of sorts, in an aggressive young woman named Laura Ashley Hall.

Hall spent her first years in Madisonville, Texas, but grew up in Crosby, twenty-five miles northeast of Houston, in a metropolitan area of around twenty-three thousand. An agricultural setting, Crosby wasn't particularly affluent, but it had a certain charm. Many of the residents were blue-collar, middle-class folks who worked hard, paid their bills, and raised their families.

Laura's mother, Carol, was a lissome woman, with short, reddish-blond hair, a fair but freckled complexion, and calm manner, who worked for a plastic surgeon. Laura's father, Loren, had a thinly trimmed beard and a dark mustache, and reddish-brown hair combed back. With a penchant for jeans, Western shirts, and loud sport coats, he made his living as a yacht broker but fancied himself a writer. He'd produced a five-book series of children's books and one work on "poetic philosophy," but none was published.

"He adored Laura," says Andrea Jiles, Laura's best friend for many years. "Her dad had her on a pedestal."

Casual, fun-loving people, Carol and Loren weren't

called Mom and Dad by their only child, but by their first names. The family lived in one of the nicer houses in town, in a good area, and Laura had the run of the second floor. As Jiles remembers it, Laura usually got whatever she wanted from her parents. When she was sixteen, for instance, Laura drove a hand-me-down Cadillac sedan. Loren and Carol Hall "acted more like friends than parents," says Jiles, a tall, slender, African-American woman with a long face and rich, dark complexion.

Always, Laura seemed in a world of her own, and she had a sense of herself that Jiles found bigger than life. As a teenager, Laura carried her small rat terrier, Sweetie, in her purse, taking him everywhere, a decade before Paris Hilton made it fashionable. Her hair dyed dark, her complexion pale, and with a long, straight nose, Hall resembled the actress Gina Gershon. She dressed vaguely Goth, in black with black makeup, but was athletic, swam, and played soccer, and beginning in her freshman year, competed on the school debate team, often placing well at competitions. The year Laura was the captain, the team competed before the American Legion and the local VFW chapter, and she took them to nationals. To the dismay of her opponents, Laura read and formed arguments quickly, taking a strong stance on whatever issue was assigned.

At times, Hall became so passionate about ideas, she acted on them, as when during one debate meeting a team member threw out a comment derogatory of the United States. The students agreed the country was "screwed up," and one said things were so bad they should refuse to stand for the Pledge of Allegiance. At the next school function, Hall did just that.

As far as Jiles knew, Laura Hall didn't use drugs in high school. The dangers of illegal drugs and guns were topics Jiles understood firsthand. For much of her life, she'd grown up in Houston's rough fifth and third wards, where gun violence was commonplace. Her biological father had been killed by drug dealers, and her mother and stepfather were both murdered. With all her parents deceased, Jiles lived with her grandfather.

In Crosby, Hall and Jiles hung out with the "smart" kids, although, in school, Laura was far from popular. She hid her athletic body under sweatshirts, and walked through the halls reading vampire novels. While Laura let her guard down around Jiles, she put on a tough front with her other schoolmates, often glaring at them with cold, blank eyes, and many questioned why Jiles befriended Hall. "Laura's not a people person," says Jiles. "She was rude without realizing it. Not many people liked her."

At the same time, Laura loved to talk. In fact, Jiles believed her friend habitually said whatever occurred to her, without self-censorship. "Laura never had a thought she didn't share," says Jiles. "If she wasn't with someone, she was talking to someone on the telephone."

When it came to boys, Laura fell head over heels, never holding back, suffering when the liaisons ended. "Laura put everything into a boyfriend. Blew them out of proportion. When they split, she was devastated," says Jiles. "It doesn't really matter how smart someone is. Relationships are a different thing."

After her junior year at Crosby High School, Carol and Loren moved the family to the even smaller town of Bedias, and enrolled Laura in Allen Academy, a small, conservative, private military school with an enrollment of 350. Like Jennifer when Sharon told her they were moving to Corpus, Laura didn't take the news happily. "Laura didn't want to move," says Jiles. "She was angry at her parents for making her do it."

The following fall, when Colton Pitonyak graduated with honors and moved to Austin intent on becoming a Wall Street whiz kid, Laura Hall also enrolled at UT, with plans to major in government and dreams of law school, perhaps at Georgetown University in D.C. "I really thought Laura could do it," says Jiles. "She was smart, had good grades, and Laura was a great debater. She was a natural."

In Austin, as in Crosby, Laura struck many of those she met as odd or eccentric. She lived in a four-plex on Twenty-sixth Street, in a converted grocery store, filling her tiny apartment with plants and a big fish tank. The car she parked outside was another hand-me-down from her parents, a 1994 green Cadillac Concours.

As a neighbor remembers her, Laura "played the rebellious, isolated chick to a T." At times, she could be friendly. At other times, she seemed defensive and rude.

By then, Loren and Carol had relocated again, this time to the small Texas Hill Country town of Tarpley, fifty miles northwest of San Antonio, and opened the Caribbean Cowboy RV Resort, a Jimmy Buffet–style trailer community aimed at active seniors. When her parents arrived for visits in an RV, Laura acted embarrassed. Such times, she'd stop the neighbors to explain that her parents owned the RV park, not just lived there.

At other times, Laura Hall walked right past neighbors, including those she'd talked to a day or so earlier, without even saying hello. "She was moody, and people didn't know how to react to her," says a neighbor. "We rarely saw anyone but guys who wore long trench coats visiting her. She didn't seem to have any girlfriends."

One day a neighbor found Laura's Crosby school yearbooks in the apartment garbage. He thought it was odd that she'd brought them to UT and then thrown them away. When he looked inside, he saw the books bore childish notes scribbled on top of or next to photos of teachers and students, everything from "bull dyke" to "shit head," along with "queer," "lesbian," and "slut." Next to some of the boys' photos she wrote "fine," and "cute."

There was more evidence that their neighbor was odd. At times, Laura suddenly screamed, shrieking so loud she could be heard throughout the apartment building. "We knew she was alone in there. It was like she was venting," says a neighbor. They smelled pot outside her door, but that wasn't unusual in Austin, and Laura didn't look high or drugged.

Off and on, Andrea Jiles and Laura talked, sometimes about one or another of Laura's love interests. At one point, Laura announced to Jiles that she was dating a woman named Ericka who went to Harvard. After her breakup with Ericka, Laura briefly attended a Mormon church. "She was always trying to shock people, talking about sex and things. We didn't know if she was kidding or not," says someone who met her there and formed the opinion that Hall cultivated drama. "She was a really fickle person, and she'd change her mind on a whim, go along with anything. Once she told us how she'd thought she was a lesbian but then changed her mind. Laura craved attention."

In the fall of 2004, Laura met Colton's friend Justin. At the time, she was dating a straitlaced UT student, a guy. Before long, Laura started hanging out at Justin's apartment, much to the dismay of his roommate and friends, who complained that she was always underfoot and depressed. They asked Justin to tell her to leave, but Justin never did. "I'm not much of a pro at telling people no," he says. "She hated being alone. Laura had to be with someone constantly."

At Justin's, Laura sat around and cried, at times screaming that she hated her life, and Justin expended more energy than he wanted trying to cheer her up. Once, after Laura's ex-boyfriend stopped at the apartment, Laura lay on the grass in the apartment's common area, sobbing and shrieking. "It appeared that she had serious emotional problems," says Justin. "She was seriously strange."

At a party at Justin's, Laura Hall met Colton Pitonyak. He came in looking every bit the gangster he wanted to be, in a black leather sport coat and jeans, and talked about guns and selling drugs. After Colton left, Laura pressured Justin for his phone number. "I realized bringing those two together was the worst idea in the history of time," Justin says with a sigh. Hoping to keep them apart, he lied and told Laura that Colton had a girlfriend, but she wasn't dissuaded.

"Dating would be a loose way of putting it," Justin would later say about the relationship that developed between Colton and Laura. "Colton didn't care about Laura except for sex. Laura was crazy about Colton. Obsessed with him."

"I don't know if Laura knew what love was, but she liked having sex with Colton," says Jiles. "And Colton used her, treated her like a muddy little dog."

At times, Laura talked to Jiles about Jennifer, once claiming Jen stole drugs from Colton and bragging that she, Laura, was going to steal them back. "Laura was fanatical about Colton, talked about him constantly. And she didn't like any other woman who had a connection to him, especially Jennifer. Laura hated Jennifer. She was jealous," says Jiles. When it came to Colton's guy friends, however, Laura couldn't have been more pleased. "Laura liked that Colton had friends, because she didn't have many, and she liked being around college guys who wore hundred-dollar jeans. She thought it was exciting that Colton was a drug dealer," says Jiles, who warned her friend how dangerous drugs and guns could be. Jiles had seen other suburban white kids who acted like gangsters. "It's a way to be part of the group. It's a game."

"It's cool," Laura told her. "It's more like a gangster movie than real gangsters. It's not real."

That winter, Laura worked at the Richard Pena law firm in Austin, where they specialized in workers' comp and personal injury cases. High-profile in Austin, Pena was a past president of the Texas Bar Association and had photos of himself with presidents Bill Clinton and George W. Bush. It was a plum job for a would-be law student, and Laura worked hard, doing everything from filing and filling out reports to running errands.

Not long after she met Colton, friends at the firm noticed changes in Laura Hall. She looked rougher, dressed sexier, talked tougher, and before long started showing up for work late. She referred to Colton constantly, calling him her boyfriend, and seeming to be fixated on him. When she dropped in at the duplex of a woman she worked with, Sammi Moore, and her boyfriend, Chris Collins, Laura was strung out. "Once she met Colton, she was messed up all the time, nearly always high," says Chris. "She was a middle-class white kid and she began jiving like a thug from a South Central L.A. ghetto."

Not long after Laura hooked up with Colton, Jiles drove into Austin to see her. She was struck by how much Laura had changed. She'd lost weight, her eyes were surrounded by dark circles and sunken; she looked like a different person. "Laura talked about drugs and money constantly. It was a terrible relationship for her. Everything was bad," says Jiles. "Colton Pitonyak used my friend for sex and turned her into an addict."

As Colton's June court date on the possession charge approached, his attorney, Hughes, still hadn't worked out a plea bargain. With the help of his parents, Colton replaced Hughes with Sam Bassett, an attorney at one of the best-known firms in Austin, Minton, Burton, Foster & Collins.

Founded in 1963, Minton Burton had a client list that included a who's who of Texas's financial and social circles. Their offices, in a converted house across the street from the courthouse, led people to call Minton Burton "the red brick firm." Over the decades, they'd defended their share of drug cases. In fact Roy Minton, the patriarch of the firm, started forty-four years earlier at a time when even the possession of a small amount of pot was a felony. "The thing with criminal law is that you often end up with very young clients," he says. A grandfatherly man, Minton was slight and frail-looking, with oversize glasses and a genteel manner. Lawyers who came up against him were wary. Minton had the ability to lull prosecutors and opposing attorneys, only to strike at the first opening and leave them wondering what had happened.

A protégé of Minton, Sam Bassett, with a high forehead; thick, reddish-brown hair; and incisive eyes, had joined the firm four years earlier. In addition to practicing civil and criminal law, Bassett taught part-time in the UT law school, where he'd earned his degree. Bassett had interned at Minton

Burton during law school, and he'd adopted Minton's calm demeanor in the courtroom.

For Colton Pitonyak, Bassett negotiated with the prosecutor's office, urging the assistant DA to reduce the possession charge to a misdemeanor. Colton was a young man with his future on the line. If convicted of a felony, it would be on his record forever. Even if he turned his life around and became a model citizen, the felony would follow him wherever he went. It could keep him from ever being licensed to work on Wall Street, even prevent him from voting.

Perhaps the least concerned was the defendant himself. That spring, Colton made no apparent attempt to change his lifestyle. He arrived at parties bleary-eyed, talked about drugs, guns, and how his attorney was going to get him out of serving time. Laura Hall came with him, hanging on his every word, arguing with anyone who contradicted him.

"She was crazy," says one of the partygoers. "She worshipped Pitonyak."

The drug business was lucrative that year. Pitonyak and a few of his friends had expanded until they were selling or trading up to four thousand ecstasy pills a week, reserving another one thousand for their own needs. They were flush with cash and throwing the best parties on West Campus. "We ate ecstasy, popped it like candy," says Pitonyak's good friend Jason Mack, who hung in Colton's inner circle. "Everyone showed up at the parties. It was wild."

That spring, however, something changed. The ecstasy and coke weren't enough for Pitonyak anymore, even when he mixed them with booze. They just didn't deliver enough of a thrill. At first Colton tried heroin, but he didn't like the way it made him feel. Instead, he became enamored with meth. Before long, he was smoking it off and on throughout the day, staying up for days on end, until his body gave out and he crashed. When he woke up, he helped himself to more. "With guys, meth gets the testosterone flowing," says Mack. "They get amped. They're on edge. Eventually they become sleep deprived and paranoid. It can drive you insane. There was no doubt that the meth changed Colton. Once he started on the meth, he was never the same."

Pitonyak traded the ecstasy pills he got from his Asian connection to a dealer who sold meth he procured from a group he described as part of the "Mexican Mafia." But since Pitonyak was using more than selling, money wasn't coming in as easily as it had in the past. As summer arrived, Pitonyak consumed up to $300 a day in meth. "Colton got spun," says Mack. "He was over-amped on the speed. He was so drugged up on the meth, he didn't know if it was up or down, night or day."

For more than a year, Colton had dropped in unannounced on Louisa, a UT student who lived in an apartment building where Colton had friends. Louisa liked Colton, thought he was funny, with a quick sense of humor. She knew he was high much of the time, but she never cared. That changed in 2005. By that spring, Colton's very presence telegraphed danger.

One morning, just after 3 A.M., he knocked on Louisa's door. He had his arm slung over a woman who worked as a topless dancer in an Austin bar, and they were both drunk and high. Colton pushed his way into Louisa's apartment without being invited and then didn't take the hint when she suggested they leave. From the moment he entered, Colton watched the door, as if he thought they were being followed. After that, Louisa stopped opening her door for Colton.

"I was worried about Colton, but I was scared of him," she says. "He'd completely changed, and I felt so sad for him."

That spring 2005, college students across America flocked to sign up on Facebook.com, an online social network started by a Harvard student. A MySpace.com-type Web site with a private club approach, on Facebook profiles were only visible to those with college or university e-mail addresses, and then only to individuals registered within the same institution. An online database where students displayed photos and profiles, on Facebook students detailed their likes and dislikes, and then posted messages on each others' walls or message boards.

Colton signed up on Facebook on May 1 of that year, describing himself as a management and French major in the UT group. Although he'd entered the university in the fall of 2001, he estimated, perhaps optimistically since he rarely attended classes, that he'd graduate in 2010. On the left-hand top of his page, he posted a smiling photo with good friends Juan Montero and Roel Escobar. Colton claimed as his screen name ILoveMoneyAndHos.

On Facebook, Colton Pitonyak defined the person he'd become with echoes of his past. He listed his interests as drinking, women, and making money, saying he was self-employed, a reference to his thriving drug business. His favorite music: rappers Paul Wall, Slim Thug, Chamillionaire, and Triple Six. And his favorite movies: *Boondock Saints*, *Menace II Society*, *City of God*, *Reservoir Dogs*, *Goodfellas*, *Casino*, and *Donnie Brasco*. In the section reserved for words of wisdom, the would-be tycoon-turned-drug-dealer quoted Warren Buffet and J. P. Morgan, alongside his gangster idols, including the infamous John Gotti. Perhaps the most telling quotes were two Colton credited to Al Capone: "I am like any other man. All I do is supply a demand," and "You can get a lot farther with a kind word and a gun than a kind word alone."

Like Colton, Laura Hall built a Facebook profile that spring. A government major, she planned to graduate from UT that coming December. In her photo, she posed playfully in a furry coat and a short skirt with boots. She credited her favorite quote to horror author Peter Straub, from his book *Shadowland*: "You're part music and part blood, part thinker and part killer. And if you can find all of that within you and control it, then you deserve to be set apart."

Laura Hall and Colton had the same photo linked to their Facebook pages, one of Colton with his bros: Juan Montero, his fists with his middle fingers extended in the universal symbol of contempt, knelt in the center. In the background, in a wise-guy pose, stood Colton, a small V-shaped beard just under his lower lip, wearing his bill cap backward and a derisive smile. In another Facebook photo, Colton, hair disheveled, wore his black leather sport coat and stared into the camera in a drugged daze.

If the profiles were windows into Colton's and Laura's souls, they were frightening. At one point Laura Hall noted: "I should really be a more horrific person. It's in the works."

That June, Andrea Jiles warned Hall that Colton had turned her into a drug addict. "Colton is cool," Hall replied. "He's a rich boy."

Jiles looked at her friend and hardly recognized her: "He'd changed her so much there were now two different Lauras."

Despite his relationship with Laura Hall, Colton and Jennifer talked almost daily. Jason Mack had no doubt about Pitonyak's feelings. "He was in love with Jen," says Mack. "Laura was the one he called if he had no one else to hang with, but Laura was in love with Colton. Jen? She thought of Colton as a friend."

Despite no longer needing him for drugs, since she used so little, Jennifer was still drawn to Pitonyak. Scott noticed that whenever Colton called, Jennifer picked up immediately, and then ran out saying Colton had a problem and "needs to talk." In May, Colton called Scott with a crisis, claiming someone was trying to kill him. Half an hour later, Colton drove up in a cab and ran to their apartment door. Scott let him in and knew right away that Colton was high, as he rattled on about how he'd been out with an escort, and that her pimp was after him. Scott thought it sounded like the plot of a bad movie.

When they were alone, Scott and Jennifer talked about Colton often, including the upcoming hearings over his possession case. One night she told Scott about a party where

Colton played Russian roulette with a loaded gun, while a group of his friends watched him pull the trigger. Rumors floated around the Delt house that summer. Someone heard that one of their inactive brothers, Colton Pitonyak, pulled a gun on a frat kid he sold drugs to.

But most of the time, Colton Pitonyak wasn't part of Jennifer's and Scott's lives, which centered on Madyson. They worked their schedules around caring for her, and Jen catered to the little girl with the big smile and the worldly eyes. Jennifer seemed to be thriving on her time with the youngster. She bought Madyson new clothes, including a pink cowboy hat studded with rhinestones. They cuddled and huddled together: the little girl looking for a mother and Jennifer living her dream of having a child.

On nights when he didn't work at the restaurant, Scott and Jen got together with friends, playing poker or going out to the Canary Roost, a strip-center bar near the apartment. They drank and laughed, Scott sang karaoke, and they danced long into the night.

One night, when the place was packed, Karissa Reine, the bartender, shouted last call, just as Jen walked behind the bar. Reine had noticed Scott with the redhead. When alcohol-fueled tensions rose in the bar, Reine saw Jennifer try to calm the other patrons down. "It struck me that she always seemed to be worried about other people," says Reine.

Reine soon found out that was why Jennifer walked behind the bar. "What are you doing?" Reine asked. "You're not supposed to be back here."

"You're working too hard," Jen said. "You need a break. You need to call me and we'll go out. You need to relax more."

She slipped Reine her phone number, and Reine did call her. They became friends, and Jennifer convinced Reine to take more time for herself. "She was right," says Karissa. "I was working too hard, too many hours."

On May 31, 2005, Jennifer and Scott went to Reine's

apartment, the one she shared with her boyfriend, Bryan Breaux, a musician. They laughed, told stories, and drank wine, until, exhausted, Scott passed out on the couch. Intrigued by Jennifer, Reine took out a camera, a new digital she'd just bought, and followed Jennifer through the apartment, snapping photos, trying to capture the light in Jen's blue eyes. The photos from that night showed Jennifer fully in the moment, holding a glass of red wine, her cheeks flushed, with a breathless smile on her face. Some were highly sensual, as Jennifer's long red hair fell over her pale, freckled shoulders, her breasts plumped by a black lace bustier.

From that night on, Jen sometimes visited Reine in the wee hours of the morning, after she closed the bar and returned home from work, while Scott and Madyson slept. At times, Karissa talked to Jennifer about the way she took on the problems of others. Jennifer told her about a friend, a "crazy guy," and how she sometimes stayed with him. He was smart and, when he wasn't high, sweet, and Jennifer saw something in him that needed to be protected. "Jennifer, you're not responsible for everyone else," Reine advised. "You can't save everyone."

Over the months, the two women drank wine and shared stories about their lives and their dreams. One night their conversation turned to premonitions. "We both believed in them," Reine says.

That night, Jennifer confided that she had the unmistakable feeling that she had to live her life quickly, that she wouldn't be around to grow old. A fear haunted her, giving her the sense that she needed to enjoy every moment, because, although only twenty-one years old, Jennifer Cave believed her time on earth would be short.

"It feels like something evil is stalking me," Jennifer said. "I have to be one step ahead; I have to run."

Twelve

On June 10, 2005, Colton Pitonyak appeared before Judge
Wilford Flowers in the 147th District Court, on the seventh
floor of the Travis County Criminal Courthouse, an under-
stated, modern structure next to the old courthouse near the
corner of Eleventh and Guadalupe. Sam Bassett had negotiated a good deal. Colton had two offers from the prosecutor
to consider: the first, Colton could plead guilty to the felony
charge and serve no additional jail time; the second, the
charge would be plea-bargained down to a misdemeanor, attempted possession of a controlled substance, but there was
a catch—Colton would be sentenced to sixty days in Travis
County's Del Valle jail. Perhaps on the advice of his attorney and parents, who worried about the effect of a felony
on his record, Colton chose the second option: the misdemeanor conviction with accompanying jail sentence.

Sixty days may have seemed formidable, but based on
good time laws in place in Texas, if Colton stayed out of
trouble in prison, he'd be out in less than a month. That
same day, he entered the Travis County jail system for the
third time and disappeared inside.

While he was incarcerated, neighbors at the Orange Tree
saw Laura Hall at Colton's apartment almost daily, watching his cable television, preferring it to her current apartment, one she'd moved into on Oltorf Street, south of the
city. "Colton's in jail," Laura told Andrea Jiles. "He just
needs to do his time, and he'll be out."

"Well, obviously he's not that smart to end up in there,"
Jiles said.

"Colton's cool," Laura said.

"He's the wrong guy," Jiles cautioned again. She knew her friend was giving Colton money, funds Laura needed to pay expenses, including rent. At times, Colton gave Laura a little back, but then quickly asked for more, and Laura gave it to him, even money her grandmother gave her as an early graduation gift. "Colton's using you," Jiles said. "And remember: A lot of people in my family ended up in prison or dead because of drugs and guns."

Meanwhile, with Colton confined in jail, Jennifer began to piece her life back together in earnest. "She really did well," says a friend. "Colton was a distraction she didn't need but couldn't seem to get rid of, and having him in jail did that for her." Jennifer applied for jobs, interviewing for one in an insurance office. She was excited about the opportunity and was disappointed when another applicant was hired. The executive who broke the bad news to Jennifer told her, "You won't stay here. You're too bright. I don't know why you're not in school."

In June, Jennifer drove with Madyson to San Marcos, the city where she'd once gone to college, and met Lauren at the vast, 130-store outlet mall, an open-air discount shopping center boasting such upscale shops as Kate Spade and Ferragamo. Despite their differences over the past few years, Lauren and Jennifer enjoyed the day together. Jennifer talked of her plans, getting a job and starting to take classes again. When she later talked to Sharon on the telephone, Jennifer sounded more positive than she had in a long time. Sharon still worried, but she began to hope her middle daughter's life had finally found its course.

"Mom, since I'm applying for jobs, I need my cell phone back," Jennifer said during one conversation from Scott's apartment, "Can I have it?"

"Sure," Sharon said. She felt as if she walked a thin line, wanting to reward Jennifer for improvement but afraid she'd open the door for more disappointment. Still, the telephone was a little thing. "Is everything okay with Scott?"

Jennifer hesitated, thinking, then admitted: "I'm starting to wonder if I'm ready to be a wife and a mother. I'm so young, and I haven't really done anything yet."

Sharon had been worried for months about little Madyson and what would happen if Jennifer and Scott didn't make their relationship work. Now Jennifer, for the first time, expressed doubts, and Sharon immediately worried about the little four-year-old. "Be careful with Madyson, Jennifer," she advised. "You've always wanted to be a mother, and that little girl needs a mother. Be careful how you handle her."

"I know," Jennifer agreed. "But I do want to be someone first before I'm a wife and a mother. I love Scott and Madyson, but I just don't know that I'm ready."

In hindsight, it wasn't just the confines of caring for a child that weighed on Jennifer. By then, she and Scott were arguing about money. When she moved in, Scott assumed Jennifer would work and help pay expenses, but in the six months they'd been together, she stayed home to care for Madyson and the apartment. Once he found her a job as a hostess at a small microbrewery, but Jennifer didn't like it and worked only a few nights before quitting.

To friends, Jennifer said she found the crush of caring for a house and child and a job overwhelming. Not realizing she was having doubts about their little family, Scott was happy when Jennifer said she wanted a real job, like the one she'd had at the bank in Corpus, where she went to an office every day.

That June, Scott and Jennifer looked at rental houses in Austin's north suburbs, not far from their apartment. Madyson was growing up, and he wanted to put down roots. Jennifer, meanwhile, felt increasingly at odds with the life she'd built for herself, the instant family she became a part of when she and Scott got together. "I love Scott," she told Laura Ingles. "I really do love him and Madyson. But I want a job, and I want to finish college."

In her Day-Timer, Jennifer recorded job interviews, at banks and small companies, charting her course through

June. Madyson must have seen Jennifer writing in the black vinyl notebook, for one day she took a black crayon and wrote her numbers on one page. It would later seem strange that the little girl used that black crayon on another page to draw a box and color it black, a box shaped eerily similar to a casket.

On June 30, 2005, twenty days after he entered, Colton left jail, his sentence completed. Someone who saw him noticed something odd. Rather than hiding his time behind bars, Colton showcased it, in the form of a jailhouse tattoo penned by a poor speller, for what he'd crudely etched on Colton's back instead of "felon" was "fell on."

Although not convicted of a felony, Colton appeared intent on achieving what, in his mind, apparently held a certain status. That duality in his personality was still front and center when, in the mold of the proper and well-mannered Catholic schoolboy he'd once been, Colton wrote his attorney a thank-you letter. "It was unusual," Bassett says. "It's not very often that a client takes the time."

Living back in his apartment at the Orange Tree, Colton registered for a second-semester summer class at UT, a biology course, The Human Body, then spent two weeks before it started drunk and high on meth, making up for the forced abstinence during his incarceration. "Colton's out," Laura told Jiles on the telephone, and in Houston, Hall's high school friend shook her head, thinking, *This is bad.*

"My friend Colton is out of jail," Jennifer told Denise at the pool, in early July.

"That's not a good thing, Jen," Denise said. Jennifer had described Colton as a mean drunk and told her about the night at Justin's when he'd come at her with a knife. "Stay away from him."

Scott's friend Laura Ingles gave Jennifer the same advice when Jen asked if Laura wanted to meet Colton. "You need to stay away from him," she said. "It's not safe."

"Oh, no, I'll be fine," Jennifer insisted. "He's really a sweet guy. When he's not drunk or high, he's great."

"He just got out of jail for drugs, Jennifer," Laura said. "Let's get real about this guy."

Like so many others, Laura wondered why Jennifer kept Colton Pitonyak in her life. Jen seemed so spunky, so strong in ways. "Colton was Jennifer's weak spot," says Laura. "She didn't seem to be able to get rid of him, even though she knew he was dangerous."

Perhaps the attraction wasn't just Colton. In July, after his release, Denise noticed that Jennifer acted differently, more keyed up, and she lost weight. "Jennifer looked jazzed," Denise says. "Something had changed."

What started as occasional questioning built into determination to step back and take a look at her situation, to reevaluate and decide if she'd chosen the right path. When Jennifer talked to Denise about her concerns at the pool one afternoon, Denise assumed Jennifer just needed a break from Scott and the responsibilities of motherhood. "You can stay with us," Denise offered. "We have a spare bedroom."

"I'll think about it," Jennifer said.

In early July, Scott took Madyson to Kansas to see family and help put a new roof on his grandmother's house. At the last minute, Jennifer decided not to go with him. Increasingly unhappy, she was thinking over options. By then a friend of Scott's, Eli Damian, a short, dark-haired, solidly built construction worker who lived in the same complex, was spending a lot of time at their apartment. Scott assumed Eli was just being a friend, but when Scott returned home, he discovered that Jen had gone to a barbecue with Eli. As Scott replayed his recent arguments with Jennifer, the tension that was building in their relationship, he wondered if Jennifer was using drugs again or if she and Eli had begun an affair. When Jennifer came home, he confronted her, but she denied both of Scott's charges. Instead, she told him what she'd been telling others for weeks, that she was too young to be a mother. They argued, voices rising, and Scott said there was no other option. If Jennifer had doubts about being Madyson's mom, she had to move out.

"She said there wasn't anyone else. Jen and I held each other and cried and promised we'd try to make it work, try to save our relationship," he says. "We agreed we'd date, and do our best to make a go of it."

Only days after July 4, Jennifer left Scott's apartment and settled in the one Denise shared with her boyfriend. Although Scott had been the one to tell Jennifer to leave, he was distraught over the breakup. "I couldn't understand what had happened. We had plans to move into a house together. I even had a place rented," he says. "I understood what she was saying, that she needed to be her own person first, but I loved Jennifer."

The afternoon Scott and Jennifer explained to Madyson that Jennifer was moving out, the little girl sobbed. Scott and Jen tried to ease the blow by talking to her together, promising that Jennifer would see her often. "I love you, Maddy, but I'm just not going to live here with you and your dad," Jennifer said, and then she added something she and Scott had decided earlier. "Instead of being your mommy, we'll be more like sisters."

"My sister?" Madyson said, intrigued with the idea. Somehow that worked for the little girl, who from that point on referred to Jennifer as "Sister." Madyson, her soft curls bouncing, hugged Scott and Jennifer. All she cared about was that Jennifer would still be in her life.

Jennifer told Sharon that she'd moved out of Scott's apartment when Sharon and Jim were in Oklahoma moving Hailey and Lauren into a townhouse in Norman, near the University of Oklahoma, where both were registered for fall classes. Hailey, who'd once been close to Jen, had become Lauren's best friend. Sharon worried about Jennifer, but her middle daughter sounded strong and determined on the telephone. Jennifer said all the right things: She was applying for jobs and she'd picked up a schedule to register at Austin Community College for the fall semester. "This time I mean it," Jennifer said. "I really am going to finish school."

"That's great, Jennifer," Sharon said. "We love you and

we're proud of you, but you need to follow through, not just talk about it."

"I know, Mom."

Sharon was troubled that Jennifer was moving in with Denise, who'd had drug issues of her own. "Jennifer, I don't know about this idea," Sharon said.

"Don't be so hard on people," Jennifer said. "She's not on drugs now. You have to give people a chance."

"Okay, sweetie," Sharon said. "But be careful."

On the drive back from Norman to Texas, Sharon and Jim took a route via Austin to see Jennifer. Sharon wanted to put her arms around her daughter, to sit and talk with her about her future. Jennifer had signed up with a temporary agency while she looked for a job, and Sharon was eager to see for herself if Jennifer was truly changing. On the road, Jim and Sharon listened to reports on Sirius radio about eighteen-year-old Natalee Holloway's recent disappearance in Aruba.

"My God, Jim," Sharon said. "How would you ever live with something like that? Survive that?"

Jim shook his head. It seemed incomprehensible that a parent could live through such a loss.

When they reached Austin, Sharon called Jennifer to tell her that they'd arrived and they were ready to meet her for lunch.

"I can't," Jennifer said. "Madyson's babysitter didn't show up. I need to take care of her."

Disappointed, Sharon and Jim continued on to the Hill Country town of Fredericksburg, to Jim's family reunion. Yet Sharon wasn't too worried; Jennifer sounded focused on the future. Sharon hesitated to open herself up to disappointment by believing that her troubled daughter had finally grown up, but she had to. As Jennifer's mother, Sharon had to believe that Jen would find her way. Only later would Sharon Cave realize that in Austin that afternoon, she'd missed her last opportunity to ever see Jennifer. Never again would she look into her middle daughter's beautiful blue eyes.

Thirteen

"I didn't know at first that Jennifer was back on the meth," says Denise, who'd noticed that her new houseguest rarely slept, yet seemed to have boundless energy. "Then one night, I stopped in her room, and she was inhaling fumes from something she was melting in this glass tube. I asked what it was and she said, 'Ice.' Jennifer wasn't using a lot, and she never looked strung out, but it was like everything started up once Colton was out of jail."

Confirming Denise's suspicions, Jennifer mentioned that she'd been out with Colton. "He got drunk and started a fight again," Jennifer said. "Colton's out of control."

That July 2005, Colton Pitonyak wasn't the only Catholic High grad out of control. On July 2, Marty Heidgen, who graduated with Dustin Pitonyak, was drunk and driving the wrong way down a Long Island, New York, expressway, when he slammed a wedding limousine head-on. The limo driver and a seven-year-old flower girl, Kate Flynn, died. "No one in Little Rock even talked about it," says a young man who graduated with Heidgen. "It was like it hadn't happened, just another rich kid having fun and getting in trouble."

Meanwhile, Scott wrestled with the breakup. Losing Jennifer had hurt Scott, and he was on the rebound. He met a thirty-four-year-old real estate agent, a pretty blond, and ended up in bed with her. "But it didn't help," he says. "I loved Jennifer."

Jennifer, too, was in a quandary. She told Vanessa she loved Scott, but worried about being a wife and mom. Yet she said being away from Madyson was the most difficult part of the breakup. "She adored Scott, but she needed space and her independence back," says Vanessa. "Jennifer was just twenty-one, and I understood that."

Jennifer settled into Denise's. She cleaned out the spare bedroom, sorted through the boxes stored there, and took the clothes inside, at Denise's direction, to Goodwill or a resale shop. Jennifer hung curtains and cleaned. She found a painting at the apartment Dumpster, one with airy pink flowers, and hung it on the wall. Within a week, the room looked feminine and pretty, bright and cheerful, with every-thing in place.

The two women got along well. "It was like having a true girlfriend," says Denise. "We'd play around with hair and makeup and clothes." At times, she ferried Jennifer and her friends down to Sixth Street for a night out. Since Denise didn't drink, she was the designated driver.

As she seemed to do wherever she went, Jennifer or-ganized Denise's apartment, cleaning closets and spruc-ing the place up, something Denise, who was constantly battling fatigue and pain from her disease, didn't have the energy for. At night, Jennifer often went out with Eli. As Scott suspected, they'd begun dating. One weekend, Jen-nifer and Eli camped on the banks of the Guadalupe River. Draped over an inner tube they brought to float down the river, she looked full of life in her swimsuit and a big floppy hat. Later Eli would remember how she'd smiled that day, content and happy. Jen had loved the outdoors since her childhood tomboy days, and fresh air and trees still invigorated her.

Back at Denise's, Jennifer worked on her résumé on the computer and posted it on Monster.com, then tracked down an old roommate who held some of Jen's things as collateral against money Jen owed her. She and Eli rushed over to the girl's apartment, and she returned to Jen the things she still had, including baby pictures, a collection of miniature frog figurines, and a star Jim's older daughter, Whitney, had made for Jennifer. The bright, cheerful wall hanging had blurbs cut from magazines pasted on it, fun and inspirational phrases: "You have to go through a little embarrassment to get what you want"; "Miracles"; "Going fast is alive"; "Flirt"; "No barriers"; and "The agony of growing up."

"The agony of growing up" certainly seemed to summarize much of what Jennifer had gone through, especially in her relationship with Colton. At times, Jennifer mentioned "my friend Colton" to Eli.

"Who is this guy?" he asked one day at Lake Travis when they'd taken his English bulldog, Stash, for a swim.

"Oh, Colton's a friend. He's depressed a lot," Jennifer said. "He wants me to go over to his place."

"Why's he depressed?"

Jennifer shrugged. "Colton hates the world."

As the days passed, neither Jen nor Eli told Scott they were dating. They weren't sure yet where it would lead, and both cared about Scott and hesitated to hurt him. Yet, somehow, Scott sensed it. Suspicious, he e-mailed Jennifer, demanding to know what had changed between them, why they rarely saw each other, but she gave no real answers. "I was hurt and angry," Scott says. "All kinds of emotions converging at once."

On July 11, Jennifer went to a career fair in Austin. That evening, she had dinner with Scott and Madyson, then the youngster stayed overnight with Jennifer, sleeping beside her in her room at Denise's. They played and told stories. Scott was still pushing Jennifer, wanting to know what had driven them apart, and Jennifer still wasn't opening up to him. "It got all weird," Scott says.

On the fifteenth, Jennifer took Madyson to see *Charlie and the Chocolate Factory,* with Johnny Depp, on its opening day in theaters. Afterward they went to the complex swimming pool and then had dinner with Scott. That night, too, Madyson stayed overnight with Jennifer. Despite everything going on in her life, Jen had made a commitment to Madyson, and she was working hard to keep it.

At Denise's apartment one evening in mid July, Jennifer returned from Colton's apartment angry. She'd already told Denise that she wasn't seeing Colton unless other people were around, that she was afraid to be alone with him. He hadn't hit her, she said, but he'd pushed her. "Why do you go there?" Denise asked.

"Because he's my friend," Jennifer replied. She hesitated and then added, "Because he's not always that way."

Another night the phone rang at Karissa Reine's house. She hadn't heard from Jennifer in a month, but when Karissa picked up, her friend sounded frightened. Someone talked in the background and Jennifer said, "I've gotta go." The phone clicked off.

Minutes later, Jennifer called back, whispering again, saying she was hiding in a closet. "Whatever's going on, get out of there," Karissa told her. "Now!"

"I can't leave. I don't have my car," Jennifer said.

"Start walking, and I'll pick you up," Karissa said, as the telephone went dead for a second time. All that night Karissa worried about Jennifer, but the next day came and went and she didn't hear any bad news, so she assumed all was well. Later Karissa would wonder who Jennifer was with that night, and if it could have been Colton Pitonyak.

"I have to stop going to Colton's," Jennifer told Denise one afternoon in late July. And then she added flatly, "If I don't, he's going to end up killing me."

Denise must have looked shocked, because Jennifer said it again: "I swear, one day Colton's just going to kill me."

The meth and Colton were connected in Jennifer's life, and she seemed powerless or unwilling to completely rid herself of either. One night when she didn't return to Denise's, she partied with her friend Nicole Ford, at an apartment where people inhaled meth fumes out of a shared beaker. Jennifer and Nicole looked around, much as they had a year earlier, and both were frightened by what they saw, hollow human beings ruled by a craving for a powerful drug, many who looked decades older than their years. That night, Jennifer grabbed her friend's hand.

"We have to change our lives," Jennifer pleaded. "Promise me we'll quit, and if one of us can't make it, the other one will go on without her."

Nicole hesitated. She knew Jennifer had been trying to rid herself of the drug. Feeling powerless to quit, Nicole feared her friend would succeed and leave her behind. The two women held each other and cried, as Nicole reluctantly agreed, "I promise."

At 12:17 A.M. on July 26, six days after the last time Madyson slept overnight with Jennifer, Colton Pitonyak logged onto his computer and went to Yahoo.com. Once the screen loaded, he conducted a search, looking for a silencer for a SW .380 semiautomatic pistol. Half an hour later, he was at his computer again, this time looking for a fully automatic Tech–9 assault gun, like the one used by the killers in the horrific Columbine school shooting.

Four days later, Jennifer was at a Wells Fargo Bank in Austin applying for a job. She didn't get it, but she wasn't dissuaded. On August 5, she was at a Compass Bank for a second interview. She kept track of each interview, every appointment in her black Day-Timer. "I really hope I get this one," she told Denise. "I really do."

Later Colton would say that he saw little of Jennifer as August began. "She was trying to straighten out her life," he says. "She was going to stop doing drugs."

Laura Hall, however, had been sucked whole into Colton's netherworld, enthusiastically, it would seem. "My boyfriend is the most powerful drug dealer . . ." she bragged.

"You're dating Al Capone?" one friend jabbed. "How's that working out for you?"

July 31, a week before Jennifer heard Compass Bank had hired someone else for the open slot, Laura Hall called her friend Sammi Moore, the woman she'd worked with at the law firm, to tell her that Colton needed money. Hall offered to sell Sammi cocaine. Sammi turned Laura down.

That month, Laura also called Said Aziz, a UT friend who'd moved back to the East Coast for the summer. When he heard the telephone ring and saw that it was Laura Hall, Aziz hesitated to answer. Laura called him often, usually to talk about Colton. Said couldn't understand why she stayed with Pitonyak, what Laura Hall got out of the relationship, and Aziz had grown weary of the phone calls. He figured this call was about another nonsensical problem, and it was.

"I think Colton is cheating on me," Laura complained.

"Yeah? And you're surprised at that because?" Said responded. It was no secret that Colton Pitonyak loved to flirt and that he was far from monogamous.

"I think Colton slept with a stripper," Laura said.

Another day, Laura asked Said if she should lend Colton $700. "Do you think I'll get it back?" she asked.

"I would consider a loan to Colton money spent," Said advised.

The next time Laura called, however, she'd made the loan, and Colton, as Aziz predicted, hadn't paid her back. "I need the money for rent," she said.

"Laura, I told you not to date the guy. I told you not to loan him money. I don't know what the hell else you want me to do," Said replied.

Said couldn't help but wish that Laura Hall and Colton Pitonyak would disappear from his radar, but that didn't happen. Instead, in early August, a new series of phone calls began. This time, Laura said Colton was in debt to some dangerous men, drug dealers, and needed cash, fast. Would their friend help him? Aziz was noncommittal, but days later, when Laura called again, she rattled off instructions on where to wire the money.

"You know, if the situation is so dire, if the guy's going to lose his life if he doesn't have the money, why don't you have Colton call me himself?" Said responded, exasperated.

"I can't do that," Laura said, crying. "I promised Colton you'd fix it."

Laura also called Andrea Jiles off and on that summer, talking about Colton.

In early August, Laura called her high school friend to tell her that Colton was so high he'd shot a gun off inside his apartment, while Laura was there. "She acted like it was no big deal," says Jiles. "But I was worried. Guns kill. It was a big deal."

Another afternoon, the subject was Colton's drug debt and a group of "Asian" drug dealers Colton owed money to. Andrea couldn't understand if Laura was trying to tell her that Colton had given them a gun as partial payment or if he'd asked her to find one for him. Either way, it didn't sit well.

Andrea was worried. Laura sounded strung out and talked constantly of guns and drugs. "Listening to her talk about her day-to-day life, it was like there was all this weirdness going on," says Jiles. "It was like, expect anything."

Still, Jiles didn't foresee what happened next, the day Laura called to say, "Colton burned me while we were fucked up." Then, to Jiles's astonishment, Laura Hall laughed.

"Burned you? Was he mad at you?" Jiles asked.

"No, he's all right," Laura said. Not sounding at all upset, she explained that he'd burned her arm with a cigarette while they were both high.

"Laura, it's not right that he took your money and didn't pay you back. It's not right that he's hurting you. This isn't all right," Jiles insisted.

"It's fun. I'm having fun," Laura said. "It's all okay."

Jason Mack didn't see what was happening as fun. He considered Colton Pitonyak a good friend. He spent much of his time at the Orange Tree, often staying at Pitonyak's apartment. He rarely saw him sleep. Instead, Colton inhaled amazing amounts of meth, and then stayed up for days at a time, becoming increasingly more tightly wound, more paranoid. The situation only worsened when Pitonyak was high and forgot to lock his door. Someone stole five hundred ecstasy tablets, and Pitonyak, who owed $3 apiece for them, was another $1,500 in debt. Upset about the theft, Colton kept two guns in the apartment.

As for Laura, Mack felt sorry for her. She loved Pitonyak so much, she'd do anything for him, including the day he sent her with a box to deliver. Mack assumed Pitonyak had a gun inside, one he was selling. Hall delivered the box and returned to the Orange Tree with $300 she gave to Colton.

Then there was the time Mack was at Pitonyak's apartment with Hall. Pitonyak hadn't slept in days, and he looked more wired than Mack had ever seen him. On edge, everything annoyed Pitonyak, especially Hall. He swore at her, and she asked him why he treated her so badly. "I've given you money and I haven't even asked for it back," she said. "Why are you talking to me like that? Why are you treating me like this?"

Colton physically threw Laura out of the apartment, into the courtyard. She sat there on a step, crying. Inside the apartment, Colton brought Mack back to the vanity area, in the hallway outside the bathroom. He pulled a pistol out of a drawer. "Should I shoot her? I should just shoot her," Pitonyak said. "She's driving me fucking crazy. I ought to just kill the bitch."

Mack reasoned with Pitonyak, urging him to put the gun away. Finally, he did. Outside, Mack collected Laura and took her to a friend's apartment, warning her to stay away from Colton. "He's too fucked up," he said. "It's too dangerous."

"I love Colton," Laura replied.

Before long, Laura was back at the Orange Tree, as if nothing had happened.

That August, Eli began to worry that the Brook Meadow Village apartment complex, where he, Scott, Jennifer, and Denise lived, had bad karma. Just looking around the complex, he felt odd, like something hung over all of them. Scott was moving into a rented house Labor Day weekend. Eager to get out as well, Eli started looking at town homes.

On August 12, a Friday, Nora Sullivan, a wispy blond UT communications major from California who'd been a friend of Colton's for a little more than a year, ran into him at the Orange Tree. She'd just moved into a condo six doors down from his a few days earlier, to get ready for the fall semester.

"Can't talk," he said. "I've got an exam tomorrow morning. I've got to study."

The following morning, Colton called Sullivan and woke her up. He'd overslept and hadn't made it to his biology final. If he drove, he'd have to find a place to park the car, and it was on the far side of campus, so it would take too long to walk. Frantic and upset, Colton wanted a ride, and Sullivan agreed to take him. They met downstairs in the complex parking lot, and she drove him and waited outside the building as he rushed in. A little while later, he walked out. The exam was over, and Colton couldn't find the professor to ask about a makeup. He was furious.

That evening, Eli and Jennifer went to a party at the home of Michael Rodriguez, a DJ she'd bumped into off and on that summer at parties with first Scott, then Eli. Rodriguez layered tracks, playing one record on top another, matching the beats, the way they did in Jennifer's favorite clubs, blending tracks into a highly rhythmic dance beat. That night, Eli and Jennifer argued, and he left early. Jennifer stayed and spent much of the night talking to Melissa Kuhl, a dark-haired girl with a half smile. They'd never met before, but as she did with many, Jennifer bonded quickly to Melissa. They spent the night telling each other their life histories. Jennifer admitted she'd used drugs.

Melissa's birthday was the following week, and someone had given her a small bag of cocaine. She didn't use drugs and didn't know what to do with it. "Do you want it?" she offered.

"No," Jennifer said. "I need to get my life together."

Off and on that night, in between sets, Jennifer flirted with the DJ, a bulkily built twentysomething-year-old with sleepy dark eyes. In addition to playing his music, Michael Rodriguez sold insurance at Progressive and worked as a bouncer at Maggie Mae's, a long-time Sixth Street club.

Attracted to her since their first meeting, Rodriguez was interested when he heard that Scott and Jen were no longer a couple. He was pleased when she handed him her cell number and said, "Give me a call." Rodriguez reciprocated with his cell phone number. While he mixed tracks, Jennifer danced, her hands in the air, looking happy and free.

The party wound down in the early morning hours, and Jennifer and Michael left in her car to meet up with a group at another friend's house. There they talked more, the flirting escalating. "I liked you the first time I saw you," she said.

"I thought we'd hit it off," Michael agreed.

They kissed and wrestled on the couch, and Rodriguez, although twice her size, let Jennifer pretend to beat him up, begging for mercy.

"You're not that strong," she said, laughing.

Later, the talk turned serious. "I've had some issues," Jennifer said, not explaining any further. "But I'm going back to school, and I've got an interview for a great job next week."

Rodriguez liked Jennifer. He watched her with his friends and saw her trying to make them comfortable, offering little things, like getting them a glass of water. Jennifer reminded him of his sisters and his mother, the way the women in his family cared about other people. "We need to get together," he said, when she dropped him back at his house.

"Definitely," she said. "I like you."

"Why?" he asked.

"You're kind of a big guy," she said. "You make me feel safe."

Fourteen

After he'd blown his biology exam on Saturday, Colton Pitonyak went on a binge, drinking vodka, popping Xanax, and inhaling the fumes from burning shards of meth. Then more bad news; Colton had lent his white Toyota Avalon to Jason Mack. While driving the car, Mack was pulled over and taken in for failing to appear at a hearing on a misdemeanor charge he had pending. Mack's mother called to tell Colton his car was towed to a lot in Cedar Park, north of Austin. That was all Colton needed. Colton's unpaid drug bills approached $5,000, money he didn't have. His parents were bound to be upset about his biology grade, and now he had to call his mother to get his car out of hock. It must have felt as if everything were falling apart around him.

Sunday after Lauren finished working at the University of Oklahoma campus TV station, the youngest Cave sister called Jennifer in Austin. Being on television as a reporter was a dream for Lauren, a career she'd wanted since childhood, and what she heard in her sister's reaction wasn't jealousy but pride. "You're so brave," Jen said.

Meanwhile in Houston, Andrea Jiles stewed over her conversation with Laura Hall, the one in which Hall confided that Colton burned her. Jiles feared Hall's relationship with Pitonyak was spinning ever more wildly out of control. When Jiles's boyfriend said he was driving to Austin for a couple of days, she decided to go along. When they got there, her boyfriend met Laura briefly but then took off, and Jiles got in the green Cadillac Concours with Laura, who rattled on as she drove about Colton and the money he hadn't paid her back. Jiles noticed a deep, dime-size wound in her friend's arm.

"Is that where Colton burned you?" she asked.

"Yeah, but it was no big thing," Laura said, with a shrug. "We were both fucked up."

"That's not all right," Jiles said, but Laura just shrugged.

The whole time, Laura talked as if everything were wonderful. But her eyes were dark and sunken, and she'd lost weight. "She looked like a drug addict," says Jiles. "I was furious with Colton Pitonyak. He'd changed Laura. He'd done this to her."

When Laura got Colton on the telephone, Jiles wanted to meet with him, to take him to task for the way he was treating Laura, but Colton was in a funk over his final and his car, and in no mood to meet Jiles.

Andrea Jiles never did talk to Colton that day. On the drive home to Houston, Jiles's boyfriend commented, "Your friend looks crazy."

"Yeah," Jiles said. "I guess she is."

On Monday, August 15, Colton had to sober up and get straight. He needed to call his parents, somehow explain what happened with the car, and get a credit card to reclaim it. He also needed a copy of the car title, which was in their names. Colton had been out of jail for only six weeks, and Eddie and Bridget couldn't have been happy.

While Colton's life crumbled around him, Jennifer pushed to improve hers. She'd offered to work in her mother's sales booth at a Houston convention the next weekend, selling Sharon's line of promotional items. Then, that Monday, something remarkable happened. Jen went for a job interview at a small law firm, Grissom & Thompson. In an old, converted house near the county court complex, the firm had two attorneys, an office manager, a full-time administrative assistant, and a part-time receptionist/file clerk. At that time, the firm had two openings to fill, both the admin assistant and the receptionist. The position she applied for was the part-time slot, and the office manager who interviewed her was impressed enough to ask her to come in the following morning, Tuesday, to meet with the lawyers. Thrilled, Jennifer agreed.

That afternoon, Jennifer called Sharon, telling her all about the law firm, how well it had gone, and discussing what she planned to wear for the follow-up interview. Sharon was happy for Jennifer but wasn't having a good day since a woman she'd hired for her promotional goods business had quit.

"Mom, please don't worry," Jennifer said. "Don't be so upset."

"Jennifer, it's hard to be an employer," she said.

"I know," Jennifer said. They talked about the coming weekend and the convention.

"Are you still planning to come?" Sharon asked.

"Unless I have a job," Jennifer told her, and Sharon knew from the sound of Jennifer's voice how excited she was about the possibility.

At 4:30 A.M. the following morning, Tuesday, August 16, one of Colton Pitonyak's old frat brothers loaded his belongings into a truck in the parking garage at the Orange Tree. Finished with classes, he was moving out and needed to rush to meet friends on a fishing trip. Colton, looking drugged, dazed, and disheveled, walked up in the dark and surprised him.

"Hey, Colton," the frat brother said.

Colton barely glanced at him, then shuffled past, incoherent, and appearing not to recognize him.

The following morning, Jennifer dressed for her second interview, putting on a gray skirt with a white shirt and a pair of small glasses. Bright and early that morning, she met with Bill Thompson, one of the firm's two partners. Jennifer looked professional, she was smart, and Thompson thought she'd be a good fit for the small office. "You're hired," he said. "Just one thing: Can you start today?"

"Yes," Jennifer said, beaming. "I sure can."

* * *

When Colton got up, he updated his Facebook.com profile. He had forty-four friends listed at schools all over the country, including Harvard and USC, some who went back to his time at Catholic High. Then he couldn't put it off any longer. He had to get his car out of hock. His parents must have been upset about yet another crisis, but his mother still got the car title to him and gave him her credit card to pay the $200 impound fee. Colton called Laura to drive him to the impound lot.

A week earlier, Jason Mack had warned Hall that Pitonyak was dangerous and advised her to stay away from him. Still Hall agreed to pick Pitonyak up in her green Caddy about three.

That afternoon, they left Colton's apartment, hit the drive-through at a nearby Arby's, then drove north to Williamson County. At the car lot, Laura dropped Colton off, and then left. During his drive home in the reclaimed Toyota, Colton took a call from Laura, who suggested they get together later that night. Apparently she'd fulfilled her purpose by delivering him to pick up his car, and Colton wasn't interested. "I'll call you later," he told her. In Austin, he stopped briefly at a liquor store to procure a fresh bottle of vodka. When he reached the Orange Tree about five that evening, he unscrewed the top and poured himself a healthy glassful. He'd had to stay sober to pick up the car, but that was over.

At six, from his apartment, Colton called Jennifer. He hadn't seen her in weeks. When she didn't pick up, he left a message. Later he'd guess it consisted of: "What's up? Call me."

At about that time, in Denise's apartment, Jennifer was jumping up and down, screaming, "They hired me. I started work and, you know what, I did such a great job that they promoted me, all in one day! I got the best job!"

That afternoon in the office, Bill Thompson watched Jennifer and realized she could do more than answer telephones and file. So, instead of the $10-an-hour job he'd hired Jennifer for, he offered her the full-time administrative assistant slot with a salary and benefits. The job required multitasking and determination, and it involved scheduling cases and motions, but Thompson had no doubt she could handle it.

"The office is near Austin Community College," Jennifer gushed to Sharon in one of their calls that evening. "I'll be able to take a class or two and get school going again. It's perfect."

"That's wonderful, Jennifer," Sharon said. "We'll get you a little one-bedroom apartment close by and fix it up really cute."

"I just want you to be proud of me, Mom," Jennifer said.

"Jennifer, we're always proud of you. We love you," Sharon said.

"I know, but I've been nothing for so long," she said. "And now, who knows. I could go to law school. I could do anything."

"Just do a good job, Jennifer. Work hard for these lawyers," Sharon said. "They're putting their faith in you. Don't let them down."

"I won't, Momma," she said. "I love you."

"I love you, too, sweetie."

When she hung up with her mother, Jennifer phoned Jim, calling him by his family nickname, "Buffalo, I'm going to make you proud of me," she said. "I got a job!"

Early that evening, Scott paced in his apartment, thinking about Jennifer.

The day before, a friend had confirmed that Jen and Eli were dating. When Scott heard the news, he was upset by what he saw as a bitter betrayal. When she moved out, Jennifer promised they would work on their relationship, try to save it. And Scott considered Eli a good friend. "Now I knew that they lied to me," Scott says. Reeling from the news, the night before, Scott had sent Jennifer a long, angry e-mail.

All that day, he chewed on the situation, thinking and

rethinking it. Although still hurt, after reconsidering, Scott regretted the e-mail and much of what he'd written. Considering all that had happened, all they'd meant to each other, Scott didn't want to be upset with Jennifer. He still loved her, more deeply than he'd ever loved a woman. So he decided to talk to her in person.

At Denise's he rang the doorbell, and Jennifer answered.

"I'm sorry for the things I said," he told her.

"I'm sorry, too," she said. They talked, and Jennifer began to cry. She knew she'd let Scott and Madyson down, but she just wasn't ready for a family. First she wanted, perhaps even needed, to explore her place in the world. And there was this other thing, the same thing she'd told Karissa Reine about months earlier.

"Scott, I feel like I'm surrounded by demons," Jennifer confided, her eyes filling with tears. "I really do. I can't shake it."

Scott held Jennifer as she cried. "It's the drugs," he said. "That's all it is. Get them out of your life, and it'll go away."

"I'm trying. I really am. But it's so hard," she told him. "I can't shake the feeling that I'm surrounded by something evil."

They stood together, silent, while she cried. Then Scott leaned forward to kiss her. As their lips met, Jennifer slid down to the floor. "I have been using meth again," she confessed, her voice quiet and ashamed. "I have, it's true. But I'm going to stop the drugs. I'm going to take this job and run with it."

Scott had never been hurt the way the breakup with Jennifer had hurt him, and he looked down at her, and then reached down to lift her up. He didn't want to let her go. It felt good to hold her.

At about 7:30 that evening, Scott turned to leave, feeling better for having forgiven her.

"I love you," she said.

"I love you, too," he responded, and then he was gone.

Later that night, Jennifer text-messaged Scott. "I'm sorry. Thank you."

After Scott left, Jennifer called friends Eli, Laura Ingles, and others to tell them about the new job. She offered to help Laura, who'd just moved that weekend, unpack, but then never showed up at the new apartment. Instead, Jennifer told Denise that she wanted nothing more than to stay home and get to bed early. By eight that evening, Jennifer had washed her laundry, dried it, and put it away. Wearing a pair of red gym shorts and a gray half T-shirt, she lay on the couch at Denise's apartment watching a Lifetime movie about two troubled teenage girls who got into drugs.

"Oh, I love this one," Jennifer said to Denise, who lay on a couch across from her.

They laughed and talked, Jennifer cluing Denise in to what to expect before it happened on the screen. "I knew a girl like that," Jennifer said about one of the characters. "She was so screwed up."

Through it all, Jennifer talked about how excited she was. She had her clothes laid out for work the next day, and her words were full of plans and hopes. Later Denise wouldn't be able to remember what time the movie ended, but when it did, Jennifer stood up and stretched. "I'm going to bed," she said. "Will you wake me when you get up at 6:30?"

"Sure," Denise said.

"Don't forget," Jennifer said. "It's important. I want to get there early in the morning."

Meanwhile in his apartment at the Orange Tree, at 8:47 that evening, Colton logged onto the UT Web site to check his summer school grade. Missing the exam had cost him dearly. The brilliant scholarship student had earned a D in his biology class. How much longer would his parents support him with such disappointments? He was already complaining to friends that his father had cut off his allowance. Minutes later, Jennifer returned Colton's telephone call.

A short time later, Nora Sullivan saw Colton outside his apartment and asked if she could watch his television that night. She wasn't unpacked yet, didn't have cable, and wanted to see *Rescue Me*, a series about New York City firefighters on the FX channel.

"I'm going out to dinner and I won't be there," Colton said. Then he thought about it, and added, "But I could give you my key."

"No," Nora said. "It's no big deal."

At 10:30, Michael Rodriguez finished his shift at Progressive Insurance and called Jennifer. She told him about her new job, excitement lacing each word.

"We need to hang out again," he told her.

No longer with Scott and her relationship with Eli casual, she replied, "We'll do lunch, soon."

"What're you doing tonight?"

"I'm going downtown to hang out with a friend," she said. "Colton's got some issues."

Michael didn't know Colton and didn't ask what kind of issues. At the time, he hadn't wanted to pry. He liked Jennifer, but they were still in the getting-to-know-each-other stage, when it wasn't a good idea to push too hard.

Although she'd told Denise she was staying in, sometime after 10:30 Jennifer left the apartment and drove to Colton's place. Perhaps she was worried about him. Between the D in biology and having to call his parents to reclaim the car, he must have been in a foul mood. That Jennifer was pulling her life together, excited about the new job, must have drawn into even sharper perspective the mess he'd made of his own.

A month or so earlier, Jennifer had called Karissa Reine in the middle of the night, frightened, saying she was in a closet and that she couldn't leave because she didn't have her car. This evening, Jennifer drove her own car. She dressed in a short khaki skirt and a striped tank top. She left her long red hair down, and got in her black Saturn to pick Colton up at the Orange Tree, then drove to Sixth Street.

Their first stop was Jazz, a cavernous Louisiana-style Cajun food place with wood floors, a long bar, and New Orleans decor.

From Jazz, Colton and Jennifer drove or walked down Sixth Street. It was quiet that night, between semesters at UT, and many of the students who habitually crowded the bars even on weekday nights hadn't returned for the fall semester. It was hot, August always is in Central Texas, and they passed old wood and brick storefronts with blazing neon signs, advertising massage and tattoo parlors, and saloons like the Chugging Monkey, The Blind Pig, and Pete's Dueling Piano Bar.

On the street, Jennifer saw a friendly face; Melissa Kuhl was celebrating her birthday with a group of friends. Jennifer had met Melissa at Michael Rodriguez's party just days earlier, and they'd spent much of the time talking. "We're going in Treasure Island, want to come?" Melissa asked.

Inside Treasure Island, a hole-in-the-wall tavern with an illuminated fish tank behind the bar and a skull and crossbones flag outside, Kuhl and four friends, three girls and a guy friend named Jeff Sanderson, along with Jennifer and Colton, pulled together stools and took over a table. In the dimly lit bar, while Jennifer talked to the others, Kuhl sat next to Colton, and began to feel an attraction. He flirted, and he was cute and funny. Before long, Kuhl and Colton huddled together. He was soft-spoken and well-mannered and seemed interested in what she had to say.

"I want to get back into school. I haven't done well," he confided. "I came to UT, did great for a couple of years and then screwed everything up by getting into drugs."

Colton told Melissa about his month in jail and insisted he wanted to get off the drugs and get back to his original goals, to finish business school and start a good career. It surprised Melissa when Colton then leaned forward and asked her if she wanted to leave with him. "I have to meet some friends," he said. "They've got an eight ball for me."

Melissa knew an eight ball was coke or meth, but she

didn't use drugs and their mention bothered her. Still, Colton was attractive and easy to talk to. When he walked to the bar to buy a drink, she asked Jennifer, "Are you two together?"

"No, we're not," Jennifer said. Then she leaned forward and warned, "But you really don't want to mess with him. He's crazy."

"What do you mean crazy?" Melissa asked.

"He's crazy. He's got a lot of emotional baggage, and you don't want to mess with him," Jennifer said. "He's weird."

"You're not going anywhere with him," one of Melissa's friends insisted. "You came with us and you're leaving with us."

When he returned, Colton said, "Come with me. We'll get it and come back."

"I'd better not," Melissa said. She'd been thinking about what Jennifer had said and wondered if Colton was clingy, one of those I-love-you-in-two-days kind of guys.

At least on the surface, Colton took rejection well. He simply shrugged, appearing not to really care.

The friends drank and talked, but Colton, who'd lost interest in Kuhl, turned to Sanderson. Jennifer seemed fine, not drunk, not drugged, but Sanderson thought Colton was high on something, "really out of it." Listening to Colton on his cell phone talking about the eight ball convinced Sanderson that he was right.

In Treasure Island, Jennifer's phone buzzed at 11:30, with a text message from Michael Rodriguez: "Why are you such a beautiful girl?"

"I get that from my mother," she responded, just minutes later.

The seven talked, laughed, and listened to music. When one of the girls struggled to pull off a plastic wristband she had from another bar, it wouldn't budge. She asked if anyone at the table had a scissors. No one did. Then Colton, a cigarette dangling from his mouth, pulled a black-handled, folding knife with a four-inch serrated blade out from his belt, reached across the table, and cut it off. The knife made Sanderson uneasy.

"Let's go somewhere else," someone suggested, and all the others nodded in agreement. Soon Melissa and her friends paid their tabs and walked toward the Cheers Shot Bar, almost directly across the street.

"Colton has to pay the bill," Jennifer told Melissa. "We'll meet you there."

About then, at 11:54, Jennifer's phone buzzed with a second text from Rodriguez: "When do I get to hang out with you again?"

"Sometime soon," was her response.

Jennifer wasn't the only one a friend wanted to hook up with that night. Four minutes later, at 11:58, Laura Hall, apparently disappointed that the guy she thought of as her boyfriend wasn't interested in hanging with her, messaged Colton: "Ugh, you should have called me back."

Just after midnight, Melissa and her friends walked across to Cheers and got a table, while she watched the door for Jennifer and Colton. Kuhl saw them show their IDs to the bouncer, and then she turned away to talk to Sanderson. When Kuhl glanced back at the door, Jennifer and Colton were gone. Kuhl looked around the bar and didn't see them. She rushed to the door, wondering what had happened, and peered out just in time to watch Jennifer and Colton walk away. They turned a corner and disappeared from sight.

"What happened?" Melissa asked the bouncer. "Why didn't they come in?"

"I don't know," he said.

Melissa thought about it, figured Colton had convinced Jennifer to go with him to get his eight ball of drugs, and went back to the table to join her friends.

Just after midnight, Jennifer called Michael Rodriguez, who lay on the couch watching television. "What's up?"

"I'm still out with my friend Colton. He's upset," she

said. "He's in trouble and the only people who can help him are in jail."

"Everything okay?" Rodriguez asked.

"Yeah," Jennifer said. "It's fine. I've got to get home soon. I've got to work in the morning."

An hour later, at 1:05, Michael's phone rang again. At first, Jennifer sounded as if she just wanted to talk. "What're you doing?" she asked.

"Watching TV. What're you doing?"

"We're leaving, I have to get home," she said.

Then all of sudden, she shouted, "Hey, that's not my car."

"My God, Colton's trying to bust in a car window," she said to Rodriguez. "He's upset because he lost his cell phone. I'm helping him look for it."

"What's happening?" Rodriguez asked.

"We're walking to my car," she said. Then, sounding exasperated, "Oh, great, now he's pissing on a car."

"Are you okay?" Rodriguez prodded. They didn't know each other well, and he didn't want to pry, but he was getting worried. Still, he'd been to Sixth Street with friends who got drunk and did stupid things. That wasn't unusual, rarely anything to be concerned about.

"Everything's okay," Jennifer said. "I'm going to help him find his phone. I'll call you when I get home."

"Okay."

With that, Jennifer Cave hung up the telephone. Michael Rodriguez thought about that telephone call for a moment. Jennifer sounded confident, insisted she wasn't in any danger. There was no reason to agonize. Feeling satisfied all was well, Rodriguez turned back to the television, and soon fell asleep. When he woke the next morning, he wasn't concerned that Jennifer hadn't called him when she got home, as she'd said she would. It was late the last time they talked, and he assumed that she probably hadn't wanted to wake him. Later, he'd look back at that night and reconsider: Was Jennifer trying to tell him something? Did she want him to look for her if she didn't call? Was she trying to make sure someone knew where she was that night, with whom, and notice if she didn't check in?

"I don't know," Michael would say more than a year later, combing through his dark hair with a thick hand, his eyes regretful. "I'll always wonder. I'll always wish I'd insisted I'd go get her. But she said she was okay. How could I have known?"

Fifteen

Less than an hour after Michael Rodriguez hung up the telephone with Jennifer, Vanessa, the oldest of the Cave sisters, woke up feeling tense and anxious. It was dark out, and she looked at the clock. Later, she'd remember it was about 2 A.M. She'd been out the night before celebrating a friend's birthday but had only two drinks. Home early and to bed, she'd fallen asleep quickly. Looking about the darkened room, she couldn't understand her apprehension. Then, suddenly, Vanessa gripped her abdomen and ran to the bathroom, with the room spinning around her. For an hour, she could barely sit up. In the wee hours of the morning, as abruptly as it started, the nausea passed.

Afterward, Vanessa went back to bed, where she fell into a deep sleep.

At the Orange Tree at 3 A.M., Nora Sullivan was wide awake, unpacking boxes, when someone knocked on her condo door. She looked out the peephole and saw Colton. She opened the door, and he burst through, looking agitated. "Did you hear gunshots?" he asked.

"No," Nora said. "Why?"

Excited, Colton launched into a tale about Mexican drug dealers and how he'd gotten into a fight where bullets were exchanged. Nora half listened. She didn't like nonsense, and that's what it sounded like to her, like fiction. She had the same impression she'd had back in California in high school, when a guy she knew insisted he'd killed a woman and dumped her body. In that case, too, Nora figured the kid was making it all up.

As he talked, Pitonyak said he'd lost his cell phone, and asked to use Nora's. He wanted to call Evan, a guy in Colton's circle of friends, one everyone knew they could count on in a jam, a nerdy kid who would do anything for a friend. Colton tried Evan's phone number twice, but his friend didn't answer. Unconcerned, Nora sat down on the floor and went through another box, unpacking, while Colton paced the small room, jabbering on and on about the gun battle. She paid little attention, scoffing at the very notion that rounds of gunfire had been exchanged just six doors from her apartment. "I would have heard it. I didn't want to waste my ears on garbage like that," she'd say later. "So I kind of tuned him out."

Despite Sullivan's disinterest, Colton rattled on, claiming he'd shot someone, one of the drug dealers. As if to prove he'd told the truth, Colton pulled a handgun out of the waistband of his shorts to show her. Holding the gun up, he slipped out the black magazine holding the bullets, saying he didn't want it to go off accidentally.

"Do I have blood on me?" he asked a short time later.

Nora glanced up and saw a smudge of what could have been blood on Colton's forearm. As she listened, Nora thought again about how close the two apartments were and concluded that she was right the first time; she would have heard shots if a gun battle had gone on so close.

"Sure, Tupac," she said, sarcastically addressing Colton as Tupac Shakur, the infamous rapper murdered in 1996 in a Las Vegas drive-by shooting.

When Colton calmed down, Nora got two beers, and they stood on her balcony drinking and smoking cigarettes. When he left, Colton said, "I'm going to my apartment, to clean up."

Later it appeared that Colton Pitonyak got little sleep that night. An hour or so later, at 4:28 A.M., he logged onto his computer and clicked over to www.sherdog.com, a martial arts Web site that promotes brutal ultimate fighting competitions. Somewhere he found his cell phone, and he used it off and on, trying unsuccessfully to reach his friend Evan. Early that morning, before the sun came up, Colton was back on his computer, this time clicking onto Facebook, working on his profile, the one where he listed his favorite gangster movies, and then at 5:34 he text-messaged Laura Hall.

"What do you mean?" she responded.

The alarm clock in Denise Winterbottom's bedroom buzzed at 6:15 that morning. She turned it off. Her boyfriend slept beside her, and she got up, grabbed her clothes, and walked through the living room to the second bathroom, the one across from Jennifer's room, the bathroom the two women shared. As she passed Jennifer's bedroom door, Denise knocked.

"Hey Jennifer," she called out. "Time to get up."

Then she heard Jennifer's alarm clock go off.

Denise ducked in the bathroom and grabbed her toothbrush. She started brushing her teeth, but still heard the alarm clock. She wondered why Jennifer didn't silence the alarm. Still brushing, she stood outside Jennifer's door, listening. "Jennifer," she called out again, knocking harder on the door. "Wake up, girl. You've got to get to work."

The alarm droned on, incessant, and Denise stood outside Jennifer's room staring at the door. For some reason, she couldn't bring herself to open it, but she didn't know why. She had the unmistakable impression that she didn't want to see what was inside. Finally, she had no other choice. She had to open the door. The last time she'd seen Jennifer the evening before, she had been going to bed, but when Denise opened Jennifer's door, the room was immaculate, the bed made, Jennifer's clothes laid out for work, but Jennifer wasn't there.

Denise scanned the room, walked over, turned off the alarm, and looked about the bedroom again. Jennifer had to be there. But she wasn't. Suddenly, Denise experienced a wave of dread. *Something's wrong*, she thought. *Something's terribly wrong*.

Yet, what? She decided to go to her babysitting job, and call the law firm later, to make sure Jennifer had arrived safely. But then, she had second thoughts. "I'll feel silly when she picks up the telephone," she told herself. "She's fine. She probably just stayed overnight with a friend."

Forty-three minutes later, Colton called Laura Hall. She'd spent the night at a friend's apartment, a thin, dark-haired guy with a manicured goatee whose name was Ryan Martindill. Laura and Martindill had worked together in the workers' compensation department at Pena's law firm and remained friends, going out off and on, sometimes with Martindill's roommate, a heavyset guy named Star Salzman. When Colton hadn't called her back to get together the night before, she called Martindill, and he picked her up at her apartment. She had a bottle of rum with her, and at his place in south Austin, they drank while they talked and watched television. Sometime between 11 that evening and 1 A.M., they fell asleep on separate couches in front of the television. Martindill was still asleep when Laura's cell phone rang.

Colton and Laura talked for thirteen minutes, and then Laura shook Martindill, eager for him to wake up. "Colton called," she said. "I need a ride to my car."

Martindill wasn't surprised. He'd watched the power Colton Pitonyak had over Laura. He'd never met him, but he believed that Hall was obsessed with Pitonyak. So Martindill got up and drove Laura to her apartment to get her car. Hall seemed intent on getting to Colton's quickly.

At 8:30 A.M., Bill Thompson was working at his desk at Grissom & Thompson, when he realized Jennifer Cave hadn't shown up for work. It seemed odd. She'd been so gung-ho the day before, so into the job. He thought about it, but assumed she was just running late. When another half hour passed and she still wasn't there, he dialed her cell phone. Her voice mail came on, and he left a message.

At 10:30, Scott text-messaged Jennifer: "Have a good day at work." He didn't think much about it when she didn't reply, assuming she was busy at her new job. He hoped it was going well, and he smiled, thinking about the night before, glad that they'd talked.

Meanwhile, when Jennifer still wasn't at the office at eleven, Thompson thought over the situation. He didn't believe he'd read Jennifer wrong; she was excited about the job, eager enough that he knew she would show up.

Concerned, Thompson called in his office manager and asked her to check on Jennifer. The woman drove north out of Austin to Denise's apartment at Brook Meadow Village, Jennifer's address on the job application. When no one answered her doorbell, the office manager wrote a note asking Jennifer to call the firm, tucked it in the door, and then drove back downtown to the office.

At 11:45 that morning, Michael Rodriguez arrived ready for his day's work at Progressive Insurance. The first thing he did was call Jennifer to make sure she'd gotten to work all right. In the back of his mind he replayed their conversation from the night before. Jennifer didn't pick up her cell phone, and it switched to voice mail. "Wondering how your day is going. Give me a call," he said.

Around two that afternoon, Bill Thompson's concern had grown into worry. Where was that girl? Why hadn't she come in? Why didn't she call? He pulled out Jennifer's application and tried her cell phone again. Still no answer. He left a message and then, an hour or so later, he called the only other phone number on the application, Sharon's cell phone.

"Mrs. Cave, I don't mean to alarm you," Thompson said, after introducing himself. "It's just that Jennifer didn't come in today. Have you talked to her?"

Sharon wasn't sure what to think. Her first thought was that she'd been foolish the day before to believe that Jennifer had changed. But then she thought back to the conversation. It was true that Jennifer had disappointed her in the past, but she didn't believe she'd lied to her about the job. Jennifer was jazzed, absolutely thrilled about working at the law firm. *She wouldn't have not shown up*, Sharon thought.

"I'm going to make a few calls," she told Thompson.

The first person Sharon called was Scott. When she told him that Jennifer hadn't shown up at work, Scott was immediately surprised, then quickly disappointed. Everything she'd said about wanting to change her life, he reasoned, was just another lie. The most likely scenario was that Jennifer had gone out after he left and gotten high or drunk and hadn't sobered up in time for work. "Jen probably stayed out late partying," he told Sharon. "I wouldn't be concerned."

"Scott, something's wrong," Sharon said. She wasn't sure how she knew that, but she did. She felt certain of it; something was very wrong.

"What are you talking about?" he asked, shrugging it off. "She's fine. She's just out somewhere with friends."

"I have to find Denise," Sharon said.

"Have you seen Jennifer?" she asked when she got Denise on the telephone.

Denise had brought Gracie to her house to nap, wanting to check for Jennifer. Nothing had changed. Jennifer's work clothes were still laid out and the room was untouched. When Denise saw the note on the door from the law firm, she was flooded with regret for not following up on trying to find Jennifer. The first one she called was Eli, but he hadn't seen Jen. When Denise thought about calling Sharon, she hesitated. She'd never met Sharon and had only talked to her on the phone, at times when Sharon called for Jennifer and took the opportunity to thank Denise for taking her daughter in. She was worried, but Denise didn't want to get her friend in trouble.

"Jennifer wasn't here this morning when I went to wake her up," Denise said.

She then told Sharon about the previous night, how Jennifer washed clothes, watched a TV movie with her, and then went off to bed, asking her to wake her the next morning.

Sharon had to ask. There was no way not to. "Is Jennifer on drugs again?"

Denise thought for a moment. Jennifer had used drugs but never seemed to be overdoing it. If she told Sharon that Jennifer was back on meth, even a little, how would it help? "No," she lied. "She's not."

"If you hear from Jennifer, have her call me," Sharon said.

About three o'clock that afternoon, Colton and Laura were both busy. They'd left unit 88 at the Orange Tree in separate cars. As if nothing were wrong, Laura called her parents to discuss her fall schedule at UT. Meanwhile, Colton drove just a few blocks to Breed's Hardware, an ACE franchise store, and walked inside. An upscale combination hardware and luxury goods store that sells everything from hammers and wrenches to Waterford crystal and Godiva chocolates, Breed's is a West Campus landmark, one frequented by students who pick up the odds and ends needed to settle into apartments, including UT longhorn salt and pepper shakers and chip-and-dip dishes. The store's owner, Jeff Breed, encountered a rough-looking young man standing in the hardware section, pushing a cart and looking at a list.

"Need some help?" asked Breed, a tall man with salt-and-pepper hair and a mustache.

When he got closer, Breed smelled alcohol on the young man. Colton showed the store owner his shopping list, and Breed guided him through the store. The store was out of one of the items on Pitonyak's list, paper towels, but Colton grabbed a roll of blue shop towels. He picked up latex gloves, ammonia, Febreze fabric freshener, dust masks, carpet cleaner, and then inquired about a saw.

"What kind do you need?" Breed asked in the saw aisle, in front of a long display of cutting implements.

"Something cheap," Pitonyak answered, as Breed pointed out a display of small saws hanging from hooks.

When the glassy-eyed young man didn't choose one, Breed asked, "What do you need it for?"

"I want to cut up a frozen turkey," Pitonyak said. "I'm frying a turkey today."

Breed suggested a utility hacksaw, and Pitonyak picked it up and made his way to the checkout.

After Sharon hung up the telephone with Denise, she considered what to do. She thought about Jennifer, how to find her. She'd already called her cell phone and left messages. What else could she do? Sharon picked up her own cell and called T-Mobile, the provider who had her service and phones for all four of her children. She explained what she wanted, and since the account was in Sharon's name, the woman in the billing department agreed to fax Sharon a printout of Jennifer's cell phone activity for the previous forty-eight hours.

Sharon paced in her office, waiting, wondering, worrying, until the fax came through. When she glanced over the records, her angst built; Jennifer hadn't made a single cell phone call since 1:05 the morning before. That wasn't like Jennifer. She was addicted to the cell phone, in love with it. She wouldn't go more than a half day without making a phone call.

Her hands trembling, Sharon called Scott and started reading off phone numbers from Jennifer's call list. When she got to one, a number Jennifer had called the previous evening, Scott said, "That's Colton's cell phone."

That name rang a bell with Sharon. She remembered Colton, the boy Jennifer talked about, the one with drug problems who'd been in jail. "Tell me about Colton," Sharon said.

"He's bad news," Scott said. "Uses a lot of drugs and sells them."

When she hung up with Scott, Sharon's head was beginning to pound, and she felt as if the world around her was out of kilter.

"Do you know anything about this Colton guy?" she asked when she called Denise back.

"I know she's hanging around with that guy, and I don't like him," Denise answered.

"I'm thinking about coming to Austin tomorrow morning, if we haven't found her," Sharon said. "I'm worried about her."

"You should come," Denise said. What she left out was, *I'm worried, too.*

As soon as she hung up, Sharon called the phone number on Jennifer's T-Mobile bill Scott had identified as Colton's. The ring immediately clicked over to voice mail, and Sharon left a message: "Colton, I'm Jennifer Cave's mom and I'm looking for her. Call me."

Eight minutes later, Laura Hall pulled into an Austin filling station where she pumped $50 worth of gas into her green Cadillac and had the car washed. Meanwhile, Colton, his purchases from Breed's Hardware in the car, drove through a Burger King on his way back to the apartment. He ordered a value meal, with medium fries and a medium Coke, asking them to hold the onions.

In Dallas, Vanessa had gone into her job at the Wyndham Hotel corporate offices only to be laid off. She'd been expecting it. The hotel chain had been talking about cutbacks for months. She drove back to her apartment and lay down on the couch. She felt hopeless and depressed, and she didn't know why. It wasn't the layoff, but something else she couldn't name. "I couldn't figure out what was wrong with me," she says. "I didn't feel sick like the night before. I felt like something wasn't right, but I didn't know what."

At five that evening, Sharon called Michael Rodriguez's cell phone. It was the last number Jennifer had called the night before. The phone went to voice mail, and she left a message: "This is Jennifer's mother. We're looking for her. Call me."

When Michael saw he had a message and listened to Sharon's anxious voice, he was worried. He thought about Jennifer out with her friend. What if they'd had a car accident? What if she were hurt? He dialed Sharon's office phone number, the one she'd called from, and she picked up.

"We're looking for Jennifer," Sharon said. "She didn't show up for work, and you're the last one she talked to on the phone records. Was she okay?"

"Yeah, she was fine," Michael said.

"Was she drunk?" Sharon asked.

"She didn't sound like it," Michael said.

"Do you know who she was with?" Sharon asked.

"She said some guy, some friend of hers named Coltran or something?"

"Colton?"

"Yeah, that's it," Michael said. "He was acting kind of weird. I don't know a lot. I wish I could give you more, but I haven't known Jennifer that long."

With that, Sharon's cell phone rang. "Hold on," she said.

"Colton?" Sharon said into the cell phone. "Have you seen Jennifer?"

"I saw her last night, but we got in an argument and she left about midnight," he said.

Colton hung up and Sharon got back on the line with Michael. "Colton says he hasn't seen her since midnight."

"He's lying," Michael said. "He was with her when she called me after one. Why is he lying?"

"Anything else you can tell me?" Sharon asked.

"That's all I know," Michael said. "I wish I knew more."

Sharon talked to Jim on and off all afternoon about Jennifer's disappearance. They were both worried. Now she did what she'd considered earlier; she called the Austin Police Department and asked for the missing persons division. An officer got on the telephone. She listened as Sharon told her what had happened, and when the officer asked, Sharon admitted that Jennifer had used drugs. Yet she felt that wasn't what was going on.

"Your daughter is an adult, and she won't technically be missing for twenty-four hours," the officer said. "If she hasn't shown up by tomorrow morning, you can file a report."

That evening, while Sharon grew increasingly anxious in Corpus Christi, in Austin, Eli, Laura Ingles, and other friends helped Scott move some of his furniture into the two-story house he'd rented, on a quiet, tree-lined street. They were all talking about Jennifer, how no one had seen her, how she hadn't returned any of their phone calls. Of them all, only Scott wasn't worried. If anything, he was disappointed in Jennifer, causing so many people such concern when she was undoubtedly out partying somewhere.

When Laura heard that Jennifer was with Colton, however, she grew instantly frightened. "He's not a nice guy," she whispered to Eli. "You need to call the police and tell them."

"No," Eli said. "Jennifer's okay."

"No, she's dead," Laura said. "I can't tell you how I know, but I know. Jennifer's gone."

Eli looked at Laura, shook his head, and then he started to cry.

Disappointed, Sharon hung up the telephone with the missing persons officer. A little while later, she called Scott back. He listened to her fears, but "blew them off." Scott didn't want to tell Sharon, but if Jennifer was with Colton, the most likely scenario was that she was high on drugs and too messed up to talk to her mother. But Scott had had enough of it. He wanted Jennifer to call her mother and keep everyone from worrying.

As soon as he hung up the telephone with Sharon, Scott called Colton. No one answered, and he left a message: "Colton, we know Jennifer's at your house, so you need to tell her that her mom's looking for her."

Colton called back. "What's going on?"

"They know Jen's at your house," Scott said. "She needs to call her mom, now."

"I haven't seen her," Colton insisted. He sounded irritated and wired.

"Her mom has called the cops," Scott said. "They're going to be looking for her."

"I don't know anything," Colton said, angry. "That bitch is going to get me arrested."

In Corpus Christi, Sharon Cave called Austin hospitals, the morgue, everywhere she could think of that Jennifer could be if she were hurt or, worse, dead. She considered driving to Austin that night, but didn't know what she would do once she got there. At least, from the house, she was busy making phone calls, not driving a car. Sharon felt certain Colton was lying, but she didn't know why. All she knew was that the radar that connected her to her middle daughter wasn't working. She hadn't felt Jennifer all day. Usually, even if they were thousands of miles apart, she felt tethered to her kids. The psychological, emotional, or supernatural rope that tied her to Jennifer had somehow disconnected. Something was very, very wrong.

At 6:45 that evening, Sharon knew little more than she had that afternoon when Bill Thompson first called her, and she was frantic. She called Colton again, but he didn't return her call.

Waiting for him to respond, Sharon and Jim walked through the house, not knowing what to do. The night yawning empty before them, he convinced her to take a drive. From the front seat of the Suburban, Jim called Colton for Sharon, and left a stern message: "Colton, this is Jim Sedwick. Her mother and I are looking for Jennifer. We know you were the last person she was seen with. The police are looking for her, and you really need to call me back."

After he left the voice mail, they drove to Havana, a restaurant they both liked. Jennifer had worked there part-time the same summer she'd worked at the bank, before she'd moved to San Marcos and her life had dissolved into drugs. At the bar, Jim and Sharon sat sipping drinks and feeling helpless.

Finally, at 8:37, Sharon's cell phone rang. It was Colton. Later they'd learn that he was at Mr. Gatti's pizzeria on Martin Luther King Boulevard in Austin with Laura Hall. "Colton, we know Jennifer was with you last night after midnight. You were the last one to see her," she said. "You need to tell us where she is."

Colton answered, his voice dripping in contempt: "Dude, I'm having pizza with my friend. Don't bother me."

"Let me tell you something, Colton," Sharon said, furious. "I called the police and missing persons. I am going to find Jennifer. So you need to just tell me what you know."

"Good luck," he said. "I don't know where she's at, dude. I'm eating pizza."

With that, Colton hung up the telephone.

For a few moments, Sharon and Jim looked at each other, neither knowing what to do. Then Jim said, "We need to get to Austin in the morning, and we need a plan. Let's go home and pack a bag."

In Austin that evening, Ryan Martindill's telephone rang. Laura Hall wanted to swing by his apartment and pick up her bottle of rum from the night before. Ryan wouldn't be home, but he called his roommate, Salzman, and filled him in on the plan. When the apartment doorbell rang, Salzman opened up, and there stood Laura with Colton beside her. They bustled in, and Salzman introduced himself and shook Pitonyak's hand. Colton seemed somewhat withdrawn, which surprised Salzman. He'd heard about Laura's boyfriend and his gangster image. Acting like all was well, Laura grabbed the bottle of rum, and she and Colton quickly left.

Meanwhile, in Corpus Christi, while Sharon packed enough clothes for a few days, Jim called Sidney Smith, a family friend and a private investigator. Jim explained only that they had "a family problem," and asked if Smith could meet them at seven the next morning at a Cracker Barrel restaurant. Smith had a busy day planned, but he quickly agreed.

The rest of that evening, Jim and Sharon walked through the house like strangers, passing each other, not knowing what to say, what to do. At one point, he grabbed her and pulled her to him. Sharon wasn't crying, but her voice was raspy and tense. "This is bad isn't it?" she asked.

"Yeah, baby," he said, in his gruff, hoarse voice, now worn thin with emotion. "This is going to be pretty bad."

As he held her, Sharon finally cried, giving in to the fear that had been haunting her all day.

Meanwhile, in Little Rock that evening, Bridget Pitonyak also appeared to be more than a little concerned about what was transpiring in Austin. At 9:20, she messaged Colton on his cell phone: TEXT ME. I'M A NERVOUS WRECK NOT KNOWING WHAT'S GOING ON.

One minute later, at 9:21, Colton responded, keying in: GOING TO HOUSTON.

Later it would seem an odd exchange, begging many questions: Why was Bridget so worried? What had Colton told her? How much, if anything, did she know about Jennifer's disappearance? What reason did Colton give for fleeing Austin in the darkness?

The evidence would later show that Colton lied to Bridget about at least one thing that night. As he typed his response, Colton wasn't barreling in the night toward Texas's biggest city. With Sharon Cave's threat of involving the police hanging over him, Bridget Pitonyak's younger son sped toward a vastly different destination.

That night, neither Sharon nor Jim slept. After a few hours, Sharon got up and went to her office. She gathered Jennifer's cell phone records and wrote down everything she'd done and discovered, documenting her phone calls with Colton. Then she made three copies: one for herself, one for the police, and one for Smith, the private investigator. It was all she could think of to do that might help find Jennifer. She knew in her heart that the road they'd take in the morning to Austin would lead to life-altering pain. One thought haunted her: Jennifer had never gone a full day without talking to her, even when they were angry with each other, even when Jennifer was deep into drugs. If Jennifer could get to a telephone, she would have called. That she hadn't meant Jennifer was either in dire trouble and couldn't get to a telephone, or dead. Throughout that long night, Sharon called Jennifer's cell phone off and on, taking what little comfort she could from hearing her lost daughter's voice on the recorded message.

While Sharon Cave waited anxiously for sunrise, at 2:41 that morning, Laura Hall's 1994 green Cadillac Concours was in Del Rio, Texas, driving on the nearly deserted bridge that crosses the Rio Grande and connects Del Rio with Ciudad Acuna, Mexico. At the checkpoint to enter Mexico, Laura stopped and handed over her passport and that of her passenger, Colton Pitonyak. She looked unconcerned, even happy. When the Mexican border patrol officer returned their passports and waved them on, Laura and Colton drove off, disappearing into the night.

Sixteen

At seven the next morning, August 18, a Thursday, Vanessa's cell phone rang in her apartment. She wasn't happy. It was her first morning among the ranks of the unemployed, and she'd planned to enjoy it at least temporarily by sleeping in. She hadn't slept much the night before, still feeling unsettled, and an extra couple of hours in bed would have felt good. "Mom, I'm sleeping," she said. "Can I call you back?"

"We can't find Jennifer," Sharon said, followed by a brief recounting of the day before. "Jim and I are meeting with Sid Smith this morning and then driving to Austin."

Now it made sense, that gnawing in Vanessa's chest, the suspicion that all wasn't well. "I'm going, too," she said. "I'll meet you there."

"No," Sharon objected. She had multiple reasons. It was a long drive, she was sure everything was fine, and it would be a waste of time if Vanessa traveled all that way. "We need you at home. You can help. Take out some photos of Jennifer and scan them in the computer for us, so we have something to e-mail to the press if we need to," Sharon said. "We'll call you from Austin."

Vanessa agreed, but she wasn't convinced.

"As soon as you leave here, call the Austin police again," Sid Smith advised over coffee at the Cracker Barrel, a short time later. Smith didn't like what he was hearing from Jim and Sharon. A family friend, Smith had met Jennifer only once, but she'd impressed him as a sweet girl. Colton Pitonyak's history was worrisome, but what bothered Smith more was that the kid lied about the time he'd last seen Jennifer. A former sergeant in Corpus Christi PD's homicide bureau, Smith had twenty years' experience suggesting that people don't lie without a reason. "No one's heard from Jennifer in thirty-one hours now, so you can file an official report," he said "Get it done and get the police looking."

At six feet and 250 pounds, Smith reminded Sharon of a redheaded Santa Claus, round and jolly, but today he wasn't smiling. "I understand what evil people can do," he says. "And I was concerned."

What he told Jim and Sharon was: "Pull everything you need together, and then drive to Austin. I have a deposition this afternoon, but if you need any help, call me."

Sharon and Jim left, and Smith got on the telephone and called Vanessa. He hoped she knew something she didn't want to tell her mother, perhaps something she'd be willing to tell him. But when they talked, Vanessa didn't have any real information for him. Yes, she'd heard Colton's name, but she didn't know much about him. What she'd heard from Jennifer was that she was trying to stay off the drugs, and that she was excited about the new job. "I want to go to Austin," Vanessa said. "I can't wait here."

"Well, go then," Smith said.

"My mom said no," Vanessa said.

"I'll take care of it," Smith said. "It might turn out that she can use your help."

As soon as she got in the car to leave the restaurant, Sharon called APD for a second time. Detective Kathleen Hector, a woman with a full face and long brown hair, answered in the missing persons department. She asked questions and took down the information, writing what would become APD report number 05–2291714. At one point, Hector asked Sharon if Jennifer used drugs.

"Jennifer has in the past," Sharon told her. "But I don't believe that's what's happening here."

Hector sounded official, and Sharon knew the officer was duly recording all the information in her report, but she didn't sense that Hector was as concerned as she'd hoped. At the end, the detective said, "We'll do what we can. You know kids. She'll probably call you soon."

"I hope so," Sharon said, but she didn't believe it.

After she hung up with Sharon, Hector logged onto her computer to check NCIC, the FBI's National Crime Information Center, and its Texas equivalent for unidentified bodies or persons found who matched Jennifer's description. Hector didn't find anything, so she put out a BOLO, a be-on-the-lookout request for Jennifer and her car.

Meanwhile, in Dallas, Vanessa hurriedly packed a suitcase. It was about noon when she got in her car to start the three-hour drive to Austin. All the way there, Vanessa's intuition whispered that Jennifer was dead. Vanessa thought about the possibility that her sister had overdosed. Despite her suspicions, Vanessa felt calm. On the road, she listened to CDs and thought about the music Jennifer liked, even considering what to play at her sister's funeral. She and Sharon called back and forth along the road, but the daughter said nothing to the mother about her fears. Vanessa knew she didn't have to. Sharon's sixth sense would be acting up, too. They were all so interconnected, three daughters and a mother, that if something happened to one of them, how could the others not know?

Vanessa never truly worried until, on the road on the way to Austin to find her sister, she had a disturbing vision. She saw Jennifer dead, but not in a peaceful sleep. "I saw Jennifer suspended in the air," Vanessa says. "She was held up by ropes tied around her wrists and her neck."

"We're coming to Austin," Sharon told Scott when she called him that afternoon from Jim's Suburban. "We should be there by four o'clock."

"Let me know if I can help," he said. "But I bet she's fine, just out partying somewhere."

"I hope so," Sharon said. "But then, why hasn't she called?"

That Scott couldn't answer. He knew Jennifer lived on her cell phone.

Sharon and Jim's drive seemed to take forever. Everything that day, in fact, would feel as if it unraveled in slow motion. Two hours after leaving Corpus Christi, Sharon's cell phone rang. Detective Hector had news.

"We found your daughter's car," she said, explaining the steps she'd taken after she'd talked with Sharon. First, she'd called Colton's cell phone, the number Sharon had given her for him. When Colton didn't answer, she called Denise and Scott, reconstructing the day before Jennifer disappeared. Then Hector pulled Colton's driver's license up on her computer and found his address at the Orange Tree. Not long after, a squad car found Jennifer's car parked across the street from Colton's apartment.

When Detective Hector arrived at the West Campus complex, she looked over Jennifer's Saturn, saw nothing amiss, and then walked upstairs to unit number 88. Once there, she rang the doorbell and pounded on the door. No one answered. She rang the bell and pounded again. Still, no one answered. She watched the mini-blinds, to see if anyone peeked outside. They didn't move.

She'd brought photos with her, Jennifer's from her driver's license and Colton's mug shot from his previous arrest. Hector looked around for a building manager to let her into the apartment, but found instead a workman with a paint bucket, who explained that the Orange Tree was a condominium project with individual owners. There was no one on-site to give her permission to enter unit 88. She returned to the station, and then realized there was something else she should have done.

"I drove back to the condo and left my card tucked in the peephole on Mr. Pitonyak's door, asking him to call," she told Sharon. "Then I went down to Jennifer's car and left one on her windshield. I wrote 'Jennifer, call me and your mother,' on the back. Maybe she'll see it and check in."

That Jennifer's car was parked outside Colton's condo suggested more to Sharon than to Hector. "You have to go inside that apartment," Sharon told the officer. "My daughter's in there. I know she is."

"We don't have probable cause to enter the apartment," Detective Hector said. There were regulations and laws that determined when officers could break into private property. This situation didn't fit any of them. "We can't."

"You have to," Sharon said. "I'm telling you Jennifer is in there."

When Sharon said she wanted to pick up Jennifer's car, Hector gave her the address, and then the detective said, "You know how kids are. Jennifer's probably fine. The best thing to do is stay with her car and wait for her to come back to get it."

"You don't understand. I know Jennifer is in that apartment," Sharon said. She didn't know how she knew, but she was certain, and she was growing angry. Her voice trembled, and she had the feeling that Hector was treating her like a hysterical mother.

"I'm sorry, Mrs. Cave," Hector said. The detective knew the law, what she could and couldn't do, even if a parent thought otherwise. "We can't go in."

When Sharon hung up, Jim said, "Well, at least now we have a plan. We'll drive to his apartment."

Jim called Sid and brought him up to date, and then Sid relayed the information to Vanessa. She was to meet her parents at the Orange Tree. Since Vanessa was an hour ahead of them, she'd arrive first.

Once Sharon had an address, she called Scott and got directions, writing them down on a pad of paper she was filling with notes. Soon after, Laura Ingles called Sharon's cell phone. Ingles was tired of trying to convince Eli he needed to call. "You need to go right to Colton's," Laura said. "If Jennifer's with him, she's in trouble."

When Vanessa arrived at the Orange Tree just before three that afternoon, she searched until she found Jennifer's car.

It didn't take long. The black Saturn Ion was just around the corner. Vanessa peered through the car's windows, but found nothing out of order. She then gazed up at the three-story condo project across the street, walked toward it, and trudged up to the second floor. As she turned to the right at the top of the stairs, she saw the University of Texas clock tower soaring above the treetops. As soon as she entered the condo's second-floor common area, she spotted a red door marked with two brass eights. She knocked. No one answered. She knocked again, but no one came. She banged on the door, hard, then on the windows, but heard nothing stir inside.

"Mom," Vanessa said, when she got Sharon on her cell phone. "I'm going to kick in a window and go inside."

"No!" Sharon shouted. "Absolutely not. We'll be there soon. You wait for us."

They argued, but Vanessa reluctantly agreed. When she hung up, she beat on the door again, to no avail. Then she called Sid Smith.

"Let's see if the kid's car is there," he said. "Call me from the garage."

In the first-floor, under-the-condo-unit parking garage, in slot 88, Vanessa found a white Toyota Avalon with Arkansas plates. "Right apartment number," she told Smith, rattling off the license plate number.

"Well, then, we'd better check that one out," he answered.

With Jim and Sharon an hour away, Vanessa didn't know what else to do. She walked back to her car, glancing at Jennifer's car on the street, her eyes filling with tears for not the first time that day. Halfheartedly, she got back in her car and drove to a friend's house, where she showered and changed clothes. Then she called someone she'd known since eighth grade but hadn't talked to in years, a lanky, clean-cut preacher's son named Aaron, who lived outside Austin. She picked him up, and they drove to the Orange Tree, where they sat on the steps that led to unit 88.

When Jim and Sharon finally pulled up in his Suburban, Vanessa ran to her mother, and they embraced. Then Vanessa showed them Jennifer's car. Detective Hector's card was on the windshield, and Sharon used a key she'd brought with her to open the door and look inside. They saw nothing that appeared strange, no signs of a struggle. From there, they walked into the parking garage, where Vanessa pointed out the white Toyota Avalon. They peered inside, hoping to find something with the owner's name on it, without luck.

Minutes later at the red door that led to Colton's apartment, the one with another of Hector's cards stuck in the peephole, Sharon, Vanessa, and Aaron stood by as Jim pounded. No one answered. He knocked again, but still no response. Worried, Sharon called Detective Kathleen Hector back, at APD. "I think Jennifer's inside that apartment," Sharon said. "I think Jennifer is being held hostage in there."

Hector reiterated that the police had no probable cause to enter unit 88, and, before she hung up, insisted again that Sharon's best option was to stake out Jennifer's car and wait for her to return.

From the lush grounds of the stately sorority homes around them, the small group gathered outside Colton Pitonyak's door heard young women chanting; pledges at houses practicing the chapter's song. On the hour, half hour, and quarter hour, the UT clock tower's melodic bells resonated, reminding them that time was passing, and Jennifer still hadn't been found. Tired of pounding on the unanswered condo door, Jim considered the situation. Not sure what they should do next, he suggested to Sharon, "Let's go to the hotel and think about this. We'll take Jennifer's car with us. If she comes back and finds it missing, she'll call you or the police."

Sharon agreed, and at the foot of the stairs, they split up. Vanessa and Aaron left for her friends' apartment, while Sharon drove Jennifer's car behind Jim in the Suburban to the Omni Hotel, where they had a reservation. At the hotel,

Jim checked in, and they went upstairs. Sharon unpacked, but they talked little. The air between them felt charged with anticipation and danger. Wanting a cigarette, Jim took the elevator back downstairs to smoke in front of the hotel.

Meanwhile, Sharon sat at the desk and called information for the phone numbers of every Pitonyak listed in Arkansas. Once she had them, she started dialing. The first to answer turned out to be Eddie's sister-in-law. Still, the woman said, there was nothing she could do to help: "The family is estranged. We don't talk to Eddie and Bridget."

When Sharon explained that she desperately needed to talk to Eddie and why, however, the woman agreed to get her brother-in-law a message. Moments later, Eddie called. Relieved to have contacted someone who could help, Sharon quickly filled him in on the situation, stressing that they'd been searching for Jennifer for more than a day. "Colton called here Tuesday night and asked to use his mother's credit card to take Jennifer out to dinner," Eddie said. "That's all I know."

Sharon wanted more information, maybe where Colton and Jennifer had gone or when Eddie had last heard from Colton, but from that point on, Eddie Pitonyak wanted to talk to Sharon about only one thing: He wanted her to stay away from his family. One parent might be expected to feel compelled or at least drawn to help another find a lost child, but that didn't appear to be the case with Pitonyak, who chastised Sharon for calling his brother's home and talking to his sister-in-law.

Jim returned, and Sharon was still on the telephone. She appeared upset, and she mouthed, "Eddie Pitonyak."

"My daughter is missing, and we're just asking your help to find her," Sharon said. But that didn't seem to imprint on Eddie, who ordered her not to call his family again. Was it possible that Eddie didn't know? Had Bridget failed to tell her husband that trouble was again brewing in Colton's life, and that their younger son had fled Austin hurriedly in the night?

"Here," Sharon said, handing Jim the phone. "You talk to him. I don't want to talk to him anymore."

Frowning, Jim took the telephone and introduced himself. As Sharon had, he explained to Colton's father that all they hoped for was a little help; they were searching for Jennifer, and Colton was the last person she'd been with. "We'd appreciate anything you can tell us," Jim said.

Ignoring Jim's plea, Eddie Pitonyak replied, "My wife tells me that when she met Jennifer down there, that she thinks Jennifer is really the whole problem on this deal."

Dumbfounded, Jim simply couldn't talk to the man anymore. It was obvious that Eddie Pitonyak wasn't at all inclined to help them find Jennifer. Quickly Jim broke off the conversation and hung up the telephone.

In the hotel room, Jim thought again about the situation unfolding around him. What if their worst fears were playing out? What if they disrupted evidence by moving Jennifer's car? "I think we need to take Jennifer's car back where we found it," he said. Sharon agreed, and she called Vanessa to say they were headed back to the apartment.

At 7:30 that evening, Sharon parked the black Saturn Ion in the same spot where they'd found it, and she and Jim walked warily up the steps to unit 88, where Vanessa and Aaron waited. Again, Jim pounded on Colton Pitonyak's door. Again, no one answered. Again, in the background, the UT clock tower marked time.

"What do we do?" Sharon said.

"Let's take another look at the car in the garage," Jim suggested.

They walked back down the stairs to the first floor and into the parking garage. There the white Toyota sat, just as before. They looked inside, but saw nothing unusual. Finally, Sharon called Scott.

"Do you know what kind of car Colton has?" she asked.

"No," he said. "But if I saw it I would recognize it."

"Is it a white Toyota with Arkansas plates?" she asked.

"That's the car," he said. "What's going on?"

Sharon told him about Jennifer's car outside and Colton's in the parking garage. For the first time, Scott began to worry. "Listen Sharon," he said. "Colton's bad news. Really bad news."

After Sharon repeated Scott's warning, Jim decided to bring Sid Smith up to speed on all that had happened: "We're back over at the apartment, and we're positive this is Colton's car, based on information from one of Jennifer's friends."

"You need to call the police again. This is not a good thing," the private investigator said, his concern growing. "If they'd gone somewhere, one of the cars would be gone."

As soon as he hung up, Jim dialed 911.

The officer dispatched to the scene arrived minutes later and listened patiently as Jim explained Jennifer's disappearance and their suspicions that Colton Pitonyak was involved.

"We have to get inside," Jim said. "This apartment is our only clue to finding Jennifer."

Looking dubious, the officer called his sergeant, who told him to find the building manager to ask permission to enter. The officer left, but he returned a short time later. As Detective Hector had before him, the officer had found out that the Orange Tree consisted of privately owned condos. Without probable cause, no one but the condo owner or the tenant, Colton Pitonyak, could authorize police to enter unit 88.

"You don't understand," Sharon pleaded with the officer. "We have to get inside. Jennifer could be in there hurt or dying."

Again, he called his sergeant. This time, when the patrol officer hung up, he informed Jim and Sharon that he'd been ordered to leave.

"What if I get a locksmith, so we don't have to break in?" Jim offered. "We wouldn't damage anything that way. We'll just take a look around and see if she's in there."

The officer seemed to consider that. He called his sergeant again, seeking advice, but the outcome was the same. "I'm sorry, but I can't go inside," he said. "We don't have probable cause to get a search warrant."

As the patrol cop walked away, Jim said, "I'm going to get a locksmith."

"I'm leaving," the officer responded. "And you should, too."

Not sure what to do, Sharon, Jim, Vanessa, and Aaron all bunched around the door, again banging and knocking, over and over. College students who lived in nearby units stopped and stared, but none of those gathered to find Jennifer cared who watched. They wanted only one thing: to get inside Colton Pitonyak's apartment.

The heat was oppressive early that evening, even as the sun dropped in the sky. On the Orange Tree's second floor, long shadows cast by third-floor staircases and balconies offered shade, including the balcony over Colton Pitonyak's front door.

"We have to get inside," Sharon said. "Jennifer's in there. I know it."

"Then let's call a locksmith," Jim said, dialing information on his cell phone. It took more than an hour to find one willing to send someone out quickly, and then they waited half an hour for the man's arrival. A man in coveralls showed up carrying a tool chest and spent another half an hour picking at the lock. Finally, he said to Jim, "This has a high-security lock. I can't get inside."

Night had arrived, by the time Jim paid the locksmith. Once he had his money, the man turned and left. More hours wasted, and nothing accomplished.

A man and a woman resembling college students walked up, out of the darkness, to Colton's apartment and looked at the small group gathered there. "Hey, is he in?" the young man asked.

Vanessa knew immediately that they were there to buy drugs. When she questioned them, asking if they knew where Colton was, they answered that they'd left some "stuff" at his place for safekeeping, and were just dropping by to pick it up. But to her, they looked "cracked up."

"Do you know Jennifer Cave?" Jim asked.

"No," one of them said. "But we really need our stuff."

"Well, then you'd better beat it and get out of here," Jim ordered. They looked at Jim, questioning, then turned and left.

At 9:45 in the evening, the small group had been at the door marked 88 for much of the past six hours, without progress. "How are we going to get in?" Sharon asked Jim for what felt like the hundredth time.

"I don't know," he admitted.

They stared at the door, then the windows, and Sharon told Vanessa to go to Jim's car and retrieve the black *Sports Illustrated* blanket they kept in the backseat. "I'll wrap it around my leg and kick the window in," she said.

"No, you'll cut yourself," Jim cautioned. "There's got to be another way."

Holding back tears, Sharon looked at the condo, searching the front of the building, sizing up the door, thinking about how to get inside. Her head ached. She hadn't eaten since breakfast, but she wasn't hungry. Earlier she'd noticed a circular crack, the kind made from a BB gun, in the third window on the right facing the door. Now she went back and looked at it again. It was directly above the window lock. *If I can just . . .* she thought. She took a pen out of her purse and removed the cartridge, then used it to start tapping on the section of damaged glass, pushing at it, nudging it, trying to get it to snap. Finally, it splintered and popped out.

The hole wasn't large enough to stick a finger through, so Sharon took the pen and tried to push open the lock. The pen slid off, rolled off, and wouldn't work. "Wait," Vanessa said, then turned and left. Minutes later, she returned with an earpiece off a broken pair of sunglasses and handed it to her mother.

"Try this," she said.

On the first try, the curved earpiece easily caught the latch and pushed the window lock open. Now they looked at one another, as if trying to decide what to do. No one talked, as Jim pulled the window open.

"I'll go inside," Sharon said.

"No. I'm going," Jim said. "It's not up for discussion."

"She's my daughter," Sharon argued.

"She's mine, too," Jim said.

Sharon was quiet for just a moment. She knew Jennifer was inside. She could feel it. There had to be some reason she couldn't get to the door to let them in. Then that nagging feeling came back, the one that said Jennifer was dead. Sharon pushed back such dark thoughts, reassuring herself that there were other explanations. Colton could have Jennifer tied up. What if he'd beaten Jennifer and left her for dead, but she was alive and needed help? Her heart pounding, all Sharon felt certain of was that Jennifer was inside that condo.

"Be careful," Sharon told Jim.

Jim reached in and pushed up the blinds, then pulled the curtain to the side. Sharon moved in quickly, grabbing both and holding them out of the way. Inside, the condo was cloaked in darkness. Taking a deep breath to steady himself, Jim turned on the flashlight he'd brought from his car and projected a funnel of light into the apartment. The place was a wreck, and Jim wondered if there'd been some kind of struggle. He put one long leg through the window, then the other, until he stood on a dark-colored sofa positioned directly below the window.

"Okay, here I go," he said.

"Jimmy, be careful," Sharon said, her voice small and frightened. "Please be careful."

"Is anyone inside?" Jim shouted. "Don't shoot. We're not here to hurt you. We're just looking for Jennifer."

As Jim entered the condo, Sharon's phone rang. It was Scott. He was home with Madyson, and he had a strange sensation, the feeling that something was about to happen.

"What's going on?" he asked.

"Jim's going inside the apartment," Sharon said. "We'll call you later."

Although she thought she had, Sharon didn't hang up, and Scott heard their voices, Jim in the apartment, Sharon calling out to him to be careful. Then everything grew quiet for a moment, and Jim said to Sharon, "I don't think anyone's here." Still, he wasn't certain. They could be hiding. Carefully, Jim walked farther into the condo. Standing outside, next to her mother and Aaron, Vanessa saw Jim pick his way through the tiny efficiency. The living room was in chaos with clothing, books, papers, debris strewn about. The kitchen was bare, the only orderly room in the house. On the wall was a poster, Al Pacino in *Scarface*. Underneath Pacino's photo, it read: "Make way for the bad guy."

From her perch in the window, Sharon relaxed a little, reassuring herself that everything was all right. Jim hadn't found Jennifer. Maybe she wasn't even in the apartment. Maybe Sharon's intuition was wrong. Perhaps they'd find Jennifer alive and well, and the fear that ached Sharon's chest would go away.

Finding nothing tied to Jennifer, Jim turned from the kitchen and walked into the bedroom nook, where the bed, too, was covered in clothes. He finally found a light switch and flicked it on. The place lit up, but no one was there. Silence.

Slowly and deliberately, Jim opened a door to the right of the bed and peered down a short hallway, just as he noticed a heavy, rancid odor. Jim had grown up deer hunting in South Texas, and this was an odor he recognized: something dead.

Another door waited at his left. Hesitantly, he opened it, this time staring into a closet. He fanned the flashlight beam through the closet, saw clothes and shoes and books, but no one hiding, nothing wrong. The odor grew more pungent as Jim walked farther into the hallway. On his right was a vanity, a sink scattered with toiletries and rubble. Jim turned to the left and faced yet another door.

As soon as he opened the bathroom door, the odor assaulted Jim, full force. Almost instantly, at the window, Sharon smelled it, too. Her stomach tightened, but she didn't yet consider what it could mean.

Sensing that he didn't want to see what waited inside, Jim felt for the bathroom light switch and turned it on. The light flashed on, and the bathroom lit up, bright. At first, Jim couldn't comprehend the horror of what was in front of him. An accountant who liked his world orderly, a man who wouldn't read Stephen King novels or go to horror movies, Jim Sedwick simply couldn't grasp what he saw.

"Oh, God," he whispered, as he finally accepted what his eyes told him. Panicking, Jim rushed from the bathroom screaming, "Call 911. Call 911. I've got a body."

In his apartment, Scott heard Jim yell for someone to call 911, and then his cell phone disconnected. What happened? he wondered. What did they find? Alone, he stood holding the cell phone, suddenly feeling queasy. He thought Sharon would call back. He waited, and the phone didn't ring. Perhaps it didn't have to. Without being told, Scott knew: *Jennifer's dead*, he thought. *They found her, and she's dead.*

After he hung up the telephone, Scott started to cry. He thought of his conversation with Jen the night before she disappeared, when she admitted she was dating Eli and using meth again. It was the drugs. It had to be. Furious, Scott called Eli. When Eli didn't answer, Scott left a message: "Good job, Eli," he said. "You put everything bad back in Jen's life that I worked to take away."

Wanting to help, Vanessa's hands fluttered over her cell phone, as she tried to push 911. She thought she did, but her call didn't go through. When someone did answer, Vanessa thought she was talking, but they didn't seem to understand her. Only later would she realize she was screaming hysterically, shrieking a painful wail that started deep inside her. She thought she was saying the address, and she couldn't understand why the operator kept asking her to calm down and repeat it again.

Inside Colton Pitonyak's condo, Jim struggled to unlock the red front door. As soon as he stumbled out, Sharon pushed forward, wanting to get past him, to go inside the apartment. "Is it Jennifer? Is that her?" she demanded.

"I don't know," he said, holding her back. "I need to go inside to take another look."

"No. I'm going," Sharon said. "I need to go inside to my baby."

"No, Momma, please don't," Vanessa begged, grabbing Sharon's arm. "Please don't go in there."

Finishing the discussion, Jim turned and walked back inside, carefully, now mindful that he was entering a potential crime scene, not wanting to disturb what could be evidence.

This time the lights were already on, and he walked directly to the rear of the condo. At the bathroom doorway, Jim Sedwick braced himself. The truth was that he didn't want to look, he didn't ever want to see it again, but he had to. He had to be able to tell Sharon if the body in the bathtub was Jennifer's. So he stood in the doorway and stared for a second time at the most horrible sight he'd ever seen, one so indescribably gruesome it would haunt him forever.

Outside, Vanessa screamed into the telephone. Aaron took it from her and started talking to the 911 dispatcher.

"Send an ambulance," he said, repeating the address to the operator. After explaining that they were looking for a missing girl, and he thought they'd found her, Aaron said, "She's either overdosed or there's something bad wrong."

"Is she breathing?" the woman asked.

"I don't think so," he said.

For the second time, Jim walked out, shaking and white, gulping the fresh air. Just outside the door, Vanessa and Sharon shrieked, unable to restrain their terror. Students from the surrounding apartments gathered staring at them, watching, their eyes wide, and their senses piqued to the prospect of danger. "Is it Jennifer?" Sharon screamed. "Is it my daughter?"

Still on the telephone, Aaron talked to the 911 dispatcher. "You need to go inside and start CPR on the patient," she ordered. "Tell everyone else to go outside and you go inside. I need you inside."

Aaron turned to Jim, and explained that the dispatcher wanted him to go inside to begin CPR. Jim said no. No one was going inside. After hearing Jim's voice in the background, the dispatcher asked Aaron to pass him the telephone.

"I need you to go inside to begin CPR," the woman told Jim. "Is she breathing?"

"She's in the bathtub, covered with blood," he said. "I don't want to touch her."

"Is she past CPR?"

"Yes, there's a crime scene here, and I don't want to disturb it . . . Please send someone over here right away," Jim pleaded.

"They're on their way," the operator said.

In the background, Sharon's and Vanessa's cries grew ever louder, screams of utter despair.

Jim held Sharon and wondered what he should tell her. When he entered the bathroom that second time, Jim thought he recognized the girl's green striped top, but he couldn't be sure. Reluctantly, he walked closer, his body shaking, his stomach churning, determined not to turn away. For there in front of him, in the bathtub, was the decomposing body of a young woman. A filthy patterned brown bathroom rug covered her arms, stomach, and right leg. On her chest lay a small red hacksaw.

When Jim looked down at the bathroom floor, he saw a large black trash bag. Without looking inside, he knew what it held. Someone had cut off Jennifer's head.

Seventeen

"Is it Jennifer?" Sharon demanded again, when he walked outside. Jim's hands shook, and he'd turned pale.

"I think so," he said. "I saw her foot."

Jennifer had freckles all over her body, even her feet, and Sharon knew instantly that must have been what Jim was talking about. That meant Jennifer's body was inside the condo. Jennifer was dead. Sharon moaned. In the back of her mind was an unspoken question: Why had Jim looked at Jennifer's feet to recognize her? Why hadn't he simply looked at her face?

Barely able to speak, Sharon couldn't ask. All she could do was cry and hold Vanessa, who trembled uncontrollably. Everything Sharon had been through in the past two days, all the fears she'd had for Jennifer since the day she was born, all the love she had for her middle daughter, the little girl with the long red hair and the big glasses, came crashing in on Sharon. It felt as if the world had caved in on top of her, and she had no place to escape. Sharon collapsed against Jim, sobbing.

"He killed my baby," she screamed. "That boy killed my daughter."

Free of her mother's arms, Vanessa felt overwhelmed by a deep sense of panic. Without realizing what she was doing, she ran up and down the stairs screaming, "My sister. My sister." She passed a young man, and he looked at her and backed away.

"Is everything all right?" he asked.

"My sister," she cried out. "My sister."

Aaron grabbed Vanessa and took her downstairs, and she crumpled in the driveway to the condo parking garage. "Jennifer's dead," she cried. She didn't know what had happened, but she'd heard enough about what Jim was saying to understand they were calling the police because it was something bad.

"You don't know that," Aaron said. "Vanessa, we don't know."

"Jennifer's dead," Vanessa screamed.

"Let's pray," Aaron said. He wrapped her in his arms, and as sirens blared in the background and the curious collected around them, the two friends stood in the middle of the street beseeching God to help them.

The call went out at 10:12 that evening as a 504, a suspicious person, at the intersection of Twenty-fifth and Rio Grande. Officer Richard Barbaria had been with APD for twelve years. In his marked squad car, along with his partner, Officer Chris Clark, Barbaria turned to drive to the intersection in the West Campus area, part of his beat, which extended from downtown Austin onto the UT campus. A muscular man with a short, buzzed haircut, Barbaria had hoped to leave early that night, to start his vacation, but instead they headed to the Orange Tree, calling along the way for an update. By the time they were halfway there, the dispatcher relabeled their assignment as a disturbance call, and Barbaria and Clark were instructed to proceed to unit number 8.

When they arrived, they saw nothing unusual. No one answered the door marked 8, and the complex appeared quiet. Then Barbaria heard sirens and saw an ambulance and a fire truck barreling down the road past them toward the other end of the block of condominiums. "Let's go," Barbaria shouted, running back to the marked squad car. The two uniformed officers followed the sirens. It was sad to say, but Barbaria knew that the EMTs often had more accurate information than APD dispatchers. He figured the paramedics in the ambulance were snickering at them for going to the wrong apartment. As they again pulled to a stop, Barbaria and Clark heard over their dispatch channel that their call had been changed to a "woman in trouble."

Barbaria grabbed his flashlight and then ran, passing the EMTs on the stairs. When he reached the tall man holding up a sobbing woman outside unit 88, a man he later learned was Jim Sedwick, Barbaria noticed the guy looked "frazzled." As soon as he saw them, Jim, agitated, excitedly babbled about someone inside the apartment. Barbaria and the others couldn't understand what he was trying to say. When the officer heard drugs mentioned, Barbaria figured they had an overdose victim in the apartment and somehow Jim was related to her. Jim stammered about something in the bathroom, so Barbaria decided to look for himself.

Not sensing anything out of the ordinary, Barbaria did what he'd always done in an overdose case; he followed the EMTs into the apartment, so he could look for narcotics while the paramedics worked on the injured party. Only Barbaria quickly realized that this call wasn't playing out like overdose calls usually did. The EMTs ahead of him walked into the apartment toward the bathroom, but none went inside. They looked in the bathroom door, and one after the other made a quick U-turn. Even odder, none of the paramedics talked. It was stone silent in the apartment. Something was wrong.

When he reached the bathroom, Officer Barbaria looked inside and understood. In the bathtub lay the body of a young woman. *Where's her head?* he wondered, thinking maybe it was covered somehow, with towels or the grimy rug thrown over her abdomen. But then Barbaria noticed the hacksaw, recognized blood and hair on the blade, and looked at the body again. To his horror, he realized the woman's head was gone, severed at the neck.

Glancing at the trash bag on the bathroom floor, Barbaria didn't have to guess any more than Jim about what most likely waited inside.

"We've got a body, everyone," he screamed. "This is a crime scene. Everybody out."

At the front door, Barbaria used not his radio, which could have been picked up by others, but his handheld computer to request backup, including homicide responders. Then he barred the doorway and began a crime scene log, writing down what Jim was telling him and listing those who had gone inside. In total, he'd later estimate that his time inside the apartment had been less than a minute, but it had seemed vastly longer, and, like everyone else who made the Orange Tree scene that night, he'd never forget what he'd witnessed.

What Jim had been trying to tell Barbaria suddenly made sense. There was a young woman inside, and somebody had murdered and butchered her.

Unable to help Jennifer, the EMTs spread out, one pairing up with each of the family members, hoping to keep them calm, away from the crowd that was gathering around unit 88 and one another. Now that they were witnesses, the police didn't want Jim, Sharon, Vanessa, and Aaron to talk until they'd given individual statements.

"Does anyone know the person who lives here?" Barbaria asked the crowd of students watching from the perimeter of the crime scene. No one answered, but there was a murmur, a buzz between the young bodies congregating around them. "Anyone who can tell us what's going on here?" the officer asked.

"You know we do this for a living. How'd you walk in there on that?" one of the EMTs asked Jim.

Outside the apartment in the common area, Jim smoked a cigarette, his hands shaking, and admitted, "It was pretty scary, partner."

Half an hour after his 911 call, Jim watched as the scene flooded with police officers. Among the responders, three counselors arrived from the district attorney's victim assistance team, there to stay with Sharon, Jim, and Vanessa, while they went through the process of giving statements and to protect them from a crowd of reporters gathering outside the police barrier on the street below.

When the EMTs half carried and half walked Sharon down the stairs, they brought her to the grass and sat her down. Police had cordoned off the area, and Sharon saw Vanessa across the street, crying. Unable to process the horror unfolding around her, the oldest of the Cave girls had begun to hope that maybe she'd been wrong. Maybe Jennifer was still alive. She lunged at everyone who passed close to her, all the firefighters and police, asking them, "Is my sister going to be okay?"

Finally, she grabbed the arm of a young man in a uniform, shouting, "Is my sister all right?"

"Your sister's dead," he said, pulling away.

When the man walked by again, Vanessa, sobbing, yelled, "You don't know how this feels."

"I do," he said, more kindly. "My sister jumped off a mountain in Greece last summer. All I can tell you is it will get better."

Nearing hysteria, Vanessa rolled onto her side and lay in the grass, wrapping her arms around her legs, in a fetal position. Sharon ached to hold her oldest daughter, to comfort her, but the police had ordered that they be kept separated until their statements were taken. Sharon couldn't help but reach out toward her oldest child, and she pleaded with the paramedic assigned to her: "Please let me go to my daughter," Sharon begged. "She needs me. I promise we won't talk. I promise."

Across the street, Vanessa gasped, as if she couldn't breathe.

"As long as you don't talk about what happened," a police officer nearby said. Sharon nodded, then stood up and ran toward Vanessa. When she saw her mother coming toward her, Vanessa ran to her. In the street, people stared, and Vanessa turned and yelled, "Stop looking at us. Stop looking at us."

Overhead a news helicopter circled, and around them TV cameras whirled. When Sharon reached her, Vanessa rested her head on her mother's chest. Wrapped in her mother's arms, Vanessa wailed inconsolably.

On the second floor of the Orange Tree, an orderly chaos was erupting around unit 88. Jim watched as gray-haired men in suits showed up, lots of them, and he figured APD was pulling out all the stops. "That's the chief," one officer whispered, pointing at a guy who looked to be in his fifties. Despite everything he'd experienced, Jim reasoned through what he saw unfolding around him. He could understand the urgency. It was the beginning of the fall semester at UT, and anxious moms and dads were bringing their sons and daughters to the university. A shocking campus murder was the kind of publicity neither the university nor the city wanted, especially an unsolved one with a killer on the loose.

What Jim didn't know until later was that questions were already being asked, like why weren't the family's suspicions treated more seriously? The commander himself, Brad Connor, called Kathleen Hector, the detective in missing persons who'd taken Sharon's report. After reviewing her report, it appeared Hector had followed standard procedure, but that didn't keep Sharon from being furious that the detective didn't take further action when she first found Jennifer's car.

Meanwhile, each time he had to explain what he'd seen inside the apartment, Barbaria looked more shaken. No one could blame him. Like Jim and the EMTs who first responded, Barbaria hadn't been able to brace himself for the shock. Now that they'd designated the condo a crime scene, no one could enter until they had a search warrant signed by a judge. To do that, police had to pull the information together to write up the warrant. With a dead body in the apartment, everyone wanted to make sure that the investigation went by the book.

The lead homicide detective on that night, Mark Gilchrest,

heard about a suspicious death about 11:15, an hour after the 911 call came in. At midnight, Gilchrest arrived on the scene, where he circulated and talked to witnesses. One of the homicide unit's senior detectives, Gilchrest was a broad-shouldered man with a mustache. At APD, the detective was known to be unemotional and precise, methodical and determined. This night, Gilchrest listened to reports of what waited for them inside Colton Pitonyak's condo. Without seeing the atrocity for himself, the detective already looked mad as hell.

Backing up Gilchrest were two others from homicide. With three years in the unit, Detective Keith Walker was younger than Gilchrest, with ears that stood out from his long face, and a chin that ended in a dimple. Walker was a new father, who was known to be obsessive about following up leads, and his role in the case would be to run the crime scene, coordinating the forensic team and guiding the search of the apartment.

The third detective, David Fugitt, would take statements from witnesses. Wearing Clark Kent glasses and a dark flat-top, Fugitt had been in homicide for four years, coming from the family violence unit. At the time he'd made the change, APD offered two options: homicide or the cold case unit. Fugitt took homicide because he wanted the experience. Being on 24/7 was one of the downsides of the job. It left little time for a social life.

By then Officer Barbaria had questioned the students in the surrounding apartments about the tenant in unit 88. Colton Pitonyak, it turned out, was well known at the Orange Tree, as he was throughout campus, as a source for drugs. When he reached unit 66, the apartment some of the gawkers pointed to as the home of a girl who knew Pitonyak, Barbaria knocked, and Nora Sullivan opened the door. By then it was the middle of the night, but Sullivan was still wide awake. Barbaria asked questions, but sensed Sullivan wasn't being forthcoming. Before long, he told her, "I'd like you to go downtown to give us a statement."

The old farmhouse on the edge of a small South Texas town where Jennifer Cave grew up.
Photo Kathryn Casey

Sharon had four children: Vanessa (rear), Jennifer (left front), Clayton (center), and Lauren (right front). For photographs, Jennifer took off her glasses.
Courtesy of the Cave family

As a little girl, Jennifer hated her freckles. Sharon told her they made her special, that they were the places angels kissed her, before God sent her down from heaven.
Courtesy of the Cave family

Jennifer and Lauren, here in their uniforms, were cheerleaders through elementary and middle school, into high school, jumping in the air, shouting out cheers, and urging the Bishop, Texas, teams to victory.
Courtesy of the Cave family

Jim, surrounded by his girls (left to right, rear row): Hailey, Jim, Sharon, Vanessa; (front row): Jennifer, Whitney, Lauren.

Courtesy of the Cave family

Lauren, Jennifer, Sharon, and Vanessa at Jennifer's high school graduation. By then, Jennifer was already changing, coming out of her shell. Her glasses and braces were gone, and she was turning into a beautiful young woman.

Courtesy of the Cave family

As Jennifer came of age, she and Vanessa (left), looked more alike. Both turned heads when they entered a room.

Courtesy of the Cave family

Nora Sullivan and Colton Pitonyak lived just six doors apart at the Orange Tree condominiums.

Courtesy of Nora Sullivan

Colton Pitonyak arrived at UT a scholarship student, but gradually refashioned himself into a drug-dealing thug.

Austin PD photo

Christmas 2004 brought an end to what was known in the Cave family as "Jennifer's dark year." That day a miracle of sorts happened—snow—in South Texas, a rarity. (Back row, left to right): Jim, Myrtle, Sharon, Whitney, Clayton; (front, left to right): Hailey, Lauren, Vanessa, Jennifer.

Courtesy of the Cave family

Living with Scott, Jennifer felt more at ease, happier than her friends had ever seen her. Yet dark fears still haunted her, and she grabbed life with both hands, fearing she had little time to enjoy it.

Courtesy of K. Reine

Scott Engle fell in love with Jennifer, and for a little while, his love changed her life.

Photo Kathryn Casey

A precocious, waifish little girl, Madyson called Jennifer "Mom."

Photo Kathryn Casey

Katrina deVilleneuve was a topless dancer with a heart of gold who grew frightened when Jennifer told her of Colton Pitonyak's threats.

Photo Kathryn Casey

Denise Winterbottom befriended Jennifer, inviting her to move into her apartment when she needed a place to stay.

Photo Kathryn Casey

Eli went with Jennifer to reclaim her possessions, including the star Whitney made for her.

Photo Kathryn Casey

Laura Hall fell in love with Colton Pitonyak, but he "treated her like a muddy little dog," says a friend.

Austin PD photo

Sharon, Jim, and Vanessa pounded for hours on the door marked 88 at the Orange Tree condominiums.

Photo Kathryn Casey

Michael Rodriguez would later regret that he didn't ask Jennifer more questions, but at the time she insisted all was well.

Photo Kathryn Casey

Colton Pitonyak's gun. A week earlier, he'd threatened to shoot Laura Hall with it.

Austin PD photo

When they opened the dishwasher, police found a machete inside, with blood on the blade.

Austin PD photo

The ACE bag inside the apartment, next to blood on the carpet.

Austin PD photo

"That's just how I roll," Laura Hall said about her getaway with Pitonyak in her green Cadillac.

Austin PD photo

At first Pitonyak and Hall looked like any other vacationing students. Then Pedro Fernandez grew worried and snapped this photo to have a record of the strange young American couple.

Courtesy of Pedro Fernandez

Despite decades as a police officer and then a DA's investigator, this was a case that Jim Bergman would never forget.

Photo Kathryn Casey

Stephanie McFarland and Bill Bishop took on one of the most gruesome murder cases in Austin's history.

Photo Kathryn Casey

From one of the best known law firms in Austin, Sam Bassett (left) and Roy Minton had to separate their client from the aftermath of the murder.

Photo Kathryn Casey

Bridget and Eddie Pitonyak, Colton's parents, kept to themselves throughout the trial, rarely talking to anyone.

Photo Kathryn Casey

Laura Hall, here in the courtroom, dyed her hair red, something those who knew Jennifer found unsettling.

Photo Kathryn Casey

Scott's shrine in his bedroom, including the prophetic painting of Jennifer's torso, praying hands, and a small plaque that reads: "Heaven."

Photo Kathryn Casey

* * *

Downstairs on the street, Vanessa and Sharon had been separated again, Sharon taken to sit in a squad car. Despite the information circulating through the clutch of officers and paramedics, Jennifer's mother and sister still didn't fully understand what had happened. They hadn't been told about the condition of Jennifer's body. Grappling with the horror of losing her daughter, Sharon was already precariously close to giving in to the urge to just let go, to give herself over to the grief. About midnight, she looked up at the Orange Tree through the car window, and thought about her other children. Clayton and Lauren would have to be told. How would she tell them? How could she? And Vanessa? Sharon looked across the street at her oldest crying on the curb and wondered if she would ever recover.

Glancing back and forth from the apartment complex, to the street, to the paramedic assigned to stay with her, Vanessa fought the terror that surrounded her that night. She knew Jennifer was dead. Not only had the firefighter she'd stopped to ask told her, but now she remembered hearing Sharon scream, "He killed her. I knew he killed her."

All the way to Austin that afternoon, Vanessa had feared that her sister was dead, but knowing was different. She'd accepted the possibility that Jennifer might have died of an overdose. Although that was horrible, murder was so much worse, nearly inconceivable. At times, Vanessa feared she would "lose it." She hyperventilated, and the paramedics talked to her, calming her down. One brought her a paper bag to breathe into, so she could catch her breath. Finally, a paramedic sat beside her and talked, in a soothing, reassuring voice, about skydiving. When she began to shake, he described how it felt to soar through the air, free, and, for a little while at least, Vanessa held on.

Eighteen

At 1:30 A.M., Jim followed in his Suburban, and the police, with Sharon and Vanessa in separate squad cars, led him to APD's brown brick headquarters building, off I–35, in downtown Austin. Once there, they were escorted upstairs to homicide, where their accounts would be taken. The events of the last two days were now evidence that needed to be documented in the search warrant application for Pitonyak's apartment. Jim worried about Sharon. She knew Jennifer was dead, but there was much she didn't yet understand.

At APD headquarters, Jim, Sharon, Vanessa, and Aaron were all ordered not to talk to anyone or one another, and then Jim was taken into one of the interview rooms to give his statement. He recounted everything that had happened the previous two days, from first learning that Jennifer was missing to walking into the bathroom and finding the headless body.

"You know he wasn't finished, don't you?" the detective remarked. "Ya'll interrupted him, so he couldn't finish."

Jim hadn't thought about it, but now that he did, it made sense. "Yeah," he answered.

At about that same time, across Austin, Denise slept when someone pounded on her door. She stared out the peephole at two police officers. "Are you Denise Winterbottom?" they asked, when she opened the door.

"Yes."

"Do you know a Jennifer Cave?"

"She lives here," Denise said. "She's a friend."

"I'm sorry to have to tell you this," the officer said. "Jennifer's dead and you need to come with us."

Shaking, Denise went into her bedroom and pulled on clothes for the drive downtown. When they walked her past the door that said homicide, Denise understood what had happened. Two plainclothes officers escorted her to an isolated cubicle. One of the officers began describing the crime scene, and Denise felt ill. Barely able to believe what she was hearing, Denise had the feeling that they were gauging her reaction.

"I don't understand why she went out," Denise told them. "She told me she was going to bed."

They asked questions about Jennifer, what she was like, where she hung out. When they asked about the drugs, Denise acknowledged that Jennifer had a history of drug use. When they brought up Colton, Denise said, "I don't like him, but I barely met him," she says. "But Jennifer told me, she said, 'Colton will kill me someday.'"

When they'd finished, the detectives walked her out, and Denise looked over and saw Vanessa crying.

Sharon saw Denise, but just nodded at her. They weren't supposed to talk, and it all felt awkward, strained. By then, Jim was finished, and the homicide department was buzzing with activity, all aimed at getting the search warrant typed up and ready to be signed.

At one point, Sharon noticed Nora Sullivan. She didn't know who she was, and later she'd feel foolish recalling how she'd worried about the young girl with the long blond hair who sat eating out of an Outback Steakhouse carryout bag, looking upset. "There's been an accident, and I'm at the police station," Nora told someone on her cell phone. Sharon kept wondering where Nora's parents were, why someone wasn't coming to help her.

Later that morning, Nora was brought into an interview room, where Detective David Fugitt waited to interview her. She still didn't know what had happened to Jennifer, and thought that perhaps there'd been some kind of an accident at Colton's, or that he was in more drug trouble. If Fugitt asked about the last time Sullivan saw Colton, she later wouldn't remember. She left without telling the detective about Pitonyak's 3 A.M. visit to her apartment, never really considering that it might be important.

In the waiting area, weighed down by her grief, Vanessa lay with her head on Aaron's lap, when a detective came about four that morning to collect Sharon and bring her to an interview room. Her mother wasn't gone long when Vanessa heard Sharon scream, "This can't be happening. I didn't even get to say good-bye."

Vanessa's entire body ached. She'd never felt so alone.

When the interviews were finally done, Sharon and Jim were taken downstairs to the lab, to be fingerprinted. Once the APD forensic team had their search warrant and could start processing the crime scene, their prints would be needed to match with those on the crime scene, to determine what they'd touched. In the lab, the girl assigned to collect the evidence walked in and said, "Hi, I'm Jennifer."

Sharon began sobbing violently, and Jim held her, then tried to reassure the startled lab tech. "It's okay," he said. "It's not about you."

Approximately seven hours after Jim discovered the body, they were leaving homicide, when Detective Gilchrest pulled Jim to the side. The detective asked if they would remain in Austin for at least one more day, to meet with him again on Saturday. Jim agreed, and then Gilchrest asked one more thing: "I don't want you to tell anyone about what you saw in that apartment, not even Sharon," he said. "Until we arrest this guy, we don't want that out there."

"Okay," Jim said. "You've got it."

As they walked through the APD parking lot to his Suburban, Jim, Sharon, and Vanessa saw two tired, tattered-looking men walking toward them, and Jim realized they were undercover officers.

"We're sorry about what happened," one said to them.

"You've been out working?" Jim asked.

"Yeah," one said. "We were looking for Colton Pitonyak down on Sixth Street. No sign of him."

In the Suburban on their way back to the Omni, no one talked. "There was nothing to say. Jennifer was dead," says Vanessa. In the hotel room, Jim and Sharon lay down on the bed, and Vanessa nestled in beside her mother. They held each other and tried to sleep.

After calling Eli the night before, Scott waited up until after midnight, hoping Sharon would call. When she didn't, he sat on the edge of his bed, closed his eyes, and tried to visualize Jennifer. All he could see were dark clouds. In bed, he tossed, unable to sleep, feeling sweaty and anxious. At 5:30 that morning, he thought he was dreaming that someone was pounding on his apartment door. He suddenly woke up and realized it wasn't a dream. He looked out the peephole and saw two police officers.

"Do you know a Jennifer Cave . . . a Colton Pitonyak?"

"Yes."

"We'd like you to come downtown with us."

After Jennifer moved out, a friend of Scott's, Maci, had moved in to help with Madyson. Scott stuck his head into Madyson's room, and quietly woke Maci, asking if she could watch the little girl. When Maci agreed, Scott went to his room to dress. Just then the telephone rang.

"Jennifer's dead," Denise said, when Maci picked up.

Maci ran to tell Scott. "Jennifer's dead?" Scott repeated to the police.

"Yes," one of them said. "We're sorry."

As Denise had earlier, Scott walked past the homicide sign and realized that Jennifer's death wasn't an accident. It was then that the horror of what had happened came into sharp focus. In the interview room, the first thing the detectives asked was where Scott had been the night Jennifer disappeared. "At home, in my apartment. Madyson, my daughter, and her babysitter, Maci, were there," he said.

The police talked, asked questions, but Scott barely listened. "All I could think of was that the girl I loved was dead," he says.

With a series of photos on the table, the detectives asked Scott to pick out the man he knew as Colton. It wasn't hard. There was the disheveled drug dealer he'd met, the thug Colton Pitonyak had become, in his mug shot, his dirty black hair wild and a goatee circling his mouth.

When Maci called Laura Ingles at eight that morning to tell her Jennifer had died, Laura screamed so loud that her neighbors from surrounding apartments rushed to check on her. She drove to the police station, offering to tell them whatever she knew. All the while, she kept thinking of that last phone conversation, the night Jennifer disappeared. "I couldn't remember if before I hung up I'd told Jennifer that I loved her," says Ingles. "I just couldn't remember."

"Did she suffer?" Laura kept asking the detectives.

"We can't tell you anything," one said.

The story of an unidentified woman's body found in a central Austin apartment broke at 8:45 that morning. "There were signs of obvious trauma," the television reporter said. "And it's being investigated as a murder, the fifteenth in Austin this year."

A short time later, Scott finished giving his statement, and the detectives said he could leave. He'd been thinking about the message he'd left for Eli. Jennifer's murder wasn't Eli's fault, Scott knew. He didn't want to hurt his friend. So he called Eli's phone number and left a second message: "Eli, I'm sorry for what I said. It's not your fault Jennifer's dead." After he hung up, Scott didn't know where to go, but he knew he had to find Vanessa and Sharon. He called and found out they were at the Omni.

"Come here," Sharon said.

Scott didn't have his car with him, so he ran to the hotel. It was a mile or so, and when he arrived he was hot and sweaty. Vanessa opened the door and wrapped her arms around him, and they both wept. When Laura Ingles arrived an hour or so later, Vanessa hugged her tight and sobbed, "He killed my little sister."

On the edge of the bed, Scott sat shaking and crying so hard he couldn't talk.

Detective Gilchrest arrived at the Orange Tree condominiums at ten that morning with the signed search warrant, and the team of APD personnel who'd been there much of the night into the morning finally began processing the evidence in Pitonyak's apartment.

Along with patrolmen who maintained the perimeter, three crime scene officers were on the scene, eager to get busy. To prevent disturbing evidence, the body would be left in place, in the bathtub with the brown rug over it, until the forensic team finished processing the scene. There was no need to hurry. The paramedic in charge had called in the information to nearby Breckenridge Hospital at 10:30 the night before, where a physician pronounced the Jane Doe dead. Despite Jim's assumptions, the police weren't yet ready to officially identify the deceased.

Everyone on the scene knew what to expect. They'd all been briefed on what waited for them in the bathroom.

Detective Walker, who'd coordinate the processing of evidence, was still on the scene, and he gave crime scene supervisor Kimberly Frierson permission to enter Orange Tree unit 88. As the first order of business, Frierson videotaped the entire scene, documenting where everything was before work began. While Frierson videotaped, Walker accompanied officers downstairs to the parking garage to inspect Colton Pitonyak's car. Along with the apartment, Gilchrest had written the warrant to include Pitonyak's white Toyota and Jennifer's black Saturn. Walker issued orders for both cars to be towed to 906 McFall, the APD forensic workshop, for processing.

Once Frierson finished the first videotape, Walker entered the apartment for the first time with Vince Gonzalez. It would be their job to identify and photograph evidence where it lay, before collection began. Gonzalez started by shooting photos of each room, then parts of the rooms, finally zeroing in on particular items. Evidence lay everywhere they looked, all around them. In the living room, Walker pointed out two spent bullet cartridges near the couch. Only in the kitchen did it appear someone had attempted to cover up what had taken place. The floors were clean, the countertops wiped down. Yet, here, too, they found disturbing evidence. When they opened the dishwasher, a machete lay across the bottom rack. Blood and hair still coated its thick blade.

One item Gonzalez decided on his own to photograph, a phone number written on the wall with the name J. Ribbit above it. It was Jennifer's cell phone number, written under a reference to the sound made by her family nickname, Frog.

What wasn't going on inside or outside unit 88 that morning was a lot of talking. Often, to keep murder scenes from weighing on them, detectives and officers banter back and forth as they work, a way of lightening the load. This day, the scene fell oddly quiet. "You could tell that everyone was upset," says one who was there. "No one felt untouched."

As he scouted the apartment, Walker placed small, hard plastic tents with numbers, the type restaurants sometimes use to mark tables, beside evidence he wanted photographed and collected. He moved a pillow near the bed and saw red stains on the carpet. Blood? He pulled out an evidence marker and placed it beside the bloodstain. That carpet section would be cut out and bagged. Beside the bed, Walker found an ACE hardware bag. With his hands gloved to protect the evidence, he inspected a receipt that lay inside. Looking it over, Walker realized that the day before Jennifer's body was discovered, Colton Pitonyak purchased items that included a hacksaw, ammonia, carpet cleaner, dust masks, blue shop towels, Febreze fabric freshener, and latex gloves. It didn't take much imagination to understand what Pitonyak intended to use the items for.

After the evidence was photographed, Victor Ceballos,

the third crime scene specialist assigned to the case, entered the apartment, carefully removing the items that were taken into evidence. An avuncular man with a wide smile, Ceballos designated each piece of evidence with his initials, VC, along with the number on the crime scene marker Walker assigned to it. VC–9 became Colton's folding knife, one the police would later call "the buck knife." Black-handled, with "Brandt, the most trusted name in farm implements since 1913, a division of Pitonyak Machinery Corporation" stamped on the serrated blade, the knife was a promotional item given away by Eddie Pitonyak's company. To prevent disturbing blood evidence he could see on it, Ceballos placed the knife inside a protective cardboard sheath and then into a ventilated white glassine bag.

From the living room, the two fired cartridges were collected. To protect markings that could tie them to a weapon, bullet casings were placed in a special box. The machete became VC–12, and the hacksaw found on top of the body, VC–34.

At the Omni, Jim and Sharon tried to sleep. Telling their families that Jennifer was dead would be one of the hardest things they would ever have to do, but they decided to wait until they had an official identification from the police. Trapped somewhere between shock and grief, Sharon had no choice but to think of others. Sharon had to notify her mother, Myrtle; Clayton; and Charlie, and she had to find Lauren. Sharon assumed her youngest daughter was in Norman, where Lauren roomed with Jim's youngest, Hailey, and they both attended the university. Jennifer and Lauren were so close that Sharon wanted to tell Lauren in person, and Jim agreed. They decided to bring her to Austin, to be with them and drive home to Corpus the following morning. They had more to do. Even in a horrific death, even in murder, there are customs that needed to be adhered to. Sharon and Jim needed to make arrangements for a funeral.

Jim called friends in Corpus, and one offered his private

plane to pick Lauren up. For hours, Jim tried to call Lauren, but she didn't answer her cell phone. When he finally reached her, he told her to go to the Norman airport, to wait for them. Lauren hemmed and hawed, at first claiming she had to work. Jim insisted, and finally the truth came out.

"I'm not in Oklahoma," she admitted. "Hailey and I are in Laredo."

They'd gone to South Texas with Hailey's mother, Jim's ex-wife, Susie, for a wedding. Lauren had talked about it with Sharon, but Sharon thought she'd convinced Lauren not to go when she'd told her about recent drug violence in the Rio Grande Valley and a spate of killings in Laredo.

"I'll get right back with you," Jim said. He called Lauren a little while later, and said, "Okay, I need you to go to the Laredo airport at about five this afternoon. Bring your suitcase. We're flying in to get you." When Lauren asked what was wrong, Jim repeated what time to be ready and asked her not to worry, but, of course, she couldn't stop wondering what had happened that was serious enough for Jim and Sharon to come for her in a private airplane.

Detective Arthur Fortune walked into Breed & Co. ACE hardware store that afternoon with a copy of the receipt found in the bag at the foot of Colton Pitonyak's bed. Hours earlier, Detective Gilchrest had stopped in and asked if Breed's had a video surveillance system. They did, one that surveyed the main checkout area.

As Fortune requested, Jeff Breed played the video from mid-afternoon, Wednesday, August 17. At one point, Fortune asked Breed to pause it. On the screen was a young man who looked like Pitonyak. When Breed saw him, he remembered the young, dark-haired man with the goatee. As Fortune took notes, Breed recounted how Pitonyak had appeared lost in the store, looking at a list. The young man smelled of alcohol but didn't seem drunk, and he'd said he needed the hacksaw to cut up a frozen turkey.

When Fortune talked to the checkout clerk who'd been

on that day, Rene Carden, she also remembered the young man, adding that she, too, smelled alcohol on his breath.

Detective Fortune left Breed's that afternoon without the video, however. Neither he nor Breed knew how to download off the digital equipment the store had just installed. Later that day, Detective Fugitt, homicide's resident tech geek, circled over to Breed's and hooked up a Sony Video Walkman to the surveillance camera, recording the segment with Pitonyak on a videocassette. The video Fugitt made clearly showed Pitonyak pushing a cart up to the checkout, waiting in line, checking out, and then leaving the store. In addition to the hacksaw, dust masks, ammonia, Febreze, and latex gloves, Colton purchased fifty-five-gallon drum liners, blue shop towels, bathroom tissue, and Spot Shot carpet cleaner.

At 2:30 in the afternoon, after he'd spent more than fifteen hours on the crime scene processing evidence, Detective Keith Walker was relieved by another detective. Walker, however, wasn't going home. Instead, he'd accompany the victim's corpse to the morgue. It was time to remove the corpse from the bathtub.

The sight was so horrific it was difficult to look at the grotesque scene as simply evidence to be collected, but that was precisely what Walker and the forensic team had to do. Walker's first order of business after videotaping and photographing the body was to have tape lifts used, strips of clear plastic tape used to pick up and preserve loose evidence, such as hair and fibers. The brown patterned rug still lay over the corpse, and everything in the bathtub had to be transported together, to disturb as little as possible.

Along with the rug, the black trash bag on the bathroom floor would accompany the body. No one had looked, but all believed Jennifer's head would be found inside. When Jennifer's arms became visible, they had their first clue that the bag might contain more. Jennifer's head wasn't the only thing missing. Both her hands were gone, severed at the wrists.

Something else became visible when they moved the body from the bathtub, a third bullet casing, found in the bathtub near the drain. Ceballos marked an evidence box and slipped it inside, one more item to be processed in the lab.

At 3:20 that afternoon, the body and the accompanying bag arrived at the morgue and was rolled on a gurney into an autopsy suite, where it was laid on trace evidence sheets, sterile sheets used to collect any remaining fibers or hairs. As Detective Walker and Ceballos stood nearby, deputy medical examiner Dr. Elizabeth Peacock opened the large, black trash bag. Inside were two black bags. When she took them out, she found a smaller white trash bag with a red pull cord inside each. Dr. Peacock, a woman with a long neck, glasses, cropped dark blond hair, and a competent manner, opened the first white bag, and found Jennifer's severed hands.

It must have been an unsettling sight as Dr. Peacock held and fingerprinted the small, delicate severed hands. The hands were photographed, and then the second bag was opened. If Detective Walker had any doubts about the victim's identity, looking inside the second white bag silenced all arguments. Jennifer's head was removed and set on the autopsy table beside her body. She still wore her earrings and her makeup, and, except for stab wounds across the side of her face, she looked remarkably like her Texas driver's license photo. Yet that wasn't sufficient.

When he left the morgue, Walker went to APD and compared the fingerprints from the corpse with those filed with Texas Department of Public Safety's drivers' license records. When they matched, the victim had an official name: Jennifer Cave.

After she heard the news that they now had a positive identification, Sharon called Clayton and Charlie, to tell them that Jennifer was dead. They cried, and when she hung up, Sharon worried, both about her son and that her ex-husband could have another stroke. She called friends and asked them to go to Charlie's house to be with them. Meanwhile, in Sinton, as soon as his mother hung up the telephone, Clayton dialed Jennifer's cell phone: "Hello, this is Jennifer. I'm not here now, but please leave a message." He called over and over again that evening, just to hear his dead sister's voice.

Two hours later, Lauren waited at the Laredo airport, worried, frustrated, and annoyed. She wondered if her father had suffered another stroke, if he had died. She kept urging herself to calm down. Jim's ex-wife, Susie, and Hailey stayed with her, trying to help but not knowing what to say. When the small plane landed and the stairway came down, Sharon, doubled over, could barely walk, and Jim looked as if he hadn't slept in weeks. Lauren noticed she and Sharon had worn the same outfits, and she made a joke of it. "We're twins," she said.

Sharon didn't even smile.

"There's been an accident," Jim finally told them as they all grouped together in a small room in the airport offices. "Jennifer's been killed."

"How?" Lauren asked.

"Somebody killed her," he answered.

Nausea welled up inside her, and Lauren hurried to the wastebasket and started retching, her whole body shaking. She screamed and cried, but it would last only minutes. From that moment forward, Lauren wouldn't cry for her almost twin for more than a year.

Along with a search warrant for the apartment and cars, Gilchrest had a signed warrant for Colton Pitonyak's cell phone records. Once they came in, showing what towers the telephone was bouncing off on the night of August 17, a pattern was easily apparent. Shortly after Sharon hung up the telephone with Pitonyak, warning him that she'd called police, he was on the run. His cell phone showed that someone had used it while cutting a southbound path through Texas, leading to the Mexican border. Calls went out to the

FBI and the U.S. Marshals office, asking for their help in finding Pitonyak, but there were problems. First, Pitonyak's cell phone calls had been recorded nearly two days earlier, giving the fugitive a formidable head start. Second, no one knew what type of car he would be in. His Toyota, after all, was locked up in APD's forensic processing center.

That afternoon, nearly three days after Jennifer's disappearance, the U.S. Marshals office, a division of the federal Department of Justice, issued a wanted poster for Colton Aaron Pitonyak, distributing it to the agents working throughout Texas, especially those on the border with Mexico. Pitonyak had blue eyes and brown hair, at five-eleven weighed 170 pounds, and he was to be considered armed and extremely dangerous. The bulletin warned, "Approach with caution."

Four years earlier, Colton had lived the cloistered life of a Catholic schoolboy. Now, at just twenty-two, he was a wanted criminal living a fantasy that matched *Scarface* or any of his favorite gangster movies. Colton Pitonyak had transcended a level most criminals never reach: He was being searched for by the FBI, the U.S. Marshals office, and Austin PD for what many were already calling the most brutal murder in the history of the University of Texas.

That evening, Jim, Sharon, and Lauren flew back into Austin. The next day, Jim and Sharon had the appointment with Gilchrest, and then they'd all drive home to Corpus. Jennifer's autopsy was scheduled for the morning, and then her body would follow. Sharon had already decided where her daughter's gravesite should be, beside her grandfather. "I had this crazy feeling that if I did that, my dad would protect Jennifer," Sharon says. "I wanted her to be safe."

Late that evening, many of Jennifer's friends congregated at Eli's, to band together to comfort one another. Many were crying, including Eli, who didn't appear to be able to stop. He lit a candle, one scented with apple spice, Jennifer's favorite. Friends noticed that he talked about her in the present tense, as if he hadn't yet absorbed that she'd died.

Meanwhile, at eleven that evening, in Piedras Negras, Mexico, a city just over the border from Eagle Pass, Texas, Laura Hall walked into the Casablanca Inn, and Pedro Fernandez, a heavyset man with glasses, looked up. He was the manager of the establishment, which had the look of a converted Holiday Inn. The place was busy that evening, and Fernandez had stayed late to help the desk clerk. When he saw Laura and the young, dark-haired man next to her, Fernandez assumed they were college students on a holiday.

"Do you have a room?" Hall asked.

"We're pretty full," Fernandez said. "I have to check."

Ten minutes later, Fernandez gave the couple the good news. He had a vacancy. Hall handed Fernandez a credit card and two University of Texas IDs. One was in Hall's name, the other was in the name of her traveling companion: Colton Aaron Pitonyak.

Nineteen

The first article on the case appeared in the *Austin American Statesman* the following morning, Saturday, August 20, 2005. In the metro section, it was small and said simply that Jennifer Cave, age twenty-one, had been found dead with obvious trauma Thursday night and that police were seeking Colton Pitonyak, twenty-two, on a first-degree murder charge.

At nine, Travis County deputy medical examiner Dr. Elizabeth Peacock again stood over Jennifer's remains in the morgue, along with two crime scene specialists: Ceballos, there to bag evidence, and James Bixler, assigned to take autopsy photographs. Detective Gilchrest, the lead detective on the case, stood by as well.

The day before, the head, hands, and body were all wrapped in sterile sheets, a final attempt to collect any trace evidence. Dr. Peacock conducted a vaginal examination and took swabs, to look for evidence of rape. No semen would be found, and there was no evidence of sexual assault. When she cut away Jennifer's halter top, Dr. Peacock, along with an assistant, rolled the body over to unhook Jennifer's bra. For the first time, Peacock saw a bullet hole, a gunshot wound in Jennifer's upper right arm, eight and a half inches below her shoulder. When she moved the arm, Peacock discovered that the bullet had exited without hitting the bone and gone directly into Jennifer's chest from the right side.

That Saturday morning, during the autopsy, Dr. Peacock cut into the body to trace the path of the bullet. She found that the incision made by the bullet entered between the fourth and fifth ribs and then sliced into the lower lobe of the right lung before cutting directly into the aorta, the body's largest artery. It was a devastating wound; Peacock knew such catastrophic injury to the aorta would kill within seconds.

Following the wound path, from right to left, front to back, and slightly downward, Peacock discovered a pool of coagulated blood inside the chest cavity and, twelve and a half inches below the left shoulder, a medium caliber, fully jacketed, minimally deformed bullet.

On the right side of Jennifer's face and upper neck, Peacock documented stab wounds, eighteen of them. She noted the pale, waxy appearance of the skin around the incisions and saw "no vital reaction" at the site of the wounds; in other words, no bleeding. That the wounds hadn't hemorrhaged led Peacock to classify them as postmortem, or after death. Other similar wounds were found on Jennifer's right forearm, her upper arm, her left thigh, and ten more to her chest and lower neck, all, too, postmortem. Most of the wounds were smooth and straight, some intersecting to form Vs.

Someone had cut repeatedly into Jennifer's body after death, for no apparent reason.

One knife wound on the palm of Jennifer's left hand, however, was different. There Dr. Peacock saw a slight pink that suggested it occurred peri-mortem, close to the time of death, while Jennifer still retained some blood pressure.

The biggest surprise of the day began when Peacock X-rayed Jennifer's severed head. On the X-ray, she saw what appeared to be a bullet inside the skull and behind the left temple. What the physician couldn't find was an entry wound. Only when Dr. Peacock inspected the cut surface of the severed head did she discern the truth: After the bullet to Jennifer's aorta killed her, someone cut off her head. Then a gun was fired upward, into her head through the severed neck.

Along with the dozens of cuts to the body, it now appeared even more certain that someone had defiled Jennifer's dead body for no reason other than amusement.

As is always done, tissue samples were taken to send for analysis, to check for substances, including toxins, drugs, and alcohol, and then, the autopsy completed, Jennifer's body was zippered into a bag to be transported to Corpus Christi for burial.

Under the heading *Conclusion* on her report, Peacock wrote: "Based on the anatomic findings at autopsy and investigation available to me at this time, it is my conclusion that Jennifer Cave, a 21-year-old white female, died as a result of a gunshot wound which penetrated the lung and aorta. There were extensive peri- and post-mortem sharp force injuries."

Just before ten that same morning, Jim, Sharon, and Lauren drove to APD headquarters to meet with Gilchrest. At this point, the detective had been assigned to the case for thirty-five hours. In any murder investigation, the first forty-eight hours are the most important. If a suspect isn't identified and apprehended within two days, statistics showed that the percentage of closed cases drop rapidly with each subsequent day. The first thing Sharon thought when she saw the bulky detective was that Gilchrest appeared to be in a slow burn. "I wouldn't want that look directed at me," she says.

During this first meeting, Gilchrest explained that the autopsy was completed and that the cause of death was a gunshot wound. The detective didn't go into any detail about the many wounds found on the body or its condition, but he reaffirmed what Jim and Sharon had been told the previous afternoon, that fingerprints conclusively identified it as Jennifer.

Angry about what she'd just learned in a text message from a friend, Lauren then claimed the detective's attention. "There's this Web site," she told Gilchrest. "It's called Facebook.com, and a lot of the college kids are on it. I'm on it, and most of my friends are. My friend says Colton Pitonyak is on it."

In truth, Lauren simply wanted Colton off the Web site.

Facebook was something she enjoyed, and she didn't want the person targeted as the likeliest suspect in her sister's killing on the same Web site she logged onto. Lauren wanted Gilchrest to make Facebook take Colton Pitonyak off. But Sharon would later remember how interested Gilchrest appeared in Lauren's information for another reason: Facebook had the potential to yield evidence.

After leaving Gilchrest, they drove to Denise Winterbottom's apartment, to collect a few of Jennifer's things. When Denise opened the door, Sharon walked in crying and nearly collapsed. Jim and Lauren brought her to the couch, and Denise ran for a wet towel to put on Sharon's forehead.

"Thank you for being Jennifer's friend," Sharon said. "Thank you for taking her in."

Once she felt up to it, Sharon and the others went to Jennifer's room. It looked like Jennifer, neat and orderly, with her clothes organized and hung in the closet and family pictures around her. Sharon sat on the bed, feeling, for the first time since her daughter's disappearance, that Jennifer was near.

Crying, Jennifer's family collected a few of her favorite things, including Jennifer's jewelry box, an afghan, and a picture of Lauren and Jennifer together, the two of them in their cheerleading uniforms. Sharon gathered Jennifer's craft box, one filled with beads and paints. Inside were *Scooby Doo* gift bags for party favors Jennifer bought for Madyson's upcoming birthday party, acrylic paints, and two unopened packs of college-ruled notebook paper. In the past two years, Jennifer had lived a nomadic life, accumulating little. For her twenty-one years of life, she'd left little behind but photographs and memories.

The trip to Corpus Christi that afternoon felt every bit as long as the journey they'd taken two days earlier to Austin. Jim led the way in his Suburban, and Vanessa followed later in her car, driven by a friend who'd flown in from Dallas. As soon as they arrived at the house, Sharon went directly to her bedroom and her bed. Jim called their family doctor and the pastor of their church, All Saints Episcopal's Father David Stringer, a kind man with graying temples and the beginning of laugh lines around his eyes. The physician gave Sharon tranquilizers and sleeping pills, and when she awoke, she saw Father David at her side, praying.

Jim and Sharon's good friend Harold Shockley, whom Jennifer once worked for at the bank, arrived that afternoon, not knowing what to say but wanting to help. Lauren let him into the house, then, a short time later, said, "My mom wants to see you."

Shockley found it difficult to walk into the bedroom. He knew only that Jennifer had been murdered, but that was enough. He didn't have children of his own, but he'd been the Cave/Sedwick family's unofficial Uncle Harold for years, and he knew that no parent ever expects to bury a child. When he saw Sharon, she was in bed, crying. "You need to watch out for Jim," she told him. "He's seen things that no one should ever see."

Sharon had reason to be concerned. Not only had Jim lived through a horrific experience, he'd been ordered not to tell anyone what he'd seen. By then, Jim realized he couldn't remain completely silent. He had to talk to someone. While Sharon lay in bed, Jim left to talk to the one person he thought would understand, Sid Smith, the private investigator friend who'd advised them throughout their ordeal. Smith was a former homicide detective, and Jim believed his friend could shoulder hearing the gruesome details.

At Smith's house, Jim described the horror of walking into unit 88 and finding Jennifer's slaughtered body, and he cried. There was little Smith could do but be there to comfort him. Underneath it all, Smith was disappointed, wondering why APD hadn't found justification to enter Pitonyak's apartment. If they'd been the ones to go inside, his friend wouldn't have had to.

"You did the best you could, Jim," Smith told him. Then he voiced a theory similar to the one the Austin officers had told Jim. "If you and Sharon hadn't called, he would have finished the job, cutting her up and throwing away her body. They probably wouldn't have ever found her."

That weekend, Jim and Sharon's doorbell rang constantly. Vanessa found herself wishing the well-meaning neighbors, family, and friends bringing food would simply go away. She was exhausted and angry and overflowing with grief. Concentrating on doing what had to be done, Lauren took over her mother's role, focusing on taking care of everyone else, greeting well-wishers and accepting their Tupperware containers of home-cooked dinners and desserts.

While the search for Colton Pitonyak continued, in Austin, the sides in the battle that would one day wage over his freedom formed. That afternoon, Gilchrest filled in the assistant district attorney who'd handle the case. Bill Bishop was in his mid-thirties, with penetrating blue eyes. With his prematurely salt-and-pepper hair and dark eyebrows, some thought he resembled a little older Taylor Hicks, of *American Idol* fame. Bishop had been with the DA's office since 1999, and he was the chief prosecutor in the court of Judge Wilford Flowers, the same judge who'd presided over Colton Pitonyak's drug charge just months earlier. Bishop's father was a well-known civil attorney in Austin, and Bill grew up wanting to be a lawyer. When he graduated from UT, he decided against civil law, because those cases rarely went to trial.

"I wanted to be in a courtroom," he says. "I enjoy it."

When he first heard about the Pitonyak case, Bishop had just returned from a month-long family leave, after the birth of his second daughter. He couldn't help but identify with Sharon and Jim. What horror to lose a daughter in such a brutal way.

As soon as Bishop's assignment came in, Gilchrest gave him a thumbnail of the case. By then many of the warrants had already been written, including permission to search Pitonyak's apartment and car and one for his arrest, charging him with murder. Gilchrest tossed the file folder of crime scene photos at Bishop. "Take a look," he said. Bishop, of course, knew what to expect. He was used to homicide cops treating the goriest photos as mundane. "It's the way they deal with it," he says. "They have to be almost intentionally callous. You have to look at it that way." The hardest part for Bishop was sitting down and watching the DVD of the crime scene, with the footage of the body in the bathtub.

After reviewing the file, Bishop agreed with Gilchrest; keeping a lid on the details as long as possible would keep the "crazies" away, the usual suspects who showed up to confess to every sensational case or habitually called in to say they had information. The murder's location surprised Bishop. He hadn't handled many cases on the UT campus, usually nothing more than drunk drivers and misdemeanors. By the time Bishop read Gilchrest's report, the detective had already amassed a full thirty pages. Bishop went through the evidence list marking, in addition to Gilchrest's orders, what he wanted tested for DNA. In this case, the forensic evidence would be vital in telling the grisly tale.

On the other side, the Pitonyaks were busy. Their call came in while Sam Bassett was in Chicago. Although Colton had yet to be arrested, Eddie Pitonyak wanted to line up his son's attorney, the one who'd been successful in plea-bargaining Colton's drug charge down to a misdemeanor. "They found a body in my son's apartment and they're looking for him," Pitonyak said. Eddie sounded baffled and worried to Bassett on the telephone. "What do we say to him if he calls?"

"He needs to call me and come to my office, and then we need to call the police," Bassett advised. After he hung up, Bassett called a cell phone number Eddie gave him for Colton. No one answered, but he left a message.

That Saturday, Colton and Laura's friend Said Aziz called APD anonymously. A friend had called him in New York, where he was getting ready to drive back to Texas to begin the fall semester at UT. "I think Jen got murdered and they're looking for Colton," the person said. "You should know that they have a picture of you. But don't worry. They asked where you are, and I told them you're in New York."

The picture was one Nora Sullivan had taken that the police found on Facebook.com, a photo of Juan Montero thugging it up for the camera surrounded by his friends, including Said and Colton in the background. Once he knew what had happened, Aziz dialed APD. He told the person who answered the telephone: "If you're looking for Colton Pitonyak, he's probably with a girl named Laura Hall."

A city of 142,000, Piedras Negras, Mexico, lies directly across the Rio Grande from Eagle Pass, Texas, and it calls itself "La Puerta de Mexico," in English, "Mexico's door." Piedras Negras translates to "black rock," referring to the region's coal deposits, but it's better known as the self-proclaimed birthplace of the nacho. It's popular for bird hunting in the fall and partying college students year round.

While Gilchrest pulled together the investigation in Austin and Jennifer's family struggled with her death in Corpus Christi, in Piedras Negras, Colton Pitonyak was interested in entertainment. That afternoon he and Laura Hall traipsed down from their second-floor room to the Casablanca Inn's lobby, where he logged onto Facebook.com, perhaps just to pass a bit of time.

As he had been the night before, Pedro Fernandez manned the hotel's reception desk, where the average cost of a room was $56 per night. He was used to Americans frequenting the place, including church members who built houses for the poor. Next to a bodega and a busy nightclub, and near a Wal-Mart, the 140-room hotel had a swimming pool, a restaurant, and a bar with video games.

As Pitonyak played around on the computer, he talked to Fernandez about the cost of booking flights to Cuernavaca, Mexico, seven hundred miles south. Hall stood protectively beside Pitonyak. From watching the two together, Fernandez assumed they were boyfriend and girlfriend.

Off and on, Fernandez talked to other guests about his plans for the night. His wife and child were visiting family, and he planned to watch his satellite television. Pay-per-view was hosting an Ultimate Fighting Championship competition, a mixed-martial-arts battle waged inside an octagon-shaped cage. It was one of Pitonyak's favorite sports, and it didn't take long for the dark-haired, scruffy-looking young American to approach Fernandez.

"Is there someplace in town I can go to watch?" he wanted to know.

Fernandez considered the possibilities but couldn't think of a bar that would air such a brutal fight. Pitonyak asked if Fernandez could tape it for him. "I could," Fernandez agreed. "You don't have a VCR in the room, but you could go to Blockbuster, across the street, and rent one."

They talked for a while, and then Fernandez made an offer. "Why don't you come to my house to watch?"

That night at 11:15, Fernandez was ready to leave the Casablanca. Laura and Colton waited for him in the lobby. Pitonyak was dressed in a navy polo shirt and shorts, and Hall had on a UT T-shirt and shorts. They both wore navy blue bill caps that sat backward on their heads. Fernandez called a cab, they stopped at a liquor store for a bottle of Bacardi rum and a twelve-pack of beer, and then arrived at Fernandez's house, where the cab let them off. A little while later, Fernandez gave his guests the house tour and poured drinks while they waited for the competition to start.

At first, all seemed well. They talked, mostly about the competition and a Web site Pitonyak liked, Sherdog.com, which profiled the fighters, and Fernandez used the time to size his guests up. They seemed like nice enough young Americans. They were happy, appearing carefree. His assessment changed, however. As they watched the fight, Pitonyak quickly showed the effects of the rum, and Fernandez wondered how much his guest had to drink before they arrived. As Pitonyak became increasingly drunk, the alcohol loosened him up, and he talked.

"Can you help us sell the Cadillac?" he asked Fernandez. "We need the money."

While they watched the battle on the screen, Fernandez asked questions. What Hall and Pitonyak told him was that they'd driven into Mexico farther west, over the Del Rio Bridge, two nights earlier, and slept in a hotel near the border the first night. When they tried to drive into the interior of Mexico, they were turned back at a checkpoint because they didn't have the title for Hall's 1994 green Cadillac Concours. They still wanted to get to Cuernavaca, fifty miles south of Mexico City. But rather than drive, they thought they'd sell the car and buy airplane tickets.

"You'll have to get the title," Fernandez said. "Then you could sell it."

Fernandez had lived in the United States, in San Antonio, for years, and he had a used car lot for a time, so he knew the ins and outs of selling cars. "Just fill out the paperwork and they'll give you a copy of the title . . ." he explained, saying that they had everything necessary to get a copy of the title just over the border, at the Eagle Pass, Texas, tax office.

"We can't go there," Pitonyak said.

Fernandez's eyes narrowed. He wondered why not, but instead said, "You can drive around the border, but you can't go farther into Mexico without the title. To sell the car, you'll need the title."

"We're not going back across the border," Pitonyak said again.

That was something Fernandez didn't understand. It was his experience that most Americans who came to Piedras Negras intended to go home. He'd never run into ones who planned to stay in Mexico. Fernandez himself hadn't wanted to leave the States. He'd been deported, much to his chagrin, after a burglary charge. Now he looked at Pitonyak again. The American kid was eyeing him strangely, his expression angry. Fernandez considered a crudely drawn tattoo on the kid's leg and began to wonder if the kid had gotten it in jail.

"Do they extradite from Mexico?" Pitonyak asked.

"I don't know," Fernandez said, feeling more certain than ever that his invitation to the two young Americans had been a mistake.

"Colton, shut up," Hall cautioned.

For a while, they sat there, watching the fighters hammer each other on the television. When Laura asked again about selling the car, Fernandez remembered he had copies of the forms they'd need in his home office. He decided he'd get the question over with by giving them the paperwork, so they'd be quiet and watch the fight. Maybe if the American kids had the forms in their hands, they'd understand they needed to cross back over to the United States to file the papers. Explaining where he was going, Fernandez got up to walk to his office desk, but Pitonyak shadowed him. Something about the way the kid looked at him bothered Fernandez. The two young Americans were beginning to scare him.

Making the situation even more volatile, Pitonyak sneered, "I could take you," then pulled up his shirt to expose a chrome knife tucked into the belt of his shorts. On instinct, Fernandez grabbed the knife. Pitonyak glared at him but swayed, obviously drunk.

At that point, Fernandez wanted nothing more than to get the two Americans out of his house.

Back in the living room, the pay-per-view fight was over, and Fernandez suggested he drop Hall and Pitonyak at a tavern, where they could continue to drink. They agreed and walked toward the door, but Pitonyak was so drunk he suddenly lost his footing, tumbling into Fernandez's son's plastic play area, filled with toys. Laughing, Pitonyak grabbed one of the child's small sombreros and put it on over his cap. Chuckling along with him, Hall got in the playpen with her boyfriend, and Fernandez took the opportunity to flick open his cell phone and snap a picture. Just in case the evening got even more out of control, the hotel manager wanted a record of his guests.

Back on his feet, Pitonyak was so drunk that Fernandez helped him walk to the car. Increasingly worried about his own safety, the hotel clerk drove the long way back to town. If they tried to return, he didn't want the two young Americans to remember how to find his house. Yet, he was curious. "What did you do in the U.S. that you can't go back?" Fernandez asked, as they pulled up in front of the bar. "Kill a cop or something?"

"Don't roll on me," Pitonyak warned, giving him a cold, hard look.

"Shut up," Hall warned. "Colton just shut up."

Later, when he returned to his house, Fernandez downloaded the cell phone photo onto his computer and noticed something chilling: In the playpen, while laughing manically, Pitonyak held one of the toys, a stuffed Mickey Mouse. Looking comical in the child-size sombrero, Pitonyak grinned, but his hand was clamped tight over the animal's nose and mouth, as if suffocating it.

Twenty

An article on the West Campus killing in the *Austin American Statesman* that Sunday identified Jennifer but had few details about her death, except a quote from Sid Smith, whom Jim had appointed as the family spokesperson. "Jennifer was a wonderful person," Smith said, "a bright kid, outgoing and a good student." Still on the run, Colton was being sought, and UT students were nervous, especially those moving into the Orange Tree, which now was known on campus by another name: "The Murder Tree."

"I need to move," one student told her parents. "I just don't feel safe anymore."

That morning, Sharon and Jim drove to the funeral home to make arrangements. When it came time to pick out Jennifer's casket, Sharon couldn't bring herself to enter the display room. It was such an unbelievable task, to have to pick out a casket for one of her children. Jim walked into the casket-lined room as Sharon stood outside. He described the ones he thought would be appropriate. From the doorway, Sharon peeked in and saw one he'd chosen, and nodded.

Little information was coming in from Austin, and it was all being funneled through Sid, who'd not only taken on the press but would act as a liaison with APD. Although Austin appeared quiet, something important did happen that day. Colton instant-messaged Nora Sullivan, nothing specific, just things like, "What's up?" She wasn't on the computer at the time he was, so they'd never actually corresponded, but Sullivan called to tell police, and two officers showed up at her door wanting to take her computer into headquarters. By then, Sullivan realized that the commotion at Colton's apartment wasn't just a drug bust but a killing, and that Jennifer, someone she liked, was dead.

The officers didn't have a warrant, and Sullivan vetoed giving up her computer. Her television hadn't arrived yet and she didn't even have a radio, so the computer was her only entertainment, she told them, but she did offer something else. "You know, the night this happened, Colton knocked on my door at three in the morning. And he had blood on him."

That afternoon, for the second time, the wispy blond college senior went to APD headquarters to give a statement, this time revealing everything, including how Colton told her a bizarre story about a gunfight with drug dealers. Why hadn't she told them before? "They didn't ask me that question," she says. "They didn't ask when I'd last seen Colton."

When the prosecutor, Bill Bishop, heard the account of Sullivan's late-night visitor, he pegged it as insight to the time of the murder. Jennifer's body was so badly abused and decomposed that Dr. Peacock hadn't been able to estimate time of death in any terms except days, but Bishop interpreted Colton's visit to Sullivan as an attempt to cover up gunshots at his condo. From that point forward, the assistant district attorney believed that Jennifer died shortly before Pitonyak showed up at Nora Sullivan's door.

In Corpus Christi, after the morning at the funeral home, Jim grew increasingly worried about Sharon. She needed to talk to someone, he decided, not just anyone but someone who'd lost a child. He could think of no one who'd had a child murdered, but a friend, a dentist, had lost a sixteen-year-old daughter to cancer. Jim called, and that afternoon the man came over and sat down with Sharon, and for a little while, they talked. Before he left, he told Sharon, "Jennifer will come to you in some way to let you know she's all right. It happened to me, and it will happen to you."

Sharon told Jim about the conversation, and he said perhaps their friend was right. Maybe, somehow, Jennifer would return to say good-bye. Sharon felt less hopeful. Since the night Jennifer disappeared, Sharon's strong link to her middle daughter had felt severed. Until the law firm called, Sharon hadn't sensed that Jen was in trouble or missing, and, except for that brief time she sat in Jennifer's room at Denise's, surrounded by her daughter's few possessions, Sharon hadn't felt Jennifer near.

A few hours later, Sharon and the rest of Jennifer's family planned her funeral. Jim, Sharon, and their children all gathered in the living room to talk with Father David, telling stories about Jennifer and laughing, keeping at bay the terror and the sadness that now stalked their lives. Looking around the room at the faces of her surviving children, Sharon felt an all-consuming anxiety, a building fear. "I started to think that Colton might come after Vanessa, Lauren, or Clayton," she says. "He'd hurt me once, and I'd told him I'd gone to the police. That's why he'd run. What if he went after another of my children to punish me?"

At 9 A.M. the following morning, Monday, a warrant for Colton Pitonyak's arrest hit the Travis County District Clerk's office. While the indictment had come down two days earlier, the contents had been kept secret. In the signed warrant were the first details: how the call from the law firm alerted Sharon to Jennifer's disappearance; the calls to missing persons; and the events that led up to Jim opening Pitonyak's window, climbing in, and finding Jennifer's body, the bloody machete in the dishwasher, and the hacksaw on the corpse's chest. The most shocking words were those associated with the condition of Jennifer's corpse: "parts severed . . . multiple stab wounds."

The charge against Colton Pitonyak was murder, with a potential range of punishment from probation to life in prison. Despite the gruesome details of the case, Pitonyak wouldn't be eligible for the death penalty, since in Texas the ultimate punishment required a murder accompanied with the commission of a second felony: robbery or kidnapping, or special circumstances such as the murder of a police officer.

That same day, Detective Walker arrived at the McFall forensic facility to execute the search warrant on Colton Pitonyak's Toyota Avalon. Crime scene specialist Kimberly Frierson was there to take photos and process evidence. Without a key at their disposal, Walker called a Pop-A-Lock technician to open the right passenger side back door, which had already been fingerprinted.

Starting from the outside, they examined the car and the contents. Inside, they found a road atlas with an interesting omission: Someone had torn out the page of southern Texas that showed routes from Austin into Mexico. When Frierson opened the center console, she spotted something else of interest, wedged between receipts and insurance information: a Smith and Wesson .380 caliber, semiautomatic pistol.

Carefully removing the gun, Frierson clicked out the magazine, removed the bullets, and bagged it all as evidence. The .380 bullets were the same caliber as the shell casings found in Orange Tree unit 88, and when inspecting the grip, Frierson noted that someone had attempted to scratch off the gun's serial number.

Finally, Frierson sprayed the interior of the car with Leuco Crystal Violet, a colorless spray that acts as a blood enhancement agent. When it comes in contact with hemoglobin, the solution turns a bright violet. Frierson noted on her report that no blood was found.

In Corpus, Lauren and Hailey went shopping. They bought Jennifer soft, baby blue pajamas to be buried in. Jim brought them to the funeral home, along with Jennifer's "blanky," the well-worn quilt Myrtle had made for Jennifer when she was a baby. Coming from her grandmother, the quilt was something Jennifer had always loved.

That morning in Austin, Scott and Denise drove to 906 McFall, the APD forensic site, to claim Jennifer's car. The police had finished processing it a day earlier, and Scott had promised Sharon and Jim that he'd drive the car to Corpus for the funeral, and then return to Austin with friends. After he threw his things into Jen's trunk, Scott brought Madyson to stay with Denise while he was in Corpus Christi. At the doorway, as he got ready to leave, Madyson looked up at her father. "When's my sister coming back?" the little girl asked. It was then that Scott and Denise realized someone had to tell Madyson about Jennifer. Still, this wasn't the time.

"Everything's okay. We'll talk when I get back," Scott told the little girl, hugging her. "I love you, Madyson."

"I love you, Daddy," she replied.

In Jennifer's car on the drive to Corpus Christi, Scott listened to an Incubus song entitled "I Wish You Were Here" on the radio, and he started to cry. It was one of Jennifer's favorites, and the words sang of forgiveness. The verse repeated the sentiment that if nothing else, they would always have each other. "But Jennifer was gone," Scott says. "And the song reminded me that she wouldn't be coming back."

A telephone rang at APD that afternoon, and Loren Hall, Laura's father, was on the line. "I'm worried about my daughter," he told an officer. Laura had e-mailed him and asked him to move her possessions out of her apartment. "I think she might be with Colton Pitonyak."

Alerted by his call, APD investigated, and then called Deputy U.S. Marshal Vincent "Vinnie" Bellino in his office in the Rio Grande Valley. By the time they gave the information to Bellino, APD investigators had found a traffic ticket issued to one Laura Ashley Hall for traveling at an unsafe speed with an expired state tax sticker. At 1:46 A.M. on the night Pitonyak disappeared, Hall was pulled over in her green 1994 Cadillac Concours in Valverde County, north of Del Rio, Texas, where a bridge spanned the river into Mexico.

Assigned to the Lone Star Task Force, set up in 2003 to return fugitives to the United States, Bellino had worked for the Bexar County Sheriff's Department for sixteen years before joining the U.S. Marshals. As part of his job, he developed relationships with his Mexican counterparts, especially immigration authorities. Still, Bellino couldn't assure APD of the Mexican government's cooperation. "It's hard to know what they'll do in a given situation," says Bellino. "But relationships have gotten better, and we do get more fugitives out."

To check out the video from the Del Rio Bridge, Bellino assigned Deputy U.S. Marshal Joseph Smith, an officer with brown hair and thin lips, to take Pitonyak's wanted poster, Laura's driver's license photo, and the information on the green Cadillac. Smith was told to concentrate on tapes from Thursday, August 18, the day Hall and Pitonyak were suspected of crossing into Mexico. One thing in particular made it easier: "Most of those who cross the border in Del Rio are Hispanic," says Bellino. "Two white kids would stand out."

Later, Smith called Bellino with good news; he'd found video of Hall driving the Cadillac license number P72BWK over the border at 2:36 that morning. Bellino and Smith now knew when and where Hall and Pitonyak entered Mexico, but that didn't answer the most important question: Where was Pitonyak now?

That afternoon, at the Casablanca Inn in Piedras Negras, Pitonyak again got on the lobby computer to check his Facebook account. By then, the friends listed on his page had dropped from forty-seven to forty-one. As news of the murder spread, more would pull off his Web page, not wanting to be associated with someone whose name filled the newspaper as a fugitive suspected of murder. When Fernandez reviewed the accounts that afternoon, he noticed the young Americans had fallen behind on their hotel bill. He needed another payment. He called Hall, who brought down cash.

Early that afternoon in Corpus Christi, Jennifer's friends began arriving for her funeral. Jim had made arrangements for them to stay in a friend's condo on the beach, one he, Sharon, and the girls, especially Jennifer, had always enjoyed. When Vanessa was in the elevator with Scott, the door wobbled, stuttering back and forth, not closing, causing the elevator bell to ring, ding, ding, ding.

"Do you see what Jennifer's doing?" Vanessa asked. "That's been happening all day."

Scott looked at Vanessa as if she'd lost her mind, but then she said, "Okay Jennifer, you can close the doors now. We know you're here."

Scott watched wide-eyed as the elevator doors slid closed.

Visitation began at the Seaside Funeral Home that afternoon at five and was set to run until seven. Sharon and the family arrived early. The casket was closed. Sharon still didn't know about the horror that had been inflicted upon Jennifer's body, and she begged to see her lost daughter one last time, to touch her and look at her face as she said goodbye. Without explaining why she couldn't, Jim insisted that wasn't wise. Standing beside the casket, Sharon sobbed and clawed at it. "I want to see my baby," she pleaded. "Please, I want to see my baby."

Thinking nothing else this awful could ever happen in his life, Jim held her. "You can't," he said. "You have to trust me on this. You can't."

The funeral home was filled with flowers and pictures of Jennifer with family and friends. When the doors opened, a long line of hundreds of well-wishers walked toward the family, wanting to shake hands or hug and share their condolences.

Pulling together her remaining strength, Sharon held on, determined not to break down. She held up surprisingly well, but then halfway through the vigil, Sid pulled Jim to the side. Moments later, Jim asked the funeral director to turn off the music and to close the doors on the line of mourners still waiting outside. When the doors closed, Jim stood in the center of the room.

"I'm sorry, but everyone except immediate family has to leave," he said. "We appreciate your coming, but ya'll need to go."

Some hesitated for a moment, unsure, looking at one another for guidance, but soon everyone followed Jim's order and left. Only immediate family remained in the funeral home with Jennifer's closed casket. In the pit of her stomach, Hailey knew they were about to hear horrific news. She looked at Lauren and worried that she simply couldn't endure more. Hailey knew Lauren well enough to understand that she handled information better if it came when she was prepared to hear it. "Please leave this room," Hailey told her.

With no alternative, Jim explained that in Austin the newspaper and TV stations had found the arrest warrant and were pushing to get Jennifer's autopsy. "I have to tell you something that's fixing to run on the six o'clock news," he said. "Anyone who doesn't want to hear needs to leave, now."

Lauren looked at Hailey, and turned and left.

After she'd gone, Jim explained Jennifer had been shot and she'd died quickly, but there was more. After her death, someone had mutilated her body, cutting off her head and hands. As he spoke, Sharon and Vanessa screamed, their bodies violently shaking. Jennifer's grandmother, Myrtle, sobbed, as Vanessa ran outside. Hailey, not able to bear more, ran out after her. When one of Jim's friends found Vanessa, she was again sitting on a curb, much as she had at the crime scene, this time rocking and staring into space.

"I'd like a cigarette," she said, although she wasn't a smoker. When the man gave it to her, Vanessa couldn't hold it, and it fell into the gutter. The man helped her up and brought her to his car, then drove her home.

One of Jim's cousins, a physician, followed them home to help, and from the house, Jim called their family doctor, who rushed over to care for Sharon and Vanessa, who were both near hysteria.

In Little Rock, Tommy Coy watched the evening news that night and heard that Texas authorities were searching for

Colton Pitonyak on a murder charge, in a horrific case in which the body of a young woman had been dismembered. Coy stared at the television. The report, he thought, had to be wrong. But the news anchor had clearly said Colton Pitonyak, who'd graduated from Catholic High School. For a little while, Coy sat and wondered, and then he went to an upstairs closet and pulled out a box of student mementos, things he'd kept from his best students.

After rummaging through, he pulled out a handwritten note from Colton dated 2001, thanking him for writing a recommendation to help him get into UT's business school. Coy read and reread the note, thinking about the kid he knew.

"I was baffled," says Coy.

Sam Bassett also heard the reports not long after he reached Austin that evening. At first, he couldn't quite believe the news about the condition of the body. Then, he thought about what this meant for the case, the publicity and the shock for Colton's parents. "This wasn't going to be your usual case," he says. "But I liked Bridget and Eddie Pitonyak, and I knew I'd do what I could to help their son."

Deputy U.S. Marshal Aaron Greenwood called Vinnie Bellino at 7:30 that evening, with more information via APD from Loren Hall. Hall had reported that he believed his daughter was contacting him from a hotel in Piedras Negras. As soon as he hung up the telephone, Bellino put in a call to his counterpart in Coahuila, the Mexican state that includes the city of Piedras Negras, asking to meet him at the border in Eagle Pass. At the international boundary line on top of the bridge over the Rio Grande, Bellino gave Mexican officers a wanted poster for Pitonyak, a driver's license photo of Laura Hall, and a description and license plate number for her green Cadillac. "This Pitonyak's tied to a really brutal murder," Bellino told those gathered. "We need to find him and get him in custody, quick."

A while later, Laura Hall called the front desk at the Casablanca Inn, and Pedro Fernandez answered.

"Are you going to help us sell the car?" she asked. "We want to leave."

"I don't want anything to do with you two and your problems," he replied.

"That's okay," she said. "But please don't tell anybody about us."

That evening in Corpus Christi, Scott, Vanessa, and the rest of the twentysomethings were on the beach. They took wine, beer, and blankets. "We were going to say good-bye," says Vanessa.

The Gulf breezes were strong, and they talked about Jennifer and played CDs, including the Incubus song Scott had heard on the radio on the way there that day, "I Wish You Were Here." As it played, they held hands and sang along, then ran out into the waves together, letting the cold water wash over their bodies.

On the U.S. side of the border, Vincent Bellino was in the department's Eagle Pass office, maintaining a vigil, hoping for word on the whereabouts of Colton Pitonyak. At 12:30 that night, the phone rang.

"We found the Cadillac," a Mexican officer told him.

The Mexicans had moved quickly, appearing to want Pitonyak out of their country as much as Bellino and a squad of homicide detectives wanted him under arrest in Austin. The plan was to take Pitonyak by surprise, before he could get to a lawyer and fight extradition. Because he was without legal status in the country, the Mexican police planned to expel Pitonyak as an illegal immigrant. For all intents and purposes, "Colton Pitonyak was like a wetback in Mexico," says Bellino. "He wasn't born there, didn't have citizenship, and could be kicked out at any time."

Dressed in jeans, boots, and a T-shirt, Bellino drove to the line down the center of the Eagle Pass Bridge, the border between the two countries. A little while later, the plainclothes Mexican police arrived in a beat-up white van. Bellino got inside, and they escorted him across the border and drove the short distance to Piedras Negras, pulling into the parking lot at the Casablanca Inn. Once there, they stopped near an old green Cadillac. Bellino checked the license plate number. It was Laura Hall's. Glancing up at the hotel, the deputy U.S. Marshal saw Hall and Pitonyak on a second-floor walkway, smoking and talking.

"That's them," Bellino whispered.

With that, Mexican officers backed up the van to transport Bellino back across the border. He had no authority in Mexico, and they didn't want him in their country when they apprehended Pitonyak and Hall. Back in the Eagle Pass office, Bellino waited with Smith, hoping Mexican authorities wouldn't hesitate too long and lose their prey.

An hour later, Pedro Fernandez was at the inn's front desk when a squadron of Mexican police entered. Without asking any questions, they proceeded directly through the hotel, outside, and into the parking lot. Fernandez followed and watched as the officers banged on Pitonyak's room. Pitonyak opened the door, and the officers rushed in and grabbed him. Colton Pitonyak said nothing as he was handcuffed and brought from the room, but Laura Hall, sounding like the lawyer she one day hoped to be, screamed: "We're American citizens. You're violating our civil rights. You can't arrest us."

At 1:40 A.M., Mexican police called to report that they had Pitonyak and Hall and were about to deport them from Mexico. Bellino and Smith rushed back to the center of the one-hundred-yard-long international bridge in two cars. At the boundary line, they waited. Again the white police van pulled up and stopped. The Mexican officers climbed out, bringing the two young Americans with them. Pitonyak looked dirty and disheveled, wearing a green T-shirt, too big Ralph Lauren Bermuda shorts, and a pair of $100 tennis shoes. Relieved to have his suspect in custody, Bellino signed the documents, and the Mexicans left.

In two cars, one of the young Americans with each, Bellino and Smith drove the short distance to the U.S. Customs office, where Colton Pitonyak was officially welcomed back to Texas, then quickly read his rights and arrested. Bellino entrusted Hall, who had no charges pending against her, to the custody of the customs officers, and Bellino, Smith, and an INS officer took Pitonyak and left for the Maverick County jail. On the way, Colton spoke for the first time: "What am I being charged with?"

"Murder," Bellino said.

"If this is a murder charge, I know what this is about," Pitonyak said.

They asked no questions, and he offered nothing else.

When they arrived at the jail, the sally port entrance, a set of two doors used to isolate and secure vehicles brought into the facility, wasn't working, and Bellino got out with the INS officer to walk inside and let the jailers know they'd arrived. While he was in the car alone with Joseph Smith, Pitonyak spoke again.

"I really fucked up," he said.

Twenty-one

"They got him. They got him," Scott heard Vanessa screaming when he awoke the next morning. Jennifer's friends
filled the condo, and Vanessa was crying and jumping up
and down on the telephone, talking to her mother.

"They found Colton," she shouted. "They arrested him!"

Scott ran to hug her, and pretty soon everyone in the
condo was awake, talking about Colton Pitonyak's arrest in
Mexico. After so much sadness, it was the first reason they'd
had to rejoice. Afterward, Vanessa went back to bed and fell
quickly to sleep, the first peaceful sleep she'd had since the
night before Jennifer disappeared.

By then, detectives Mark Gilchrest and David Fugitt
were en route to Eagle Pass to interview Pitonyak. They'd
considered flying, but Gilchrest didn't trust small planes,
so they drove south, heading toward the Maverick County
jail, figuring that without airports to contend with, it would
be almost as fast. By the time they arrived, Loren Hall had
already come and gone. Bellino had called him as soon as
he'd finished turning Pitonyak over to the jail guards, to let
Hall know they had his daughter at the point of entry. While
they were on the telephone, Hall confided in Bellino. "He
sounded upset and frustrated, and he said that Laura was
trying to grow up on her own," says Bellino. "I had the impression that he thought this was all rebellion, and that he
was trying to hold on to her."

While she waited for her father, Smith watched Laura
Hall pace the facility, talking to herself and acting strangely.
She wanted to call Colton's attorney, saying she had to get

him out of jail. At one point, an agitated Hall said, "I'll kill anyone who hurts Colton."

Whatever the issues between the father and daughter, when Loren Hall arrived, Laura ran to her father and threw her arms around him.

Loren Hall asked Bellino about reclaiming the car and Laura's things, along with Colton's possessions still at the Casablanca. Bellino advised Hall to wait to drive into Mexico until daylight, when it would be less dangerous. But Hall and his daughter didn't take the advice, instead leaving immediately for Piedras Negras. Customs called Bellino two hours later. Laura Hall was coming back across the border in her Cadillac.

"Do you want us to detain her?" the border patrol officer inquired.

"No, APD didn't ask us to hold her," Bellino answered. "There are no charges pending against her."

After checking in with the Maverick County Sheriff's Department, Gilchrest and Fugitt went directly to the jail. Because of the severity of the charges against him, Pitonyak was on a suicide watch, his shoelaces and belt confiscated. Guards brought a handcuffed Pitonyak to meet with the two detectives, and Gilchrest read Pitonyak his Miranda rights: He had the right to an attorney, and anything he said could be used against him. The talking ended quickly, when Colton Pitonyak asked for a lawyer.

At 6:30 that morning, Said Aziz was in his car driving to Texas. He planned to stop in San Marcos before continuing on to Austin to get ready for classes to start at UT in a week. Following reports of the news unfolding in Austin, Aziz had thought a lot about Jennifer, whom he considered a friend. That morning a long article had run in the *Austin American Statesman*: "Police: UT Student Used Saw to Butcher Body."

When Said's cell phone rang and he answered, he heard

Laura Hall's voice. "You wouldn't believe the shit coming down," she said. "Colton's been arrested. The Mexican cops broke our hotel door down. I can't believe they found us so fast."

Telling him about the early-morning raid, Hall sounded excited, elated at the drama she'd become enmeshed in.

"How long have you been involved in all this?" Said asked.

"I have been up in this shit since like two hours after the shit started," she crowed.

"Well, what's going on?" he asked.

"Basically, I'm fucked," she said, but then she went on to explain that she had a plan. Her intention was to tell police that she believed she and Colton were on a vacation, and that she knew nothing about Jennifer's dismembered body in his bathtub. "I'll be okay."

At eight that morning, the U.S. Embassy in Mexico City issued a press release: "Thanks to quick action on the part of Mexico's immigration authorities and the US Marshals service, Colton Pitonyak will be held accountable in the US for one of the most horrific murders ever committed in the state of Texas."

By then, Andrea Jiles's cell phone was ringing in Houston. "You wouldn't believe what's happened," Laura said, again sounding excited. "Check the Internet."

Laura hung up, and Jiles, who was recovering from foot surgery, got up and logged onto her computer. She typed "Colton Pitonyak" into Google and felt queasy as a list of news articles appeared, including the wanted poster from the U.S. Marshals office.

"My phone is probably tapped," Hall said, when she called back. "Colton's in jail."

"Why aren't you in jail?" Jiles asked.

"They aren't going to get me," Hall said. "I didn't do anything. We were just on vacation."

"You're going to go to jail," Jiles warned. "They're just

working on gathering enough evidence to book you."

"Don't say that," Hall said, for the first time sounding worried. "They aren't going to get me."

Laura Hall made at least one more call that Tuesday morning, phoning Colton's attorney, Sam Bassett, to tell him of the arrest. Bassett immediately contacted an Eagle Pass attorney, hiring him to meet with Pitonyak. Bassett needed to make sure his client didn't talk to police. Then he went in to talk to his mentor, Roy Minton.

Gracious and old-fashioned, Minton had headed the go-to firm in Austin for decades, and Sam Bassett was one of the old man's favorites. "He's one of the best young lawyers I've known," he says. It was Minton's opinion that defense lawyers could be too aggressive, too caustic, and that doing so only backfired on their clients. Bassett respected the older man. Often dressed with a bit of Texas flair, Minton had an optimistic attitude and appeared comfortable in his own skin. Bassett had seen other criminal defense attorneys eaten up by working with clients who'd done terrible crimes or by being unable to free clients they believed innocent. Minton wasn't like that. "You do the best you can for the client," Minton says. "And you accept that there are a lot of things you don't control."

At about that time in Corpus Christi, there was a silent ceremony unfolding at Jim and Sharon's home, on a quiet street surrounded by trees. Hailey, Vanessa, and Lauren pulled out Sharon's clothes, looking for something for her to wear to the funeral. They found a black dress, and then slipped her into it. Lauren sat her on a stool in the bathroom, and Sharon tried not to look into the mirror while her daughters curled her hair and applied her makeup. Later, Sharon wouldn't remember what she'd worn, and she wouldn't care.

In honor of Jennifer, who'd loved sexy, strappy shoes, all the Cave and Sedwick women wore "girl shoes," high heels. Vanessa's were gold stilettos. And Sharon asked them to wear something blue, Jennifer's favorite color.

As they were leaving for the funeral, Sharon looked at Hailey in her black dress. "You're not wearing any blue?" Sharon asked.

"Yes, I am," Hailey said. "I'm wearing a blue thong Jennifer bought me."

At 11:30, Laura Hall called Aziz again. The conversation lasted about ten minutes, and much of it was dedicated to Laura's angst about protecting Colton. She was in love with him, and said she would do anything she could to help him.

"Colton doesn't merit loyalty. He's an axe murderer who killed a person we both knew," Aziz argued. "A girl a lot like you."

"You shouldn't judge Colton," Hall replied. "Colton told me what happened. It was an accident . . . Colton said I could help by sticking up for him . . . There's a difference between manslaughter and first-degree murder . . . If I help him, he might walk."

"I might believe it was an accident if Colton just shot her, but look what he did to her," Aziz said. "How did you get to Mexico?"

"We just hauled in my Caddy," she said.

"Colton killed a girl, someone like you," Aziz said again. "Why would you help him?"

"I love him," Hall replied. "And that's just how I roll."

To Said Aziz, Laura Hall sounded as if she thought she were involved in a romantic getaway, a grand adventure with the man she loved. When Aziz referred to them as gangsters "like Bonnie and Clyde," Hall laughed.

After his 11:30 call from Laura Hall, Said Aziz didn't know what to do. It seemed she was pulling him into the murder case, somewhere he had no desire to be. He picked up the telephone and called APD, where an officer asked him to skip San Marcos and drive directly to Austin, to give a statement to police.

Meanwhile, with Colton Pitonyak lawyered up, Gilchrest and Fugitt decided to go back to Austin via Tarpley, Texas, to stop at the Caribbean Cowboy RV Park to interview Laura Hall. When they got there, Hall did as she'd told Aziz she would; she wrote and signed a statement that said she knew nothing of a killing and that she'd thought she and Pitonyak were on a romantic getaway. When Gilchrest asked if Laura knew what had happened at Colton's apartment, she answered, "I wish I did."

During the course of the interview and statement writing, Laura Hall claimed that Jennifer's body in Colton's bathroom could have been "a set up."

"I would like to say for my statement that Colton wasn't a sicko," she said. "He would not shoot this girl on purpose. That's my opinion."

Gilchrest and Fugitt did one more thing; they confiscated Laura Hall's green Cadillac.

At one that afternoon, All Saints Episcopal Church in Corpus Christi overflowed with hundreds of mourners, there to pay their last respects to Jennifer Cave and grieve with her friends and family. The church full, many stood outside, where reporters from both Austin and Corpus congregated as well. Television cameras rolled and still photographers snapped photos.

"Hallelujah, praise the Lord," Father David Stringer called out, beginning the ceremony. "Police caught the man they sought, the person they believe killed Jennifer."

A cheer rang through the church's high, A-framed ceiling, where a cross hung suspended over the altar.

The ceremony was at the same time joyous and sad, a bittersweet parting.

Matthew 5:9 filled the church: "Blessed are the peacemakers, for they are called the children of God." Jennifer, Father David said, had been a peacemaker, a girl who wanted the happiness of others more than her own. It was so ironic that she'd died of violence.

The crowd recited the Twenty-third Psalm, "The Lord is my shepherd, I shall not want . . . ," Jennifer's favorite, and

Father David told the warm and sometimes funny stories he had compiled from Sharon, Jim, Clayton, and the girls during the Sunday visit to the house. He talked about Jennifer the bookworm, the little girl who loved to dance, the cheerleader in her green and gold uniform with an ear-to-ear smile on her face.

In the front pew, Jim wrapped his arm around Sharon, and Scott and Vanessa held tight hands. Lauren, Hailey, Clayton, Whitney, Charlie, Myrtle, the entire family was there, along with their extended family and friends.

"We all just latched on to one another," says Scott.

Throughout the ceremony, music filled the church. Perhaps more than anything with the exception of her family and friends, Jennifer loved music. Sharon knew "somewhere Jennifer was probably rolling her eyes," but she included Andrea Bocelli and Sarah Brightman's melancholic "Time to Say Goodbye." Most of the songs, however, were favorites of Jennifer's. When Josh Groban's "You Lift Me Up" filled the church, Jim stood and motioned for others to follow. Soon everyone was on their feet, but Jim had to help Sharon and support her. Memories of the little girl with red hair who'd grown up scanning the flat Texas plain and dreaming of Oz filled the church, along with Kenny G's "Somewhere Over the Rainbow."

"Don't ever let life pass you by!" an Incubus song called "Warning" urged, as Jim helped Sharon walk from the church. A motorcycle escort and a line of cars waited to spirit them away to George West, the cemetery where Jennifer would be laid to rest next to her grandfather. The graveside funeral would be only the immediate family, and they'd taken pains to escape the clutch of media.

There, in the near one-hundred-degree heat, they stood beside Jennifer's open grave, the casket perched over it.

"Did they find Jennifer's hands?" Sharon asked Jim. "Is all of her in the casket?"

In the back of her mind, she remembered a photo she'd seen on the news in Austin of a police officer searching the

Orange Tree Dumpster. Was it impossible to think that there were parts of Jennifer that hadn't been found?

"Yes," he whispered. "All of Jennifer is in the casket. I promise."

Still, it was in the back of Sharon's mind. Colton Pitonyak had cut her daughter up. She wanted her whole again.

Said Aziz was in the APD parking lot getting ready to give a statement when Laura Hall called again, at 3:35 that afternoon. By then, she'd talked to the two detectives, and her demeanor was far less jubilant than in the morning. She sounded distraught and confused, retracting much of what she'd told him in the morning. Aziz had the impression that the seriousness was finally sinking in and that Laura wanted to limit the damage.

"I had no idea what was going on," she told him. "I thought we were just going to Mexico for fun."

The statement she gave to Gilchrest and Fugitt that day said, "basically the deal was, 'Let's go to Mexico.' It may have been my idea. I can't recall. I wanted to go to Rio de Janeiro. I was excited that he wanted to go on a trip with me . . . I was in love with him. I liked the idea of a road trip."

Around that time in Mexico, Pedro Fernandez walked across the Eagle Pass Bridge to talk to the border patrol agents who manned the crossing. "I work at the Casablanca," he told them. "I know something about those two kids from Texas."

At four o'clock, Sharon and Jim returned home. Sharon walked over and picked up a photo of Jennifer, a happy, smiling photo taken before she'd left Corpus Christi. "Jim, look," Sharon ordered.

As much as he wanted to support her, Jim couldn't look at it. In his mind, he couldn't erase the memory of what he'd seen in Colton's apartment, the horror of Jennifer's death. Needing to feel normal if even just for a little while, he left and drove to a restaurant where many of their friends congregated. He had a drink, talked, and tried to relax.

Meanwhile, Jennifer's two sisters mourned her in very different ways.

For her part, Lauren couldn't get over being angry with Jennifer. She kept thinking of all the things she'd planned to do with her, to stand up in each other's weddings, share raising their children, living their lives, celebrating their successes, and comforting each other through their failures. Jennifer had been stupid, and she'd used bad judgment. She trusted someone she shouldn't have, and she'd let the drugs take over her life. "I kept thinking that I'd never see her again, and I was mad about that, but I also felt guilty for being angry," she says. "I thought we'd be old ladies together, telling stories about old times."

Vanessa's anger was aimed more at herself, the guilt of not protecting her little sister. She found a poem that reminded her of Jennifer, an e. e. cummings poem, "i carry your heart with me." It expressed her innermost feelings, her determination to have Jennifer with her, if not physically, then spiritually. No matter where Vanessa went or what she did, Jennifer would be with her. "When I marry and have children, they'll be Jennifer's, too," she says. "For the rest of my life, I will share everything with her."

Already, there was something Vanessa knew she needed to do for Jennifer.

When Scott left for Austin, Vanessa followed him. Madyson needed to be told that Jennifer was dead, and Scott confided that he couldn't imagine being the one who told her. He simply didn't know what to say. Wanting to protect the little girl Jennifer loved, Vanessa offered to help. So they sat together in Scott's apartment, where Jennifer had been so happy, and talked, Vanessa using the story her mother had told Jennifer when she was a little girl.

"Madyson, you know how Jennifer has all of those freckles?" Vanessa asked.

The little girl nodded.

"She hated those when she was little because they made her different. But Jennifer didn't know that the freckles made her special. They're angel kisses," she said. "The angels loved Jennifer."

"Uh huh," Madyson said, with a nod.

"Well, honey, all the angels just missed Jennifer so much. They loved her so much, that they asked her to come back to heaven to be with them, and Jennifer said she would."

"When will she come back here?" the little girl asked, looking concerned.

"Once you go up to heaven, you can't come back," Vanessa said.

"What if I want to talk to her?" Madyson asked.

"Anytime you want to talk to Jennifer, close your eyes and think of her," Vanessa said. "Think really hard, and tell her whatever you want. She'll hear you."

"But I want to talk to her here," Madyson said. "I want her to be with me."

Tears filled the little girl's eyes, and she sobbed. "Don't cry, Madyson," Vanessa said, holding her. "Jennifer's not gone. She'll always be with you. Now you have your very own guardian angel."

Later that day, Vanessa was driving back to Dallas when Scott's friends gathered to finish moving him out of the apartment. He had the house rented, and he didn't want to stay any longer. The apartment reminded him too much of Jennifer.

The following Friday night, many in the circle of friends gathered for a memorial service of their own for Jennifer at Scott's new house. From there, they went to the Canary Roost, the bar where Karissa worked. Laura Ingles, Eli, Katrina, many who knew Jennifer and loved her were there, and the night felt strangely subdued. The friends talked, listened to music, and laughed. Scott got up on stage and sang a song and dedicated it to Jennifer.

Before Jennifer entered his life, Scott and Katrina had

dated, and this night they fell easily into bed together. It was familiar and comforting. They held each other, and soon they were making love. At one point, Scott looked up, and Katrina's eyes were closed and she seemed far away.

"Look at me," he said, but her eyes remained shut. Scott felt something odd was happening, believing that Katrina couldn't open her eyes.

They made love with more passion than ever before, more than Scott had ever experienced. When it was over, Katrina rolled off him, trembled, and opened her eyes. They lay there for a minute, and then, for no apparent reason, Katrina jumped up and screamed.

"What's wrong?" Scott shouted.

"I know this is strange, but that wasn't me," Katrina said, trembling. "It felt like I wasn't in my body. It felt like Jen was here."

Just then, they heard a crash.

Scott rushed downstairs, found nothing wrong, no reason for the loud noise, and then stood in the kitchen, staring out a window into the backyard. Suddenly, he noticed a shadow in the distance. As he watched, the shadow drifted toward the house. "It came through the closed door into the kitchen, and then it circled past me," he says. "I got this chill, felt a cold breeze, like a whoosh. Every hair on my body stood up, and I had an overwhelming feeling that it was Jennifer. I started to smile, and I couldn't stop."

As quickly as it appeared, the shadow vanished, and the house was quiet.

Upstairs, Scott told Katrina what had happened, and she, too, believed that Jennifer had been with them. Then, as suddenly as the first time, it happened again, another crash. Scott ran downstairs, but this time found nothing. Scott stood in the living room and laughed.

"Scott, did that really just happen?" Katrina asked when he returned to the bedroom.

"Yeah," he said. "I think it did."

Twenty-two

Within days of the first *Statesman* articles on the case, blogs,. chat rooms, and message boards filled with Laura Hall and Colton Pitonyak postings and chats. The bloggers dissected the case, culling through everything they could find in the newspapers and on television for fodder. Hornfans.com, a Web site for UT sports fans, had multiple threads where all aspects of the news coming out in the papers were bantered about. At the same time, two groups sprang up on Facebook: "I'm scared of Colton Pitonyak," and "Laura Hall is insane."

Seeming to not be able to keep herself from responding, Hall shot e-mails back. "Hey Fuckface," she wrote to one. "I just found your cutesy groups. I'm sure you will post this message. You know nothing about me. You know nothing about Colton. And if you're not careful, you're looking at a lawsuit. For the record, I think your smartass approach to our legal problems is about the sickest thing I have ever seen anyone do. You disgust me. So tell all your buddies who think he's scary and crazy, that I messaged you.

"Yes, I admit, people like you bother me. Maybe that makes me weak, but I don't care. I just can't let this kind of stuff go. I had to say something. If nothing else, respect me for that . . ."

Someone posted a response: "She thinks posting on a website is sick? What is killing a girl and cutting up her body?"

Not long after, a friend called Hailey. "Log onto Facebook, and look at Laura Hall's page," the girl said. There,

Hailey read a posting Hall must have done as soon as she returned to Texas: "Colton is innocent. He's the most generous, kindest person that I have been blessed to spend time with. There is no way he is anything but innocent. If anyone has anything to say to the contrary, I dare you to say it to me."

Under the heading *Status*, she wrote: "In a relationship," next to *Location:* "Deported," and under *Summer Plans*: "Police ruined my summer."

By then, Laura had called Andrea Jiles again, furious with her parents. "My dad was the one who called the police," Hall fumed. Jiles tried to explain to Hall that her parents were worried about her, but Hall wasn't listening. "My parents are bitches," she said. "I'm leaving."

Within days of being expelled from Mexico, Laura Hall was on her way back to Austin. Since the police still had the Cadillac, she took the bus. Once she arrived, she called Ryan Martindill, the friend she was with the night of the killing, and asked him if he would pick her up at the bus station, and if she could stay with him for a while. Martindill agreed and picked Laura up, but he and his roommate, Salzman, had tickets to hear a band that night at Stubb's, a legendary Austin barbecue joint with live music. Afterward, they hooked back up with Laura, who showed off how she'd spent her time while waiting for them. On her ankle, she had a new tattoo, one that read: "Colton."

On Thursday, August 25, a week and two days after Jennifer's disappearance, detectives Gilchrest and Fugitt returned to Eagle Pass to pick up Colton Pitonyak at the Maverick County jail and transfer him back to Austin. First, however, they had someone to talk to: Pedro Fernandez. They met Fernandez at the border and listened as he detailed his encounters with the two young Americans. Fugitt's ears picked up when the desk clerk mentioned he'd taken a photo of them the night at his house.

"Can you e-mail it to me?" Fugitt asked.

"Sure," Fernandez agreed.

When Gilchrest and Fugitt drove into Austin, they took Colton Pitonyak to the Travis County jail, where he was fingerprinted, photographed, and booked under a million-dollar bond. Sam Bassett arrived hours later, eager for his first interview with his infamous client. When Bassett asked what happened, Colton said, "I don't remember."

Blaming a fog of drugs and alcohol, Pitonyak maintained he recalled little about the entire two days, from going out with Jennifer the night before, through the shooting and dismembering the body. But he was sure of one thing. Jennifer was his friend, he said, and he wouldn't have shot her on purpose.

"What were you thinking?" Sam Bassett asked. "If you shot the girl by accident, why didn't you call the police?" If Colton had picked up the telephone and called 911, the defense attorney believed prosecutors would have had little evidence to suggest it wasn't accidental. At most, Pitonyak would be facing manslaughter charges, not murder.

"I don't know," Colton replied.

Bassett didn't soft-pedal the odds for his young client, and later when he and Minton talked with Bridget and Eddie, they laid out the problems with the case as well. The condition of Jennifer's body would infuriate a jury, and that Colton said he didn't remember what transpired that night would only make it doubly hard to defend him.

In 2003, two years earlier, an infamous case had gone to trial in Galveston, Texas, that of New York real estate heir Robert Durst. Represented by a dream team of Houston attorneys, including Dick DeGuerin, Chip Lewis, Brian Benken, and Mike Ramsey, Durst was accused of murdering Morris Black, his neighbor in a dilapidated apartment building. At the time, Durst was living as a woman in Galveston, hiding out after he left New York under a cloud of suspicion involving the disappearance of his wife, Kathie, and the California murder of a family friend, Susan Berman. After shooting Black, Durst cut up the body, put it into garbage bags, and then took it one step further, throwing the bags into Galveston Bay.

At the trial, Durst took the stand and testified that he shot Black in self-defense, and then, assuming no one would believe him, disposed of the body in a state of panic. By consistently separating the shooting from the dismemberment, Durst's lawyers won an acquittal for their mega-wealthy client.

That strategy, however, wouldn't work in Colton Pitonyak's case. Since he insisted he didn't remember the shooting, Bassett and Minton couldn't argue self-defense, because their client couldn't get up on the stand and describe what happened.

"This was going to be tough," Bassett said. "Really tough."

Still, there were things the two defense attorneys could try. Their first effort would be to try to exclude the evidence from the apartment by filing a motion challenging its admissibility. If they convinced Judge Flowers that Jim Sedwick entered Colton's apartment illegally and that his entrance constituted an illegal search, none of the evidence from the apartment, including Jennifer's body, would be admissible in court. If successful, the tactic could essentially wipe out the prosecutors' case.

Meanwhile, more trouble brewed for the defense attorneys that day at the McFall facility, where crime scene investigator Lee Hernandez processed Laura Hall's green Cadillac. The car was cluttered with papers and fast-food debris. In the back right seat lay a dark maroon sombrero. During the search, Hernandez found a receipt from a Valero station where Hall filled up the tank and had the car washed before the trip to Mexico, nineteen gallons purchased at 3:47 that afternoon, and a copy of the traffic ticket from the Valverde County Sheriff's Department.

In the backseat, Hernandez also found a backpack filled with men's clothing. The contents were those of a privileged young man, one who wore Ralph Lauren underwear and socks, shirts, and slacks; and the Bank of America credit card and the passport in the backpack were both in the name of Colton Pitonyak.

The day after Colton's return to Austin, ballistics came back on the gun found in his car and the bullets removed from Jennifer Cave's body. They matched. The SW .380 found in the Toyota Avalon's console was the weapon that shot both the bullet that killed Jennifer and the bullet found in her skull. The remaining bullets in the gun and those in Jennifer's body also matched a box found in Pitonyak's apartment, zipped inside a purple camera case. They were copper with exposed lead bases, full-metal jacket design.

When the cell phone photo arrived from Pedro Fernandez in Detective Fugitt's e-mail, he pulled it up. On the screen, he saw Colton Pitonyak and Laura Hall hamming it up in Mexico, looking like two college kids on vacation. Like Fernandez, however, Fugitt noted something particularly odd: Colton gagging the nose and mouth of the stuffed Mickey Mouse. Even then, in Mexico, after Jennifer's death, Pitonyak mimicked the tough guy.

Since they'd discovered her involvement in Pitonyak's attempted escape, there'd been talk at APD and in the Travis County District Attorney's office about what if anything to do with Laura Hall. Once the news broke about Hall's flight with Pitonyak into Mexico, Ryan Martindill told APD she was at his apartment the night Jennifer died, so it seemed doubtful that she was involved in the actual killing. Still, there were other possible charges besides murder.

That same day, the twenty-sixth, Detective Gilchrest called Laura Hall and told her she could pick up her car at the McFall unit. APD had finished with it. First, however, she needed to stop at his office. When Hall called Andrea Jiles to tell her, Jiles scoffed, "They're not giving you your car back. They're going to arrest you."

"No, they're not," Laura insisted.

When Hall walked in, however, instead of handing her

the keys, Gilchrest presented her with a warrant for her arrest. The charge: hindering apprehension, a third-degree felony. Her bail would be set at $175,000.

"Do you understand how serious this is?" Gilchrest asked. " . . . Do you have $175,000?"

If not, Gilchrest informed her, she was going to jail.

Looking back, Gilchrest would say that Hall looked surprised and rattled. She'd already refused to talk to them without a lawyer, but now she insisted she wanted to give a statement. Gilchrest left to ask the advice of others, then returned and said she could talk if she wanted to, but she'd have to sign a form waiving her Miranda rights.

At first, Hall seemed uncertain about what to do. Gilchrest reviewed the charge with her and talked about the options for her sentence, from probation to ten years in prison. "Do you understand the gravity of the charges against you?" Gilchrest asked. "Do you want to make things right?"

Hall said she did, and signed the Miranda document.

When Gilchrest asked about Colton's emotions when he talked of Jennifer's killing, Hall said that he repeated over and over that he'd killed his best friend.

"Was he excited, bragging, remorseful kind of . . . ?" Gilchrest asked.

"Remorseful, definitely," she said.

"Are you trying to protect him again?" Gilchrest said, with a slight laugh.

Hall laughed along. "Yeah," she said. "He was real upset about it, but I don't know if that's because he got caught . . . he cried over what this would do to his family. He was real messed up over that."

At the end of a more than nine-hour session with detectives, Laura Hall signed a statement that rivaled the graphic, horror-filled vampire novels she had loved in high school. Colton Pitonyak, Hall maintained, had forced her to help him. When she arrived at the apartment, she said, Pitonyak whispered, "There's a body in the bathtub."

He brought her to the bathroom, "pulled back the shower

curtain and showed me a body." Although he didn't say who the victim was, he claimed it was one of three people who had come into his apartment brandishing guns. Deranged, in Laura's account, Pitonyak was the epitome of a villain, even licking a bloody knife and cackling. In this new version, Laura portrayed herself as a victim, bullied into helping Pitonyak, who threatened to push Hall into the bathtub with the dead body. With the body in the next room, Hall said she and Pitonyak had sex on the couch. At one point, Pitonyak, Hall insisted, threatened her with a knife and a gun.

There were many inconsistencies that called the truthfulness of the statement into question. Hall admitted she left the apartment and went to the bank, put gas in the car, called a friend, and even took a nap in her apartment. If she'd cooperated out of fear, why hadn't she called police? And Hall's statement didn't match the physical evidence, as when she claimed a cackling Pitonyak stabbed Cave in the heel. No such wound was noted on the autopsy.

In Laura Hall's new version, it was entirely Colton Pitonyak's idea to flee to Mexico.

When Gilchrest asked why Pitonyak murdered Cave, Laura first said Cave owed him money, and then later that Colton killed Jennifer because she didn't want to "be around him" anymore.

In the signed statement, Hall talked of Pitonyak's emotions about the killing again: "[Colton] said it was hard, it was weird . . . It was like he cared; but then he didn't."

Hall's new statement didn't keep Gilchrest from acting on the warrant for her arrest. Bill Bishop would later say that he never offered Hall any kind of deal to testify against Colton. "I didn't trust her to get up on the witness stand and tell the truth," he says.

That day, Laura Hall was booked, her bail was set at $175,000, and she was assigned a cell in the main jail downtown. When her parents didn't come up with bail money, she was moved to unit E at the Del Valle satellite jail, a sprawling facility on the city's southern outreaches. Perhaps not surprisingly, Hall didn't mesh well with the other women on the unit. They made fun of her, and some, although she wasn't charged with murdering anyone, called her "that serial killer chick."

A few weeks later, Hall was escorted to unit C and taken to the second floor. For the coming weeks she'd share her small living quarters with a grandmotherly woman named Henriette Langenbach.

Twenty-three

At first, Henriette Langenbach didn't understand why the other inmates gestured as guards escorted the young woman up the stairs to her second-level cell, number 9 on the unit. Clearly enjoying the diversion the new inmate offered, the women sliced their hands across their throats, in a cutting motion, and laughed wildly behind the new inmate's back. Then Langenbach got a good look at her and recognized Hall's face from news reports.

In their cell, Laura unpacked her jailhouse supplies. Langenbach had the bottom bunk, and Hall claimed the top. As she settled in, Hall threw a black-and-white photo of a girl in a business suit and white blouse at Langenbach. "Do I look like her?" she demanded.

Nearing sixty, with black hair and sad brown eyes, Langenbach looked at the girl. It seemed an odd thing to do. "Yes, kind of," she said. Hall took the photo back. It was her high school graduation photo.

They were an odd pairing. Langenbach's crime was white-collar, a felony involving her role as chief financial officer of a defunct real estate venture. It wasn't the first time she'd been in trouble. Years earlier in New Zealand, the Indonesian-born Langenbach had been convicted of attempting to help a friend obtain false documents for a baby the friend wanted to adopt and bring into the United States.

Hours drag in prison, and Langenbach was never sure which of the two Laura Halls she'd share her cell with: the closemouthed girl who seemed leery of talking, or the ranting young woman who blew up and stormed about the cell, saying, it seemed, nearly anything that popped into her mind.

Most often, Laura railed against her father, calling him obscenities, blaming him for calling police. She was furious that Loren hadn't bailed her out and that he refused to hire a "real lawyer," leaving her to be represented by Tom Weber, a former assistant district attorney turned defense lawyer who'd been appointed by the court. Although Weber had a good reputation in Austin, his efforts on her behalf didn't sit well with Hall. One day Langenbach listened as Hall recounted a conversation with her lawyer, in which Weber called Hall the "weirdest" client he'd ever had.

"Why did he say that? What did you say to him?" Langenbach asked.

"I want a lawyer to help me and Colton concoct a story, so that we can get Colton off on a lesser charge and me on a misdemeanor," Hall said. She talked about O. J. Simpson, whom she said was obviously guilty but had walked with the aid of a high-priced and high-profile band of attorneys.

"Lawyers don't do that, Laura," Langenbach said. "They're not even supposed to put you on the stand if they know you're lying."

Laura's attorney, Tom Weber, would later say that he did tell Hall she was the oddest client he'd ever had. Although she'd never even been arrested before, Hall reveled in her role in the sensational murder case and its accompanying publicity. When he looked in her eyes, he saw no feeling. Laura Hall cared for no one but herself and Colton, whom she talked about constantly, professing her love. When Jennifer Cave's name came up, Laura fumed about the dead girl, expressing no sympathy for either Jennifer or her family.

Early on, Weber talked to Hall about working a deal with the prosecutors by agreeing to testify against Colton, but she refused. "That's my homeboy," she said. "I love him, and I stand by him."

Weber, chief prosecutor in Judge Flowers's court until

1996, warned Hall not to talk with anyone about the case, especially in jail, but she didn't listen.

"That fucking bastard," Hall said, and Langenbach knew her cellmate meant her father, Loren. "He wants me to talk to the police, tell them what they want to know, but what the fucking bastard doesn't get is that I'm federally fucked if I do."

Although Langenbach spoke six languages and had lived all over the world, throughout their weeks bunking together, Hall treated the older woman as if she were an inferior human being, someone with limited intellect who couldn't understand those with superior intelligence. "I don't know why they're making such a big deal about Jennifer Cave. She wasn't anything," Hall said more than once. "Colton's brilliant. He had a full scholarship at UT, in the business school. Jennifer Cave was a fucking waitress ho."

At times, Hall talked about the night Jennifer died. As she portrayed it, Colton and Jennifer argued, Hall said, over money Jennifer owed Colton for drugs. "The next thing he knew, she was dead. He shot her."

Colton was in a frenzy when Hall arrived at his apartment that morning, crying, screaming, irrational, drunk, and high on drugs. At first, Pitonyak didn't tell Hall whom he'd shot, but instead took her to the bathroom to show her the body. "I didn't realize who it was until he lifted up her head and I recognized her," Hall said.

"We have to get rid of the body," Hall said she told Colton. From that point on, Langenbach had the impression Hall was in charge, making the decisions. When she used the toilet, Colton pulled the green vinyl shower curtain to hide the body.

"How could you use that bathroom with a body in there like that?" Langenbach asked.

"When you're very intelligent, you're able to compartmentalize things," Hall bragged.

The gun was in the living room, on the cocktail table, and Colton sat on the couch playing with his machete and the buck knife with the folding blade that locked into place. Hall claimed Colton put the machete to her throat, laughing.

"Stop fucking around," she told him. "We need to concentrate on getting rid of the evidence."

"Weren't you afraid of him?" Langenbach asked.

"Absolutely not," she said. "I love him, and he knows it."

Langenbach had the impression that Hall wrote the shopping list Colton took to Breed's that afternoon. She was furious that he'd gone to the small neighborhood store, instead of a large hardware store where he might have gone unnoticed. "Had I taken control of everything, that would not have happened," she said. "Getting caught on camera buying the stuff."

While she was running her own errands, filling the Cadillac with gas and getting it washed, Hall said she stopped for a hamburger. Then she met Colton at a Mr. Gatti's pizza restaurant. Hall recounted being furious that the waitress tried to charge her when she wasn't eating. While they were there, Sharon Cave called, saying she'd called the police, and Colton again "freaked out."

Back at the apartment, they grabbed Colton's things, and then ran to Mexico.

"Why would you cut up a human body?" Langenbach asked.

"Think of it," Hall said dreamily. "How many grandmothers can tell their grandchildren that they cut up a body?"

"But how could you eat knowing that you had a dead body, cutting it up?" Langenbach asked.

Again Hall talked about compartmentalizing. "Dead body in one compartment; my hunger in another, and so forth."

Over the weeks they shared the cell, Hall explained that their plan had been to cut off Jennifer's head, hands, and feet, the parts of her that were most easily identified, and then throw them in a lake. The rest of her corpse, they planned to dump in Mexico.

When it came to her six days with Colton in Mexico, Hall described the time as "the happiest of my life."

Sickened by what she heard, Langenbach used her "rack-up" or quiet time to make notes on Laura's statements. She wrote them into letters she sent to her attorney, asking him to keep them for her. At times, she stayed up after Hall went to sleep, writing.

In addition to emphasizing that Langenbach was her intellectual inferior, Hall crowed that she was smarter than Travis County prosecutors and APD. She laughed about the offer she'd made to APD to take a lie detector test, and boasted that she knew how to lie and pass it. She had ice water running through her veins, she bragged, and had no trouble masquerading her emotions. Still, she looked for other ways to ensure that she passed the test. She talked about taking a jail meditation class to learn how to rein in her emotions even further, and one day returned from the jail infirmary drugged up on what she told Langenbach were antipsychotics. The medicines, which she claimed she lied to get, would mask her reactions and help her sail through the lie detector.

For hours on end, Laura droned on about getting two tattoos, one with her and Colton's initials entwined, and the other the letter "F" for felon. Perhaps she was emulating Pitonyak with his "fell on" tattoo from his drug-charge jail stay. As Langenbach watched, Hall spent hours scribbling on sheets of paper, trying to design just the right tattoos.

At times, Hall frightened Langenbach. The girl seemed out of touch with reality, devoid of any normal human emotion. Then, the night before Hall's first court appearance, something even more bizarre happened.

In her upper bunk, Hall slept, doped up on the antipsychotic medicines. Sometime after eleven, she thrashed about, appearing to be in the throes of a nightmare, crying out, "Get away bitch. You're dead. You're dead."

Langenbach got out of her bunk and sat in a chair opposite the bunk beds watching Hall scream at no one. The younger woman writhed in the bed, shouting and cursing, then, suddenly, Hall dove off the top bunk, smashing her head against the edge of the wall and the floor.

The next day, Hall had two black eyes and a lump on

her forehead. Laughing it off, Hall told Langenbach that
she planned to sue the jail, claiming they had unsafe beds,
hoping to make enough money to "pay for a good attorney."

The day after Hall's nightmare, she was transferred to a
unit with an open lower bunk, near the guard's station, where
she could be monitored. From that point on, Langenbach
says, her former cellmate fared poorly in jail, refusing to do
her work, such as helping to clean her unit, offering other
inmates candy and chips to pay them for doing her wash,
and then refusing to give them what she'd promised. More
often than not, Langenbach heard Hall was in solitary.

Despite having her out of her cell and her life, Langenbach thought often of Hall, her ice-cold emotions, her un-
feeling references to Jennifer as no more important than
garbage to be disposed of. And Langenbach would always
remember the night Hall plummeted out of the top bunk
as the night Jennifer Cave's spirit haunted Laura Hall's
dreams.

Twenty-four

West Campus was still percolating with the aftermath of the killing. News reports offered tips on how women could stay safe, including advice from a private investigator on how to do background checks on potential dates. Meanwhile, Gilchrest and Walker searched Pitonyak's apartment one last time before releasing it to his parents and the landlord. In particular, they hoped to find the missing bullet. While three casings had been found, they'd discovered only two bullets: both removed from Jennifer's body. Where was the missing bullet?

Gilchrest paid particular attention to the torn-up couch, where a bullet could wedge inside cushions and be hard to find, but never discovered what they'd come looking for. Instead, the detectives recovered an orange, barrel-shaped purse from under the bed, one with Jennifer's cell phone and wallet inside.

One other thing they logged into evidence that day, found near the coffee table, was a Burger King bag with a receipt attached, for a $6.16 meal purchased the day Jennifer disappeared. Just after Colton Pitonyak left Breed & Co. Hardware, he bought a value meal with a medium Coke and fries, requesting no onions.

When Bishop saw it, he shook his head. Minutes earlier, Pitonyak was shopping for tools to cut up Jennifer Cave's body, which lay decomposing in his bathtub, but he obviously hadn't let it spoil his appetite.

* * *

"In Arkansas, Those Who Knew Suspect Are Baffled by Arrest" read the *Statesman* headline on August 28. Neighbors and friends of the Pitonyaks talked to the reporter about the Colton Pitonyak they knew, the brilliant student and seemingly happy young man. "We've known that child forever," said one woman. "It could be any one of our kids. That's what's most frightening."

For their part, Bridget and Eddie Pitonyak weren't talking. As soon as the publicity hit, they'd built a wall of sorts, keeping to themselves. "We'd see them and it was the eight-hundred-pound gorilla in the room," says one of Bridget's friends. "No one mentioned Colton sitting in a jail in Austin or what he was accused of doing to that poor girl."

In South Texas, Jennifer's family tried to come to terms with her death. Clayton, at times, wondered if it were all a bad dream. He sometimes woke up mornings and, for a little while, forgot. Then it came flooding back. Jennifer was dead.

Hailey felt guilty, wondering if she might have been able to protect Jennifer, if she'd stayed closer to her. And Lauren scanned the Internet, looking at the articles on nights when Hailey was out of their apartment, when she was alone and could absorb it on her own terms. Afterward, she felt sick and awkward, as if everyone watched her. At times, Vanessa thought of something funny and wanted to tell Jennifer, only to remember she couldn't.

Sleep was difficult for Sharon, and when she did, there were the nightmares. In them, she saw Jim's frightened face as he emerged from the apartment. And she dreamed of Jennifer, how angry she must be that she was robbed of the opportunity to prove herself. More than anything, Sharon longed to touch her daughter's long red hair and whisper good-bye.

In early September, after the chaos had started to settle, Jim drank coffee on the patio, covered with potted plants from Jennifer's funeral. Since they'd moved into the house, he and Sharon had been attempting to lure hummingbirds to the yard, planting flowers to attract them and hanging a hummingbird feeder. All without luck.

On this morning, however, Jim looked up and saw one of the tiny, vibrating birds hovering next to the feeder. Fascinated, he watched, and the bird left the feeder and flew directly over to five brightly painted angel figurines he'd picked up a year earlier on a trip to Colorado. The angels were supposed to ward off evil spirits, and he and Sharon had hung them across the back of the house, at the time dedicating one to each of their girls. To Jim's surprise, the hummingbird went from angel to angel, as if kissing them.

This is crazy, Jim thought.

The next morning, however, it happened again. And then, in the afternoon, the hummingbird was back. This time Sharon was outside with Jim, and it appeared the bird was talking to each of the angels, facing them and flitting from one to the other.

"She's right here," Jim said.

"What're you talking about?" Sharon asked.

"That little bird is Jennifer," Jim said. "She's come to check on us."

Her heart breaking, aching for any connection to Jennifer, Sharon didn't believe the bird was her daughter, but she did want Jim to find what peace he could. He'd been so brave, so wonderful, and they had both been through so much.

For nearly a month, the hummingbird visited daily, watching Jim drink his coffee. Then it left and never returned.

Twenty-five

In October, two months after Jennifer's death, Sharon saw Colton Pitonyak for the first time, in a courtroom at a motion hearing. She would later remember staring at the man accused of murdering her daughter. One question nagged her: Why? She left feeling physically ill and couldn't eat for days.

Andrea Jiles visited Laura Hall in jail that fall. Her friend had bruises around her eyes and a lump on her forehead.

"What happened?" Jiles asked.

"I fell out of bed," Laura replied, without elaborating.

The two friends talked, and Laura told Jiles that it had been her idea to flee to Mexico, and she was still standing by Colton.

"How can you do that? He killed a girl," Jiles said. "That girl is dead."

"Well, this is all bullshit," Laura said. She'd already told Jiles the plan she and Colton had agreed on before his arrest: that they'd blame each other for the killing, and the jurors, unable to discount reasonable doubt, would have no choice other than to let them both go. "I have to do everything I can to help Colton," she said.

"My friend was no longer my friend," says Jiles. "I didn't go to the jail to talk to her again."

That November, Sharon and Jim flew to Norman to attend a football game with Lauren and Hailey, and Sharon noticed a young cheerleader on the field, a pretty girl with long red hair and freckles. Sharon wanted to talk to the girl, to touch her, and Jim had to explain to her that she couldn't, that she'd scare the girl.

The holidays came, and at Jim and Sharon's house, neither one could serve a turkey for Thanksgiving dinner. They kept recalling Colton's words to the hardware store owner, Breed, that he needed the hacksaw to cut one up. Neither could eat steak, either. The sight of blood turned their stomachs. Christmas was subdued, Sharon spending much of it in bed, and at one point, nine-year-old Hannah, Jennifer's young cousin, the one she'd played with so happily coloring the year before, nudged Vanessa.

"I really miss Jennifer a lot," Hannah said.

"It's okay. I do, too," Vanessa replied.

In Austin, another little girl talked of Jennifer often. At times she said Jennifer came to play with her. And each night, Madyson insisted she had a visitor. "My sister comes and tucks me in," she said.

As 2006 began, Jim had to have another talk with Sharon. For months, he'd been spoon-feeding her details on the case on a need-to-know basis, before they hit the newspapers and television stations. It was all he could do to protect her.

The press had been clamoring for Jennifer's autopsy, and now they had it. No longer under wraps, the report was being released, including the drug and alcohol screening. Not surprisingly, Jennifer's remains had tested positive for meth, pot, and alcohol. Yet the amounts were small. "Recreational levels," the medical examiner would classify them.

As Jim had told Sharon earlier, the cause of death was the gunshot wound to the torso that severed Jennifer's aorta. But along with severing her head and hands, there were cuts to her face, neck, and chest. They were postmortem, but troubling. "I wondered what they did in that apartment to my baby's body," Sharon says. "I didn't want to think the awful things I was thinking."

In January, two weeks after being released from jail when her parents paid her bond, Laura Hall moved in with

Sammi, her friend from the Pena law firm. Sammi's boyfriend, Chris, was unhappy with the arrangement, but went along with it because Sammi felt strongly that they needed to help her friend. Much of the day, Laura spent lying around the house, often high. Sometimes she talked about the flight to Mexico, describing it the way one might a honeymoon. One night, Sammi pulled Chris to the side.

"Laura said she helped Colton cut off that girl's head," Sammi said. Hall had said she and Colton were both high on drugs at the time. Later, Laura made a joke of the whole thing, laughing as she jeered, "Don't worry, I won't cut off your head."

Melancholy for Colton, Laura found a photo of him in a Spanish-language newspaper, cut it out, and carried it with her. "This is the only photo I have of my boyfriend," she said.

Despite her avowed devotion to Pitonyak, Hall briefly dated a friend of Chris's. "This girl's fucking crazy," the guy told Chris one day, saying that Laura had been making some odd statements. She'd said she'd seen the inside of a human being, and one day, while drunk and high, asked, "Do you know what it's like to take somebody's life?"

"Have you gone to visit Colton in jail?" Hall demanded when Nora Sullivan answered her cell phone.

"Yeah," she said.

When Hall asked how Pitonyak was, Sullivan answered, "Fine."

"Don't tell me he's fine," Hall chastised. "I just got out. Jail is a hellhole."

Alarmed by Hall's accusatory tone, Sullivan explained that she meant Colton was well *considering the circumstances*. In fact, the last time they visited at the jail, they spent most of the time talking about the UT football team, which had just won the national championship. Even watching from jail, Colton was excited about the win. Looking at him in his jailhouse uniform, Sullivan asked if she could bring him clothes, maybe a Ralph Lauren sleeveless "wife beater," to wear underneath. Colton explained he wasn't allowed clothes from the outside.

That day on the telephone, Hall said that the regulations of her bail didn't allow her to visit Colton, but that she'd like to go along the next time Sullivan went, to wait in the lobby, hoping he could see her through a window as she arrived and left. Although it seemed odd, Sullivan agreed, and not long after, Hall went with her to the jail. While Sullivan talked with Colton, Hall waited in the lobby.

As always, Colton seemed in good spirits. He told Sullivan that he was studying Spanish, and teaching some of the Hispanic inmates English. His mother had been sending him books. He seemed to be settling in well, and, at one point, he told Sullivan a story about his roommate, how the prison guards had asked the inmate if he'd share a cell with Pitonyak. With such a grisly murder charge against him, the guards weren't sure how comfortable the other inmates would be around him. "A couple days later, the guy admitted he was concerned," Pitonyak said, laughing. "He said, 'Dude, you're cool, and I thought you'd be some kind of a freak.'"

Sullivan thought that her friend Colton, with his brilliant intellect and his private school education, must have been an unusual inmate in many ways.

After Sullivan brought Hall to the jail, Laura peppered Nora with questions about Colton. Later, after another such visit, Sullivan became so worried Hall was depressed that she took her to the student health center.

In February, Colton appeared at a hearing. He looked pale after spending nearly six months in jail, and his mop of dark hair was gone. He'd shaved it off.

By then, Bill Bishop had police collecting everything they could on Pitonyak, from his school records to his rehab records. Officers combed through cell phone records and downloaded the information off Colton's cell phone, retrieved from his backpack in Hall's green Cadillac. On it, they found photos of the wares he sold, mounds of ecstasy pills.

Meanwhile, Roy Minton spent time with Colton at the jail. His assessment hadn't changed. This was going to be a tough case. That his client was younger than some of his grandchildren upset Minton. At Minton's age, it was tough to see someone in his early twenties with his life altered forever. To prepare for the trial, Minton had hired Edward Hueske, a gun expert. If and when the case went to trial, the .380 Smith and Wesson would be a big piece of evidence for the defense. They needed someone who could explain the weapon's flaws, to convince jurors it could easily be unintentionally fired.

The main focus, however, wasn't trial preparation, at least not yet. Both sides were busy researching and writing briefs and motions on the central issue to the entire case: the legality of Jim Sedwick's entrance into Pitonyak's apartment the night he discovered Jennifer's body. If Judge Flowers sided with the defense, without the evidence from the apartment, there might never be a trial.

In March, Sharon spent Jennifer's birthday lying on the floor crying. She wondered what Jennifer looked like inside the coffin and if they'd sewed her hands and head back on before they buried her. At times, Sharon fought back a sense of dread and sheer terror, wondering what would happen if Colton Pitonyak was released from jail, worried that he'd come after her or her surviving children. "I screwed his plan up by calling and saying I'd call the police. He didn't have time to finish with Jennifer," she says. "Colton blames me. He hates me. I know."

At times, Sharon wondered if she carried some of Jennifer's grief with her. She didn't believe her daughter had found happiness in heaven. "She died so sad," Sharon says. "She wasn't ready to go."

Searching for answers, Sharon called a psychic. "I wanted

to know if Jennifer cried out for me," she says. "All he told me was that there was a lot of blood and violence."

All along, Jim and Sharon assumed that Pitonyak would face charges not only for murder but for what he'd done to Jennifer's body. "I'm surprised there aren't any additional charges on here," Jim said, one day when they met with the prosecutor in the DA's offices in Austin. Bishop frowned. Then he explained: In Texas mutilation of a corpse was only a misdemeanor. When the legislature passed the law in the 1800s, they envisioned grave robbers, not would-be gangsters on drugs attempting to dispose of evidence.

On the way home to Corpus Christi in the car, Sharon and Jim talked about the unfairness of the law. The dismemberment of Jennifer's body had hurt them all deeply. Jim had the horrible memory of discovering her body, and Sharon had to live knowing what they'd done to her child, that they'd butchered her. She wasn't allowed to see Jennifer one last time, even in her casket. She never again touched her hair or kissed her good-bye. Sharon still had nightmares that all of Jennifer hadn't been found. "It wasn't right," Sharon says. "It just wasn't right."

Meanwhile, in Dallas, Vanessa had nightmares of the night they found Jennifer's body. She heard her mother screaming over and over, "He killed her. I know he killed her."

"Don't come in. Don't come in," Jim cried out in her dreams.

After her stay at Chris and Sammi's place, Laura, going by her middle name, Ashley, subleased a unit at the Gazebo Condos, on Twenty-eighth and Rio Grande, just a few blocks from the Orange Tree. Hall was back in school at UT, taking classes, getting ready to graduate, and working at a restaurant, Baby Acapulco, a loud Mexican place. She'd dyed her medium brown hair red, jarring to those who remembered Jennifer's long red tresses.

One of her new neighbors, Will Gallahue, a twenty-one-year-old UT journalism major, noticed her early on. The

Gazebo's residents were nearly all students, a close-knit bunch who often got together on weekend evenings, when they sat in the open courtyard in lawn chairs, drinking beer and relaxing. At first, "Ashley" kept to herself, not really socializing. She posted a note on her door, asking anyone wanting to reach her to call before knocking.

Before long, Gallahue, an intense young man who composed electronic computer music, began noticing other odd things about his new neighbor. Ashley nearly always appeared angry and, more often than not, high on drugs. At times when he knew she was alone, he heard her shrieking in her apartment, as if venting emotional pain. Once, early on, she stopped to talk to him, complained about her parents, and then out of the blue asked, "Do you know anybody who can get rid of evidence?"

Assuming she was joking, Gallahue responded, "No, but if anyone comes around, I'll give you a call."

As she met people around the complex, Ashley began seeing one of Will's friends, a guy who had his own drug problems. He had a girlfriend, but hung out with Hall on the side, doing drugs. One night, Will awoke at four in the morning to the sound of shattering glass. Out in the courtyard, Laura raged. Will's friend had gone out with his girlfriend that night, instead of spending the time with her. "I'm going to kill him," Ashley screamed.

To Gallahue, Ashley's anger didn't seem normal. "There was a constant barrage of threats," he says. "She didn't calm down."

Before long, word spread through the complex that Ashley was Laura Ashley Hall, and the other residents began calling her "the Mexico chick." At times, one or another ventured a question about the case against Colton. Laura answered that Colton would be freed on technicalities, that he'd never be found guilty.

At the end of March, a new thread popped up on the Hornfans.com Web site: "Pitonyak (West Campus Murder Suspect) Trial Set." Four days earlier, Judge Flowers had scheduled the Pitonyak trial for October 9, 2006, seven months in the future. But first, there would be an important pretrial hearing on June 9, one to hear arguments and testimony on the defense's motion to exclude the evidence from the apartment.

A poster on the Web site who called himself PatronSaint noted: "I rarely root for the death penalty. Right now I am rooting for death."

Eastside wrote: "Jennifer Cave. Jennifer Cave. Jennifer Cave. I hate that I knew the story just by reading his name and I couldn't remember hers."

Another poster wrote: "No evidence = No Trial. To get a murder conviction the case needs the apartment evidence."

"I know the big problem here is my going in the apartment," Jim told Bill Bishop that spring, as the date for the pretrial hearing approached.

"We don't think it's going to be a problem," Bishop responded. "Let's not worry yet."

"Okay, but what if we lose?" he asked.

"That could be a problem," Bishop said.

Twenty-six

On Friday, June 9, 2006, Austin temperatures crept up, flirting with one hundred degrees, unusual for so early in the summer. "A scorcher," Officer Barbaria said in the elevator on his way to the courtroom. "Makes me glad I work nights."

Meanwhile, inside the 147th District Court, the two sides took their places: Jim, Sharon, Vanessa, and Scott Engle on the right, behind the prosecutors, and Eddie and Bridget Pitonyak on the left, behind their son's lawyers. Both families appeared heart-flutteringly anxious. Everyone gathered in the packed courtroom understood how important this hearing would be. If Minton and Bassett succeeded, some questioned whether the prosecution would still have a case.

Winning, however, wasn't an easy matter; the defense attorneys had to show one of two things: either that Jim Sedwick didn't have a reasonable reason to be concerned for Jennifer's safety and well-being when he broke into Colton's apartment, or that he'd done so at the suggestion of the police.

At 1:35 that afternoon, all in the crowded courtroom stood, and Judge Wilford Flowers entered and took his place behind the bench. Moments later, Jim and Sharon were ushered from the courtroom, to await the call to take the stand and testify. Then the side door swung open and two deputies walked through, with Pitonyak between them. Colton's wrists and ankles were chained, his hair little more than stubble, and he wore a loose-fitting prison uniform, with thick black-and-white horizontal stripes. Yet he still had a slight swagger, the bravado his friends would recognize. The guard took off his handcuffs, and Pitonyak glanced at his parents and then sat down next to Sam Bassett.

"We're here to hear testimony on defense motions," Judge Flowers read. "Mr. Bishop, are you ready?"

"Yes, your honor."

"Mr. Bassett?"

"Yes, your honor."

"Let's proceed."

As the prosecutor's first witness, Sharon Cave took the stand.

"Are you the mother of the victim, Jennifer Cave?" Bishop asked.

"Yes, I am," Sharon answered, her voice strong despite appearing uncertain, even frightened. Jim, who often testified as an expert witness at trials, had coached her about what to do on the stand, principally to listen carefully to the questions and to concentrate on the person asking them.

From his seat at the defense table, Colton stared down at the sheet of yellow legal paper before him. Occasionally, he'd glance up long enough to catch a glimpse of Sharon, quickly returning his eyes to the paper, scribbling notes to Bassett and Minton.

"When is the last time you talked with Jennifer?" Bishop asked.

"Tuesday, August 16th," Sharon answered, wiping away a tear. "About 5:45 that evening."

With Bill Bishop in the lead, asking the questions, Sharon told the story of that horrible two-day period a year earlier: from Jennifer's joyous news about the new job, to Jim's dreadful discovery inside condo number 88.

"Did you ever go in that apartment?" Bishop asked.

"No, sir," Sharon answered in a sad, hoarse voice. Neither did Vanessa.

"Did anyone you talked with on the seventeenth or eighteenth give you permission to enter that apartment?" Bishop asked.

"No," Sharon answered, her voice again firm.

Why had they gone in? he asked.

Because Colton Pitonyak was the only link they had to Jennifer, she explained. "He was the last person to be with her. Her car was there."

When Roy Minton took over, he smiled, his manner courteous and a bit folksy, with a soft Texas accent. His summer-weight suit hung loose on his wiry frame when he placed his hands on his hips, and his graying hair was carefully combed back. His glasses were thick, but behind them his eyes had a slight twinkle. Minton asked what Michael Rodriguez had told her about his conversation with Jennifer after midnight on the night she disappeared.

"That Jennifer was with a friend. That the friend was very upset and that she was going to take him home," Sharon answered, looking over at Pitonyak, who continued to write on his sheet of paper.

"Rodriguez told you that she was with a friend?"

"That she was with her friend Colton," Sharon answered.

"Did the officer tell you that he didn't have probable cause and he couldn't enter the apartment?" Minton asked, referring to the first APD officer to respond to the scene, the one who refused to help Sharon and Jim open the door.

"He said, 'I can't help you. I'm sorry. I'm leaving,'" she answered, looking directly at Minton.

"Did he tell you what you could do?" Minton asked. This was an important question; to get the judge to rule in his favor, Minton needed evidence that the officer suggested Sharon and Jim act on their own.

"The officer made it very clear that he had to leave, and he couldn't help us," Sharon said.

Sharon was excused from the witness stand. She walked from the courtroom, and Jim entered. Bishop didn't ask him to repeat all the court had already heard from Sharon. Instead, he centered on a few issues. He got into the record Eddie Pitonyak's comment on the telephone, when Sharon called asking for his help to find Jennifer. Pitonyak "said that Bridget thought Jennifer, not Colton, was the problem," Jim said.

For a moment, the courtroom was silent, and Eddie Pitonyak's words hung in the air. It sounded as if even at that late date, after all they'd been through with their son, they were still in denial about what he'd become.

"What was your purpose when you entered the apartment?" Bishop asked Jim.

"I was looking for Jennifer," he explained, sadly.

"Were you worried that something might have happened to her?"

"Absolutely."

"Did you think you might have to get to Jennifer to help her?"

"Absolutely."

"Did Colton Pitonyak's father give you permission to enter that apartment?

"No, sir," Jim said.

When Sam Bassett took over, he asked Jim where the car was.

"Less than half a block" from the apartment, Jim said. If it had been farther, perhaps Bassett could have claimed Jim and Sharon didn't have reason to suspect Jennifer was inside the condo. Jim admitted he saw no indications outside the apartment of foul play, and that he'd initially moved Jennifer's car, then returned it. "I thought I made a bad decision," he said.

"Did you tell the police officer you were going to call a locksmith?" Bassett asked.

"Yes," Jim said.

The odor in the apartment came up when Bishop put Mark Gilchrest on the witness stand. The detective first entered the apartment at 10 A.M., the morning after the body was discovered, after he'd brought a copy of the search warrant to the site. Based on his experience, he said, if Jim hadn't entered, within a day or two, by August 21, police would have been on the scene anyway, called by neighbors who smelled the heavy, sickening stench of decomposing human flesh.

"When was Colton Pitonyak arrested?"

"Colton was deported on the 23rd of August," Gilchrest said. The implication was clear: Whether or not Jim had gone inside, police would have been looking for Pitonyak by the twenty-first, and he would still have been arrested.

"The body would have been detected before the twenty-third?" Bishop asked.

"Yes, sir," Gilchrest said.

With the case's lead detective on the stand, Minton went through the search warrant paragraph by paragraph, asking where the information had come from. Bishop objected, but Minton argued that he was entitled to continue his line of questioning, if not today, then at a future hearing, and Judge Flowers ruled that he could continue. When it came to writing the search warrant, Minton made it sound as if everyone at APD had his hand in it, relaying information to the detective who typed it up, and Minton pointed out that the search warrant described an unnamed victim.

"You knew the deceased was Jennifer Cave, didn't you?" Minton asked.

"No, I did not," Gilchrest responded.

Minton wanted to know if Gilchrest had gone inside the night the body was found.

"No," he said. The information in the search warrant had come from the first officer on the scene.

An afternoon break in the hearing was called, and the courtroom cleared. Colton was removed, taken back to a holding cell. With the courtroom nearly empty, Roy Minton took the opportunity to explain to the Pitonyaks that some of the issues he'd brought up, including how many people had worked on the search warrant, weren't really significant. Judges, he said, had boxes in their heads that they checked off, but they would do so only if they heard an indication that a law was broken.

"We have one issue, and that's if a police officer told

them they could go inside," he said. "Sometimes you'll get a young, inexperienced officer, and he'll say, 'I can't go in there but you can.'"

No one had testified that had happened in this case. Sharon and Jim both insisted the officer had said only that he couldn't help them, and that he had to leave. "You understand what I'm saying," Minton asked, looking directly at Eddie.

"Yes," he said, appearing stunned. "I do."

Minton was preparing his clients for failure.

Not ready to give up, Bassett told his more senior colleague that he wanted to call Officer Barbaria to the stand. Minton shrugged. "Have at it," he said.

The officer who'd first entered Pitonyak's apartment was then called, and he described the evening the body was found. When he arrived on the scene, he walked toward Jim, but had not been able to understand what the excited man was telling him, if someone were hurt or having a drug overdose. Barbaria entered the apartment, he said, believing he'd find a woman overdosing in the bathroom, not a headless body.

"What was the first thing you noticed in the apartment?" Bishop asked on cross.

"The kitchen was empty, but there was a poster of Al Pacino as *Scarface* on the wall," he said. "I thought it was odd."

As the Pitonyaks and their attorneys left the courtroom, it appeared they hadn't found an argument to hang their motion on. Neither Jim, Sharon, nor the police who testified described anything likely to convince Judge Flowers to set aside the warrant and suppress the evidence. Still, there were no guarantees. Who could say what Judge Flowers might do? Both families had eight nervous weeks to await his decision.

At the Gazebo condominiums, Ashley, a.k.a. Laura Hall, became increasingly reclusive. During the hearing, when the case was again in the newspaper and on television, she hung blankets over her windows to prevent unwanted eyes from peering in. Reporters knocked on her door, then turned to leave when no one answered. Judge Flowers's decision could impact her future as well. It was likely that if the charges against Colton were dropped, those against her would be abandoned as well.

As the months passed, Laura looked thin and sickly. Her neighbor Will Gallahue knew she took drugs, and he sometimes thought of the photo she'd once shown him, her graduation photo from high school. The pretty girl in the photo with her whole life ahead of her was now an emaciated woman with black bags under her eyes. "She looked like she was decaying," he says.

At times, she left her front door open, and he looked in and saw her sitting alone on the couch, watching television.

By then, Laura had changed her screen name on Facebook to Ashley Holiday. On June 18, nine days after the hearing, Ashley posted on Colton's "wall," the message thread on his page. "I can't stop crying over you, babe," she wrote. "I should have taken you to Paris."

When Lauren visited friends in Austin, she got the "heebie-jeebies." Whenever she went, Sharon called constantly, unable to shake her fear that she'd lose another daughter in the shadow of the UT tower. At times, Lauren dreamed of Jennifer. In her dreams, she heard Jennifer's voice, and they were holding hands, as they did as children.

In Corpus one day, Sharon was unpacking groceries when Jim walked in. She'd bought a box of white kitchen garbage bags, with red drawstrings.

"You can't use those," Jim said, suddenly upset.

"What's wrong?" she asked. "They're just trash bags."

"Okay, but those are the trash bags Colton used."

Sharon threw them away.

Concerned, Harold Shockley, their banker friend, had been watching Jim and Sharon, since Jennifer's death, wondering how parents survived such a devastating loss. Sharon had become his hero. "She was so strong," he says. "There were times I broke down and she didn't. Instead she worried about everyone else, especially Jim."

Time passed quickly as the defense attorneys and prosecutors worked on discovery, handing over seized evidence to the defense to be tested by their experts. Then, on the afternoon of August 4, nearly one year after Jennifer's death, they were in the courtroom again. This time the Pitonyaks took the back aisle on the defense side, the last before the courtroom doors. Next to Sharon and Jim sat Leah Smith, a victims' advocate from the district attorney's office.

Vanessa had to work, and Lauren was in Spain, a study trip that had been in the planning for months. Still, she hadn't wanted to go. Sharon had to convince her youngest daughter to leave, telling her Jennifer wouldn't have wanted her to change her plans. The first weeks overseas, Lauren called home crying, afraid that while she was gone someone would kill her mother. "I got to the point where either I was flying her home or I was going there," Sharon says. "Jim was the one who calmed her down and convinced her to stay."

As at the previous hearing, Judge Flowers was punctual, walking into the courtroom precisely at 1:30. He looked about, from Colton Pitonyak in his prison uniform to the reporters scattered throughout the room.

After listening to a few more brief arguments, Judge Flowers cleared his voice. He'd considered the motion to suppress, he said, and didn't agree with the arguments put forward by the defense. "Actions on the part of Jim Sedwick were not the result of any assistance or direction by the state," he said. He also decreed that Jim had a legitimate reason to break into the apartment: concern that Jennifer could be in danger. "The motion to suppress is denied," he ruled.

In the front row, Jim dropped his head down, in relief, and Sharon's eyes filled with grateful tears. The prosecution had its evidence. The trial, set for October 9, would proceed.

Twenty-seven

A year after Jennifer Cave's death, at the start of the fall 2006 semester, the University of Texas installed emergency call boxes throughout the West Campus area. Students were still on edge, and many didn't feel as safe as they once had on campus. One site seemed particularly scathed; although good rental units were scarce, condo 88 at the Orange Tree remained empty and up for rent. Even the sought-after location and convenient parking didn't make up for being the scene of the most gruesome killing in UT's long history.

In Little Rock, those who knew the Pitonyaks marveled at the tight lid they kept over the case, appearing to confide in few. When Tommy Coy, Colton's math teacher from Catholic High School, saw Bridget at a Weight Watchers meeting, he asked about Colton. She explained that all hadn't gone well for her younger son, and for the first time Coy heard that at UT Colton had become deeply involved in drugs. Later, he'd say he was stunned, finding it hard to picture his star student as an addict. "As a teacher, you think you know what lies ahead for students," he says. "But no one can really look into the future."

Just after one on the morning of Thursday, August 25, a UT student named Matt logged onto Facebook.com and e-mailed Laura Hall/Ashley Holiday: "Did you help Colton hack that girl up?"

At 9:34 that morning, Ashley e-mailed back: "I'm not snitching on my boy and don't accuse him of doing anything illegal right now, or I'll hack you up."

That evening at 5:57, Matt e-mailed again: "Laura, I'm shocked. I can't believe you'd threaten me. : ("

"Ugh, Matt," she responded. "I'm half kidding. Why would you even randomly ask me such an awful question? I don't think you are a friend of Colt's."

"You seem like the kind of person who would help Colton do something like that," Matt responded.

The conversation went back and forth, and then Hall, posted: " . . . I made him leave the country with me. What does a hacksaw have to do with a death by gunshot? What passion? That girl was a whore . . . Besides you asked if I helped. That would involve me confessing to something I did. Never ask that. Why are you asking me stuff that just makes me angry? Why are you doing this? Do you have a death wish? BTW, where do you live and who put you up to this? . . . You read like a nice guy, Matt, but you're starting to piss me off."

In early September on Facebook, Nora Sullivan and Juan Montero posted birthday greetings to Colton, who turned twenty-four in the Del Valle jail. On September 12, Laura Hall logged on to update her "Ashley" profile, posting "God is dead," under *Religious Views*. As to her relationship status, "It's complicated." She defined her residence as "Sell-out," her activities as "Living a double life," her interests as "I'm just way, way to [sic] serious about everything to be writing personal shit like that up here." Under work information, she listed her company as "Waste of my life," her position as "Lazy," and her description as "Being a bad kid."

"Ashley is not giving a fuck," she noted.

Meanwhile, DNA evidence funneled into Bishop's office. The salt-and-pepper-haired prosecutor had a mountain of reports to go through. Looking at the forensic evidence, in Bishop's opinion, it wasn't hard to see what had happened. Colton had left blood and DNA on the tools used to carve up Jennifer's body, from the machete to the bathroom faucet he used to wash his hands.

One thing, however, was surprising: Colton's DNA was on

the gun, the murder weapon, but so was Laura Hall's. "That certainly added a twist," says Bishop. He reasoned that Hall couldn't have been the killer, since she was with Martindill at the most logical time of the murder, between 1:05 A.M. when Jennifer talked to Michael Rodriguez and just after 3 A.M. when Colton banged on Nora Sullivan's door. But Dr. Peacock hadn't been able to determine a firm time of death. Hall's DNA on the murder weapon could give Colton's defense attorneys leverage in front of a jury, the ability to argue that perhaps she pulled the trigger and fired the lethal shot.

There was also the word "motive" to consider. So far, Bishop didn't have one. Later, he'd say that no one told him that Colton thought of Jennifer as any more than a friend or that he'd once professed his love and then come at her with a knife. Bishop wondered if maybe Colton was angry at Jennifer because she wasn't buying drugs from him any longer. He was in money trouble, and if she'd been a good customer . . . ?

With two hundred cases on his schedule, Bishop couldn't yet devote his full attention to the case. Sometimes victims' families resent that. But when Sharon and Jim called, they never pushed too hard. Since their first meeting, Bishop had prepared them for the realities of a murder trial. "Time will drag. At points, you won't see anything going on. It's going to be a long process," he said. "You have to hang in there and trust me."

Meanwhile, Bassett and Minton worked on preparing their case. They, too, saw the forensic evidence, including Laura's DNA on the gun. That was enticing. What had she done with the gun? The forensic evidence had just become interesting.

In response, Minton and Bassett asked for a delay in the trial, to do their own DNA testing. "We wanted to see what else was out there," says Bassett. "We wanted a careful look."

At an October 4 hearing, Judge Flowers agreed, and Colton Pitonyak's trial was reset for January 22, 2007.

A few days later, Marty Heidgen, the Catholic High grad charged with driving drunk the wrong way on a New York highway, hitting a bridal limo head on, and killing two people, was found guilty and sentenced to eighteen years to life in prison. The impunity the rich kids in Little Rock felt they had didn't appear to be playing out well outside Arkansas.

In November, Laura Hall was back on Facebook.com, this time changing her favorite movie to one of Colton's: *Scarface*. She typed under *Activities*: "Avoiding APD, posting bond." Her favorite books? "The entire criminal law section." Under *Interests*: "Escalades, Ferraris, alcohol, rap music." Under *About Me*, her profile read, "I am w/o ? the Mouth of the South."

A week later, she logged on again, and the *About Me* section changed to: "Don't fucking talk to me about Colton. If you have something stupid to say, you're not qualified to talk, and you'd never have made it through my door and never will. Fucking die. I hope it hurts."

"I hate it when skanks think they are allowed to have dinner with my lovers," she added the following day. She still had a photo of Colton with his bros, including Juan Montero, posted on the Web site. Underneath it, she'd written: "Whether or not they changed my life, for the better of course, love ya, boys."

About that time, Hall/Holiday posted on Colton's wall: "Guessed your music!"

That Thanksgiving in Corpus Christi, Sharon and Jim still couldn't serve turkey, and Sharon cried over the buttermilk pie, Jennifer's favorite. A few days later, Hall again updated her Facebook profile, changing her employer to "Brilliant," and her position to "Baller." She noted: "I get paid a shit load."

As the leaves turned gold and red in Little Rock, one of the Pitonyaks' old neighbors took out stationery and a pen and sat down to write them a note, something supportive, something to let them know that she thought of them as good people, that Colton had been a good kid, and that it must have been "all the drugs."

The woman sat there for a while, looked at the clean sheet of paper, and then put it back in the box and put the box back in the drawer. "I didn't have the foggiest idea what to say," she says. "What do you say to someone whose son cut a girl up?"

Meanwhile in Corpus Christi, Jim worried about Sharon. The trial was coming up after the first of the year, and although he hadn't seen them, he knew the crime scene photos would be horrific. "You've been remarkable the way you've handled this without going crazy," he said. "But seeing something is more acute than imagination. If you stay in the courtroom and see the pictures of Jennifer's body, they could put you over the edge."

Sharon nodded; she understood. "I'll think about it," she said. Part of her still felt she needed to see Jennifer, to witness all that had happened.

At the district attorney's office, Bill Bishop wasn't letting himself feel any too confident. Sure he had a lot of DNA evidence, but as he saw it, the Pitonyak trial could still be lost. "Everything we had was circumstantial," he says. "No one saw Colton Pitonyak point the gun at Jennifer Cave and pull the trigger."

Then, just before Christmas, a switch at the DA's office brought a new prosecutor into Bishop's court, Stephanie McFarland. With straight dark hair and a heavy fringe of bangs, a trim figure, and a pale complexion, she was a new mom who spent weekends caring for her son, reading, or working on the old house she and her husband had bought.

Although he'd never tried a case with her, Bishop heard that McFarland was good in the courtroom, able to evoke emotion. He tended to be forceful but analytical. He thought they would work well together. All McFarland knew about the Pitonyak case came from office scuttlebutt and the media. She knew it was gory and would take mountains of work, a conclusion confirmed when Bishop showed her the boxes of crated evidence covering his office wall and a timeline that filled up most of a yellow legal pad.

"It was awkward," recalls Bishop. "I said, 'Welcome to the 147th District Court, and we need to talk about Colton Pitonyak.'"

"I definitely wouldn't use the word 'excited,'" she says, about hearing she'd been assigned to the case.

The third person on the prosecution team would be Jim Bergman, a broad, tall, white-haired, retired APD patrolman, who worked as an investigator in the DA's office. A Vietnam veteran with a booming voice, he says, "What I was qualified to do when I got back from Nam was to be either a cop or a hit man. I decided to be a cop. I'm not smart enough for anything else."

Born and raised on a Blanco County, Texas, cattle ranch, he kept a dummy grenade in his office. "That's my complaint department," he growls. "Take a number."

Bergman had one gripe in particular. After nearly three decades in law enforcement, he believed the world was only becoming more violent. And when it came to the Pitonyak case? "It's one of the most gruesome ones I've seen. I'm always amazed at what we human beings do to each other," he says.

The defense, too, was getting ready for battle.

After the first of the year, Minton and Bassett sat down with Pitonyak again at the jail. "It looked very difficult," says Bassett. "How much more evidence can someone possibly leave behind at a crime site?"

"We were concerned that the jurors would think that Colton's memory loss was feigned," says Minton. "I wanted to make it clear that if it was feigned, it wasn't to our advantage." There was a time, early in Minton's more than four decades of practicing law, when some defense attorneys didn't ask defendants what had happened. Not knowing left them free to form their best arguments. But with modern forensic tools like DNA testing, techniques that can sometimes pinpoint what could or could not have happened, not knowing a client's version was a disadvantage.

That fall, Jim Sedwick didn't go on his annual bird-hunting trips: "I didn't have the heart to kill anything anymore," he says. "I couldn't even pick up a firearm." Meanwhile, in Little Rock, Tommy Coy talked to Eddie Pitonyak. When Eddie said he was looking forward to the trial, Coy wondered if the case wasn't as open-and-shut as it seemed in the newspapers. Perhaps Colton was innocent. "Eddie was upbeat," says Coy. "He expected an acquittal. After the trial, he said he was planning to bring his son home."

Right after the first of the year, Bishop and McFarland took over the war room in the DA's office, a nondescript, windowless beige conference room reserved for trial preparation, moving in the large stack of Pitonyak evidence boxes and lining them against the wall. Above the boxes, Bishop hung brown paper to compile the final version of the case's timeline, covering eight days, from August 16, 2005, the evening Jennifer disappeared, through Colton Pitonyak's arrest on the twenty-third. The timeline would be their guide to what they needed to present, an outline of the case they'd put before the jury.

That done, Bishop and McFarland culled through the pile of boxes, containing everything from witness statements and the striped halter top Jennifer wore to go out with Colton the night of her death, to the hacksaw and machete, deciding what evidence to place before the jury. As they discussed the condition of Jennifer's body, McFarland examined the gruesome crime scene and autopsy photos, her mind filled with questions about what happened in that condo at the Orange Tree after the killing. Who'd dismembered the body?

Neither prosecutor had interviewed Laura Hall, whose attorney said that if called she would take the Fifth and not testify. But they had read her two statements to police: the first claiming she knew nothing about the killing, and the second describing Pitonyak as a bloody knife–licking fiend who threatened her life. Considering the evidence, McFarland thought the truth lay somewhere in between. "It looked to me like they had fun messing with the body, taking drugs, and cutting it up," she says, with a disgusted frown. "Some things were clearly done for amusement, like the bullet shot through the severed neck into Jennifer's skull. It was sick."

As the chief prosecutor in Judge Flowers's court, Bishop understood they would have to put on a lean case, one without superfluous evidence. "Judge Flowers doesn't put up with bogging trials down," says Bishop. "He's all business, and he expects us to be as well."

When it came to which of the hundreds of crime scene and autopsy photos to enter in evidence, honing them down would be a challenge. The photos would be incredible evidence before a jury, but Bishop understood that they had to put on just enough to tell the story. Any more and, even if Judge Flowers didn't object, a guilty verdict could be overturned by an appeals court if it deemed the number of photos and their content as less informative than prejudicial to the defendant.

As the days to the trial counted down, Bishop and McFarland interviewed witnesses and organized their case, while Bergman hunted for witnesses. Many of them college students, they'd spread out across the state and even the country. Some didn't particularly want to be found, hoping to avoid testifying. Meanwhile, McFarland had her hands full working with federal authorities trying to get permission to bring Pedro Fernandez into the country. With a felony on his record, Immigration and Customs Enforcement, ICE, the branch of the U.S. government that oversaw such matters, didn't want to let him back in the United States.

When Bishop and McFarland discussed the case, they agreed that for the most part, it was straightforward: Two people were behind closed doors when one shot and killed the other. The more experienced prosecutor, Bishop had handled dozens like it in the past, albeit none with such a bloody aftermath. Still, neither he nor McFarland could guess what tactics Bassett and Minton had in mind. The prosecutors bantered about the defense's possibilities, agreeing that the most likely arguments were that Pitonyak shot and killed Jennifer Cave in self-defense or by accident.

There was one other tactic Bishop thought the defense might try; he kept thinking about Laura Hall's DNA on the murder weapon and a medical examiner who couldn't pinpoint time of death. "Laura Hall was the biggest question mark," says Bishop. "We'd heard she'd take the Fifth, but what if she changed her mind, got up on the stand, and said just enough to make the jury suspect she was the killer?"

One piece of the puzzle, however, was still missing: The prosecutors hadn't discovered a motive. Seventeen months after Jennifer's death, they still didn't know about Colton's feelings for Jennifer. Somehow, that piece of evidence was lost. Many insisted they told police, but somehow it hadn't been related to Bishop. The prosecutors didn't know about the night Colton professed his undying love, and then came at her with a knife. Although the law didn't require prosecutors prove one for a murder conviction, in a trial, a motive was strong evidence. Would a jury convict without an answer to the basic question, why?

Twenty-eight

As she got ready to leave for Austin for the trial, Sharon felt anxious and frightened. She'd have to testify, and she'd have to sit in a courtroom hearing horrible, graphic testimony about how her beautiful young daughter died, while the man accused of murdering her sat just steps away. Uncertain she'd get through it, Sharon confided in Father David, her pastor. He understood. But then he said something about her participation in the trial that gave her courage: "This is the last gift you can give Jennifer."

When they arrived from Little Rock, Eddie and Bridget Pitonyak sat down with Sam Bassett and Roy Minton. In the months leading up to the trial, the defense team had considered and abandoned tactics, including suggesting the fatal shot could have been fired by Laura Hall. Despite her DNA on the gun, they decided, the evidence just wasn't there, and the testimony of Martindill, that Hall was at his house the night Jennifer died, made that seem unwise. Both defense attorneys feared that if they angered or alienated the jurors, the jury could come down hard on Pitonyak.

Instead, Minton and Bassett attempted to prepare Colton's parents for the likeliest outcome: Their son would go to prison. Although they'd argue Pitonyak's innocence, the victory Minton and Bassett hoped for was the same outcome they had engineered four years earlier for a young man named Brandon Threet.

The case was another sensational one. Threet, a nineteen-year-old San Antonio college student, was accused of murdering Terence McArdle, a UT student. At a party, Threet and

McArdle wrestled, at first playfully. At some point, however, Threet lost his temper, hitting McArdle in the face and kicking him. McArdle suffered brain damage, then died a few days later. Williamson County prosecutors charged Threet with murder. During the trial, Minton and Bassett convinced the judge to include lesser offenses in the charge, giving the jury the option of finding Threet guilty of not murder but manslaughter. The major difference: A murder conviction had a maximum sentence of life, but manslaughter only twenty years.

During the closing at the Threet trial, Roy Minton argued, "There is no excuse, nor have we suggested an excuse. This was one moment that has made an impact on his life. Do you believe in salvaging youth when they make a mistake?"

Minton and Bassett prevailed, convincing jurors to find Threet guilty on the lesser charge and sentencing him to twenty years. Could they do as well for Colton Pitonyak?

Finally, on the morning of Monday, January 22, 2007, Judge Flowers called the 147th District Court into order, for the purpose of seating the jury that would hear the case against Colton Pitonyak. A panel made up of eighty-eight citizens of Travis County, Texas, filed through the door. In some cases, voir dire, the questioning of potential jurors, is relatively uneventful. That would not prove true in this trial. Instead, it would be an interesting day, with the word "intent" playing a major role. The reason: the prosecutors' lack of a motive.

To gauge reactions, Bishop and McFarland explained the law and then peppered the men and women with questions directed at giving insight into whether each individual would be able to look beyond the question of why Pitonyak killed Jennifer. The prosecutors did not have to prove motive, Bishop said, why on that particular night Colton Pitonyak decided to kill Jennifer Cave. The law required only that prosecutors show "specific intent": that Colton Pitonyak meant to kill Jennifer Cave. That intention didn't have to exist for any explicit length of time, not for days, hours, or even minutes. It could be formed in the split second it took for Pitonyak to point a loaded gun with his finger on the trigger.

When they took over the floor, Bassett and Minton discussed another issue: Pitonyak's high consumption of drugs. Their approach begged the question: Foggy from the drugs, was Pitonyak capable of making an intentional decision to kill Jennifer Cave? And if he wasn't, was it murder?

"If you're leading up to making the case that the drugs did it, I'd have a very difficult time finding reasonable doubt," one potential juror said.

"I am not saying that at all," Minton countered.

The bombshells for the prosecution started even before the trial, when while questioning jurors, Roy Minton gave a preview to the week ahead: Jennifer and Colton, Minton said, were best friends, and he had no reason to kill her. Yet Pitonyak would not dispute that he was the one who fired the fatal gunshot. He took responsibility for firing the gun that killed Jennifer; but it wasn't murder, rather an unfortunate accident.

One other thing Bassett said caught Bishop by surprise: Colton Pitonyak planned to testify.

For months, Minton and Bassett had suggested that with so much pretrial publicity, seating an impartial jury in Austin could be difficult, but that didn't prove the case. By the time they left the courtroom that day, prosecutors and defense attorneys had agreed on six women and eight men, including two alternates, who would be charged with deciding Pitonyak's fate.

Still, as he picked up his files to put them in his briefcase, Bishop wondered: Could he rely on what the defense attorneys seemed to be indicating, or was Roy Minton introducing one approach to mislead him, only to argue another during the trial?

Usually the opening day of a sensational murder trial is marked by a static excitement, but the Pitonyak case broke that mold. Although the courtroom filled with reporters, lawyers, and spectators eager to hear the evidence and judge for themselves, the tenor was subdued, unusually quiet. Even when the judge wasn't on the bench, talking was muffled. The horror of what had been done to Jennifer's body permeated the proceedings. One spectator came strictly to get a look at Pitonyak. "I wanted to see for myself what kind of an animal could do that," she said. "When I looked at him, he looked normal. It was terrifying."

Sitting in the defendant's chair that morning, Pitonyak resembled the young businessman he'd once planned to be. He wore a gray suit and dark tie, his hair was cut short, and his face had broken out, perhaps from stress. The blemishes only made him look younger than his twenty-four years. As he waited for opening statements, he rarely glanced at his parents, who clustered together, leaning on each other, on a bench two rows back. Instead, the young defendant stared straight ahead, has face placid and unemotional.

Meanwhile, Bridget looked tired and sad. At times, Eddie appeared angry, as if he reined in deep frustration. Dustin sat beside them. Anyone seeing the two young men would have quickly realized they were brothers; they looked so much alike. By then, Dustin, who'd been the lesser high school student, had earned a master's degree and gone to work with his father, while Colton, the family star, faced up to life in prison.

From her perch beside the judge, Rita Grasshoff, the court reporter, turned on her computer and set up her supplies. Over the years Grasshoff, a woman with a kind smile and a warm manner, had seen a parade of defendants, some found guilty, some innocent; some that never made a headline, and others, like Pitonyak, whose crimes made them infamous. One of the first trials she worked was in Florida, that of America's most famous serial killer, Ted Bundy. Decades later, Grasshoff would remember Bundy as "cavalier," a "showoff." At times, he huddled so close to her during bench conferences that she felt the warmth of his breath, sending chills through her.

Big cases attract crowds, and Grasshoff wasn't surprised that the courtroom for the Pitonyak trial was standing room only. As jurors took their seats, Judge Flowers called the case to order. He looked pensive behind the bench, listening to last-minute motions.

TV and print reporters filled the courtroom and the hallway outside. Both families kept their distance from the press, but the Pitonyaks nearly flinched when a reporter walked past. Outside the courtroom, they walked briskly, rarely looking up, often turning away to hide their faces from the camera. As they had in Little Rock, Colton's family fought to wall themselves off from prying eyes.

At the prosecutors' table, Bishop and McFarland worried. Pedro Fernandez was an important witness, and arrangements still weren't in place to bring him to the United States. McFarland had been negotiating for much of the month, but federal authorities wouldn't bend. If he came, they wanted Fernandez kept in jail during his stay in the United States. The Mexican hotel clerk balked at the idea and refused to come. Fernandez wasn't a U.S. citizen, and Bishop had no legal authority to force him. "I'm a Travis County prosecutor," says Bishop. "I can't make either Fernandez or the U.S. government do anything."

Behind them sat Jim, Sharon, Vanessa, and Scott, waiting for the first day of a trial they hoped would finally bring justice if not closure. Jim's cousin, Jack Bissett, M.D., with his dark hair streaked gray, and his wife, Tracey, sat beside them. An Austin infectious diseases expert, Bissett had grown up with Jim, and he'd been there to support him throughout the ordeal since Jennifer's death. At the trial, he'd be able to answer Sharon's and Jim's questions about the medical testimony.

Once Judge Flowers called the court to order, Stephanie McFarland read the charge against Colton Pitonyak to the jurors: murder. Then Bill Bishop began his opening, setting the stage for the case he and McFarland would put before the jury.

"Evidence will show . . ." Bishop began. Hands behind

him, pacing in a short line in front of the jury, the solidly
built prosecutor outlined the evidence. Bishop planned
to take the jurors on a journey, from Jennifer's first exciting day on her new job, through her final evening on Sixth
Street with Colton, to Bill Thompson's call to Sharon to tell
her that her daughter hadn't shown up for work, through Jim
Sedwick's gruesome discovery. "Jennifer Cave died as the
result of a gunshot," Bishop said. "After her death, Colton
Pitonyak dismembered her, cutting off her head and her
hands . . . based on the evidence you will hear, I believe you
will find the defendant guilty."

Next up was Sam Bassett, who got quickly to the point
by emphasizing that for a murder conviction, Pitonyak had
to have acted knowingly and intentionally. Pitonyak stared
blankly at the defense table as Bassett said, "This isn't
going to be a 'who-done-it.' Colton will tell you he caused
the death of his friend, Jennifer Cave." But then the caveat:
"He'll also tell you there's no reason in the world he would
have done that intentionally or knowingly."

From the defense's opening statement, the second defendant in the case, Laura Hall, entered the courtroom, although not physically, but rather by name and implication.
"You will hear from Colton. You will not hear from Laura
Hall . . . [but] Laura Hall's DNA *was on the gun*," Bassett
said, emphatically slapping his hands. Colton could try to
implicate others, "but he's not going to do that."

In a forceful voice, Bassett talked of Colton's growing-
up years, the bright scholarship student, and the Catholic
school kid from a good family. "How did we get from there
to here?" he asked. The blame lay with Colton's addiction
to alcohol and drugs.

The cause of death, Bassett pointed out, was a single
gunshot wound. The "horrible situation became worse"
when Laura Hall arrived on the scene. Colton accidentally
killed Jennifer, Bassett insisted. As for the atrocity of the
mutilation, the defense laid all the blame on Hall. "You'll
hear Colton say, 'There is no way I would have intentionally

and knowingly caused the death of my good friend Jennifer Cave,'" Bassett concluded. "That's why I'll ask you to find the defendant not guilty."

Although Bassett spoke of guilt and innocence, seated behind the prosecutors' table, Bishop and McFarland realized that the defense's plan was no longer in question: Bassett was admitting Colton's guilt and instead was laying the groundwork for a lesser charge and a shorter sentence. Yes, Colton Pitonyak was guilty, Bassett was saying, but not of murder. At the most, his client had committed the lesser crime of manslaughter.

In the audience, Sharon leaned against Jim, while Vanessa held on to her mother's arm. Both women fought back tears. Something Bassett said stung Sharon: Colton, drugged and drunk the night of the killing, didn't remember shooting Jennifer. "I hoped he'd remember every detail," she says. "I hoped he'd never forget, that not a day would go by when he didn't relive what he did to Jennifer. That's my wish for Colton Pitonyak."

"Did [Jennifer] ever call you?" Bishop asked his first witness, Thompson, the attorney who'd hired her the day before her death.

"No, sir," Thompson said. He'd just detailed August 16, Jennifer's first and only day on her new job. She'd done so well that Thompson had offered her a better position. Then, on the seventeenth, Jennifer never showed up and never contacted the office.

While Bishop laid out the timeline for Jennifer's disappearance, Minton and Bassett had points of their own they hoped to make. "Let me ask you a few questions about your conversation with Jennifer," Minton said. "Did you have any information on her at all?"

Thompson explained that his administrative assistant weeded through the job applicants. That responsibility wasn't his.

"[Jennifer] was a bright, attractive girl?" Minton asked.

"Both those things, yes," Thompson agreed.

"Since then have you had occasion to look into her background, how many jobs she had?" Minton asked. Although Jennifer wasn't on trial, her history of job hopping and drugs was something Minton wanted before the jury. This young woman was troubled, he was suggesting.

"No, sir," Thompson said.

From that first witness, Roy Minton tried to humanize Colton in front of the jury. He put his hands on his client's shoulders, calling him a "boy," and a "young man." Old enough to be Pitonyak's grandfather, the lead defense attorney acted the part, scolding his client at times, as if Pitonyak were an errant child. This was not a hardened criminal, a cold-blooded murderer, Minton's words and body language implied. Colton was simply an inexperienced young man who'd briefly lost his way.

Looking somber in a black dress, Denise Winterbottom then took the stand. Stephanie McFarland rose to ask the questions, expanding the timeline of that fateful day. When Denise awoke that morning around six, Jennifer was missing. "The room was empty," Denise said. "I felt something was wrong."

"It's fair to say that you observed Jennifer using drugs?" Sam Bassett asked.

"Yes," Denise said. She'd seen Jennifer smoke pot, and she knew she used meth.

"It wasn't a secret, was it?" Bassett asked.

"She was honest with me," Denise said.

The day would dissolve into a parade of witnesses, all setting the stage for the horror that took place in Orange Tree unit 88. Three of those who gathered on Sixth Street that night testified, including Jeffrey Sanderson, who relayed how eager Colton Pitonyak seemed to procure an eight ball of drugs and how he pulled a knife out to cut off a girl's wristband. Yes, Sanderson admitted, he'd described Colton to police as seeming as if he'd "fried" his brain with drugs.

"That's a descriptive way of saying his brain wasn't

working right?" Minton prodded. The defense wanted jurors to see Colton as unable to make a rational decision.

"Yes, sir," Sanderson agreed.

When Melissa Kuhl took the stand, the girl whose birthday was being celebrated on Sixth Street that Tuesday night, she described how Jennifer confided Colton "is crazy," and then how she watched Jennifer and Colton walk away from the Cheers Shot Bar and turn the corner, disappearing from her sight.

A break was called, and Sharon left the courtroom, followed by Ellen Halbert, the head of the DA's victims' assistance office. In the women's restroom, Sharon washed her hands, when Bridget Pitonyak bustled in.

"Sharon, Sharon, please I want to talk to you," Colton's mother pleaded.

To avoid her, Sharon rushed into one of the stalls and closed the door. The last thing she wanted to do was talk to Colton's mother.

"I'm so sorry . . ." Bridget began.

Standing between Bridget and the bathroom stall door, Halbert put up her hand. "This is inappropriate," she said. "It's not the time or place. Please leave."

Bridget looked flustered and upset, disappointed. Jennifer's death must have been weighing heavily on her. Ever since testimony began, she'd stolen quick glances at Sharon, perhaps identifying with the pain Jennifer's mother endured. Certainly the Pitonyaks were suffering. But then, as Sharon would later say, "their child is still alive. They can still talk to him, still tell him they love him."

When testimony resumed, the chronicle of Jennifer's final night continued to play out. Michael Rodriguez recounted how Jennifer complained Pitonyak was acting up, urinating on one car and threatening to break the window of another. Colton's cell phone was missing, Jennifer had said, and she was helping him find it before she took him home. "I'll call you when I get to my apartment," she promised. But Rodriguez fell asleep, and his phone never rang.

"You didn't sense any fear in her voice?" Bassett asked, making his point that Jennifer had no reason to fear Colton, that they were friends.

"No . . . if I would have, I would have made plans to meet her somewhere," Rodriguez replied.

Two hours later, Colton banged on Nora Sullivan's door. Pitonyak had been drinking, and he babbled about a gunfight with Mexican drug dealers. "Did he seem . . . highly intoxicated?" Bishop asked Sullivan.

"He was functioning fine, talking fine," Sullivan said.

Sullivan insisted she didn't worry about Colton having a gun in her apartment at three in the morning. "Were you ever concerned for your safety?" Bassett asked.

"No, not at all," she said.

At times, Sharon Cave's face so reflected her grief that it was painful to watch her on the witness stand. When the questions became too agonizing and her emotions too raw, she paused, grimaced, and took a deep breath. Then, remarkably, she went on.

"Are you close to your children?" Stephanie McFarland asked.

"Yes," Sharon said. McFarland brought a framed photo to the witness stand, and Sharon identified the fresh-faced high school senior with bright blue eyes as her dead daughter, Jennifer. The prosecutor placed the picture on a ledge in front of the judge, facing the jury. For most of the rest of the trial, when the jurors looked at the judge's bench, Jennifer looked back at them.

Throughout her testimony, Sharon appeared as vulnerable as an open wound, bleeding sorrow. She recounted her last conversation with her daughter, how happy Jennifer had been that day, her disappearance, and Sharon's frantic rush with Jim to Austin. What did Colton Pitonyak say to Sharon when she pleaded for information about her daughter?

"Dude, I'm having pizza with my friend," he told her. "Don't bother me."

When Sharon repeated his words, she looked over at the defense table. Colton stared blankly down at his hands, and Sam Bassett seemed to bristle. She looked back at Pitonyak and he looked up, but Sharon saw no emotion in his eyes. They looked dead and cold.

With Sharon, McFarland took the jury to the Orange Tree and condo 88. Sharon recounted knocking on the door, calling out the name of the daughter everyone in the courtroom knew was already dead and mutilated, Jim entering the apartment, the horrible smell of decomposing flesh, and the frantic call to 911.

"I knew it was Jennifer when Jim came out and said he saw her feet," Sharon said, sobbing. "Jennifer had freckles on her feet. I knew then." In the gallery, Jim and Vanessa helplessly watched. Sharon's face was a mask of utter misery.

"I feel sorry for both of us," Minton said, when he stood up to begin cross-examination. "I hate like the devil to ask you questions."

Despite any reluctance, Minton had a job to do, and he started his inquiry where it would tell the most about what had transpired in Jennifer's life, the path she took from high school to college to Austin. School, work, drugs, and partying, Jennifer's life seemed in chaos at times.

"Jennifer was having a hard time finding herself," Sharon admitted. Minton handled her questioning gently, calmly, and before long she'd returned to the gallery, where Jim slipped his arm over her shoulder and she cried.

On the stand, Scott Engle talked about the "connection" he and Jennifer felt the first time they met and how the relationship ended. He left a voice mail on Colton's telephone the day Jennifer disappeared. When Colton called him back, Scott mentioned that Sharon had called the police.

"What did he say?" Bishop asked.

"[Colton said,] 'That bitch is going to get me arrested,'" Scott repeated.

In the jury box, one of the men turned and looked at Colton, his eyes boring into him.

"You knew she was using methamphetamines," Minton said to Scott. "People on that can get aggressive."

"I never saw that," Scott said. "I've never seen a problem with her thoughts . . . her way of doing things . . . she took great care of my daughter."

What about Colton? Minton wanted to know. In his statement to police, Scott had written, "Colton is crazy."

"Was that the drugs or was he psychotic?" Minton asked.

"I could never balance the two," Scott responded.

When the prosecutor questioned him, Jim kept his eyes on Bishop. Articulate and calm, Jim described the terror of walking into Pitonyak's dark apartment and the horror of finding Jennifer's decapitated body.

"There's a body," he repeated, looking weary. He'd told this painful story too many times, relived the nightmare too often. "Sharon asked, 'Is it Jennifer?'"

On cross-examination, Sam Bassett asked questions. No, Jim wasn't concerned about Jennifer's use of drugs the night that she disappeared. He'd talked with her, and she was excited about her new job. As he answered, Jim glanced at Colton seated beside his attorney. Like Sharon, he searched the younger man's face. Like Sharon, Jim saw no emotion and nothing to indicate remorse.

After Jim left the witness stand, a parade of investigators testified, from Richard Barbaria, the first APD officer to enter the apartment, through the forensic investigators who photographed and collected the evidence. "Were you made aware that there was a decapitated body in the apartment?" McFarland asked crime scene specialist Victor Ceballos.

"Yes, ma'am," he responded.

"Let's take them one at a time," Judge Flowers ordered with Vince Gonzalez, the crime scene specialist who'd taken the photographs. Bishop had labeled each photo he planned to bring into evidence, organizing them to take the jurors through the apartment, just as Gonzalez had experienced the scene, through Colton Pitonyak's front door, the debris-strewn efficiency with an ACE hardware bag near the bed and fired shell casings on the cocktail table, into the kitchen where the bloody machete waited in the dishwasher, toward the bathroom, where the full horror awaited them.

Sharon and Vanessa left before the photographs of Jennifer's mutilated body were displayed on a screen behind the witness, for the entire courtroom to see. They'd decided Jim was right, that there were images they were better off not seeing. Jim and his cousin Bissett stayed. "I thought I'd seen it all before, and I could stay for this as well," says Jim. At times, he didn't want to look, but nothing the prosecutors displayed on the screen rivaled the horror of being in the apartment that day, seeing Jennifer's poor, mutilated body.

The last thing the jurors witnessed as the first day of testimony came to an end was a photo of Jennifer's dismembered body: her hands and head in trash bags and her violated body in Colton Pitonyak's bathtub.

Austin was in a drought, and few complained when rain soaked the streets and impeded rush hour traffic the following morning. Outside, I–35 was clogged with a river of cars, while inside the courtroom, more of the investigators took the stand, including Detective Keith Walker. He'd accompanied the body to the morgue, where Dr. Peacock fingerprinted Jennifer's severed hands.

When Maurice Padilla, the DNA specialist, took the stand, he testified that Colton's DNA was all over the bathroom and the tools used to dismember Jennifer's body. But then he testified to the test results that worried Bishop and McFarland: Laura Hall's DNA on the gun and on the outside of the magazine that held the bullets. It wasn't surprising, Bassett pointed out, that Colton's DNA was on the gun. It was his gun, and he'd handled it often. But why was Hall's on the gun? "Mixtures [of DNA] don't indicate how much someone has handled an item?" Bassett asked.

"Correct," said Padilla.

Bassett put a photograph of the black-handled knife on

the screen, the one prosecutors labeled "the buck knife." On the serrated blade was the logo for Eddie Pitonyak's farm equipment company, and in the gallery, Sharon's throat tightened. It was a promotional knife, and she recognized the model as one she sold through her business to clients who used them for advertising.

Then Bassett turned his attention to the DNA evidence, not what was before the jury but what was missing. APD hadn't swabbed the handles of the hacksaw or the buck knife for DNA. How else could they know who was holding them? "Was any portion of the handle [of the hacksaw] before or after the fingerprinting swabbed?" Bassett asked.

"Not by me," Padilla answered.

On the witness stand, Jeff Breed testified that Pitonyak had a list of cleaning supplies when he entered the hardware store the afternoon after the killing. When Breed asked him what kind of saw he needed, the disheveled young man asked for something cheap to "cut up a turkey."

"Did he act intoxicated?"

"No," Breed answered. "I smelled alcohol, but he didn't act intoxicated."

Jurors and the crowd of spectators watched as on the screen the hardware store surveillance tape played, showing Pitonyak pushing a shopping cart up to the checkout to pay for supplies he planned to use to clean up evidence and dismember Jennifer's dead body.

Before the medical examiner took the witness stand, Jim brought Sharon to a small room outside the courtroom. There was something he hadn't told her, something about the autopsy. "I need to tell you something that's about to come out. They found a bullet," he said, not wanting to go on but needing to. "Someone shot into Jennifer's head through her neck, after they cut her head off."

"What?" Sharon sobbed, and Jim held her. "How many things did they have to do to my child's body? Why did they have to keep hurting her? She wasn't doing anything but lying there dead."

It seemed the horror of Jennifer's death had no end.

When Dr. Peacock took the stand, she and McFarland went over the main findings, concentrating first on the gunshot wound that killed Jennifer. As Peacock demonstrated the path of the lethal bullet through Jennifer's body, Colton Pitonyak looked away. Then she talked about the cuts to Jennifer's face and chest and the bullet lodged in her skull. All were postmortem, after death, and those listening knew what they meant. Pitonyak, Hall, or both, most likely high on drugs, had not only dismembered but played with the corpse, toying with it, slicing into Jennifer's cold flesh and shooting into her skull. In the gallery, Sharon Cave seethed, believing that perhaps she understood why they'd done it. Colton and Hall were angry with Jennifer, furious that her body lay there taunting them.

"It was pure evil," says Sharon.

Again, Sharon and Vanessa left the room, this time while McFarland used Dr. Peacock on the stand to introduce the autopsy photos. Jim had intended to stay, as he had while the crime scene photos were up, seated next to his cousin Dr. Bissett for support. "I figured that being a doctor, Jack could take the photos," said Jim. "It didn't occur to me that I wouldn't be able to."

But when McFarland put up a photo of the pieces of Jennifer's body lined up on a cold, steel autopsy table, Jim's stomach lurched. "I'm out of here," he stood up and whispered to Bissett. "I can't do this."

Jim wasn't the only one that photo affected. The autopsy table photo hit the jurors hard. One, a thirtysomething woman in a matronly quilted vest, covered her mouth with her hand, while an older woman turned away. A third woman started to cry, while some of the men stared at the photo and others looked at Colton Pitonyak in disbelief.

As the second day of testimony ended, Bishop set the stage for Pitonyak and Hall's flight from Austin. A cellular telephone expert explained how on the evening after the killing, the path of Pitonyak's cell phone cut across Texas into Mexico.

Bishop had predicted that the trial could take up to two

weeks, but it was progressing quickly. The main reason: Minton and Bassett asked few questions of the witnesses on cross-exam. Since the defense attorneys admitted Colton fired the fatal shot, they had no need to. The only witnesses the defense attorneys seemed interested in were two: With the DNA expert, they stressed what items had traces linking them to Laura Hall, and with the gun expert, Minton argued that the SW .380 could have accidentally discharged.

As the crowd filed from the courtroom, Jim Bergman drove south toward Eagle Pass, Texas, to pick up Pedro Fernandez. In a last-minute deal, U.S. immigration authorities agreed to allow McFarland to bring the hotel clerk into the country, but he'd be kept under guard in a hotel. McFarland and Bishop had Fernandez for one day. By the following midnight, Bergman had to have Fernandez back at the border, ready to turn over to an INS officer, to be returned to Mexico.

On the witness stand the next morning, Detective David Fugitt testified about what he'd discovered on Colton's cell phone, including a text message to his mother: "Going to Houston." In truth Pitonyak and Hall were on their way to Mexico. Photos showed the contents of Pitonyak's backpack, everything he'd taken with him for the journey, from his collection of high-priced Ralph Lauren clothing to his passport and cell phone.

Listening to the witnesses on the stand, many wondered what Colton Pitonyak had told his parents when he was leaving Austin, especially regarding Bridget's text message at 9:20 the night after Jennifer died. Colton's mother told her son, "I'm a nervous wreck not knowing what's going on . . ." It seemed that at least Bridget knew something troubling had happened in Austin. Yet the following afternoon, Eddie barked at Sharon and told Jim that Bridget thought "Jennifer was the problem."

When Gilchrest, the case's lead detective, took the stand, he brought in what at the time seemed an inconsequential piece of evidence, the Burger King bag he discovered on his final walk through the apartment, a $6.16 value meal without onions. Then, Bishop flashed the booking photo of Colton Pitonyak on the screen, for the detective to identify. The prosecutor wanted jurors to see the defendant as he was at the time of the murder, not the clean-cut, quiet young man in a suit sitting next to his attorneys, but a thug with glazed eyes and unruly hair, a goatee around his mouth, and dark stubble on his cheeks. Roy Minton asked Gilchrest no questions.

If the defense attorneys were restrained throughout the first two and a half days of the trial, their self-control ended when Deputy U.S. Marshal Vincent Bellino took the stand. He and his fellow deputy, Joseph Smith, had damaging statements to put before the jury, words Colton Pitonyak had uttered after his expulsion from Mexico and his arrest. Minton and Bassett insisted that they hadn't been warned, as the rules required.

"Judge, we weren't told about this," Bassett argued. "We were supposed to have been told about any statements."

"It was in my bucket for more than a year," Bishop responded, referring to the container of evidence he shared with the defense during discovery.

Both sides argued, the defense attorneys maintaining the statements were inadmissible because they weren't advised earlier of their existence, and Bishop and McFarland countering that they supplied the defense with the information along with all the other reports and interviews, and it couldn't be held against them if Minton and Burton missed them in the pile of evidence.

"What irritates the hell out of me is that you gave a specific discovery order to the state to disclose statements," Bassett objected.

The defense attorneys were angry, and Judge Flowers frowned, saying he could understand their sentiments. Flowers glared at the prosecutor, but said, "I am going to let those statements in."

After the break, Bellino described Pitonyak's arrest at the Casablanca Inn in Piedras Negras, Mexico, and what he said on the drive to the Maverick County jail: "If this is a murder charge, I know what this is about."

What had Pitonyak told Deputy Smith? "I really fucked up."

Afterward, on the video screen, jurors watched Hall in her green Cadillac driving Colton across the border at Del Rio into Mexico.

It was then that Pedro Fernandez, bulky in his sport coat, glasses perched on his nose, took the stand.

As a rapt audience listened, Fernandez described the two young Americans as looking like vacationing students. From the beginning, the things they said struck Fernandez as odd. They'd wanted to sell the Cadillac, and their plan was to disappear into Mexico's interior. "I never met somebody who would come to Mexico and wouldn't want to go back to their hometown of the U.S.," Fernandez said, with a shrug, still appearing perplexed at the prospect.

At his home that night, watching the fighting match, Fernandez took a knife away from an agitated Pitonyak and snapped a cell phone photo of his two guests. In the picture McFarland displayed on the screen, Pitonyak and Hall smiled as if they hadn't a care in the world, in a child's playpen.

"Why did you take a picture?" Minton asked, appearing irritated, his voice booming through the courtroom.

"Because I was suspicious of them," Fernandez said.

When Minton pressed, asking how Fernandez had been able to take the photo without Pitonyak and Hall objecting, the hotel manager pulled out his cell phone and flipped it open. "It's easy, you take out your phone and snap," he said, demonstrating.

Minton scowled, while Fernandez looked over at Pitonyak. He recognized the hard, cold look on the defendant's face. It was the same one he'd seen on Pitonyak in his house that night, the one that frightened him so much that he took a circuitous route from his home to prevent Pitonyak and Hall from showing up at his door.

A short time later, at 11:40 A.M. on the third day of the trial, Fernandez stepped down from the witness stand and Bill Bishop stood before the crowd and announced, "Your honor, the state rests."

A buzz went through the courtroom after the prosecutors announced the conclusion of their case. While Bergman ushered Fernandez to his county car for the 450-mile round trip to return him to the border, word spread outside the 147th District Court that at 1:30 Laura Hall would appear with her attorney, Tom Weber. On the chance that it might be true, a barrage of cameramen and reporters staked out the entrance. At 1:15, Hall, wearing jeans and a gray sweater, sunglasses on top of her head, walked beside Weber toward the courtroom. She glared at the reporters recording her every move.

"On behalf of my client I am going to assert our Fifth Amendment rights," Weber said, as he and Hall stood before Judge Flowers with the jury box empty.

"We ask the prosecutors to offer Laura Hall limited immunity so she can testify," Bassett said.

Bishop had thought long and hard early on about offering Hall some kind of a deal, but he saw no advantage. He had two diametrically opposed statements from her, which meant she'd have no credibility in front of the jury. And he personally didn't believe that Laura Hall recognized and would tell the truth.

"The state is not going to grant immunity in this matter," Bishop said.

As quickly as the hubbub over Hall's arrival began, it ended. Cameras rolled until she made her way into the elevator and the door closed.

From their arrival in Austin the Monday before the first day of testimony, Sharon and Jim stayed at a downtown Radisson hotel. That afternoon, after Bishop rested, Sharon went to their room to change into her tennis shoes, while Jim stood in the open parking garage, smoking and talking to his office on his cell phone. A white Toyota Sequoia drove in, and Jim glanced at the driver and thought it looked like Bridget Pitonyak. He looked down and saw Arkansas license plates.

A little while later, Sharon arrived, and he told her that the Pitonyaks were staying at the same hotel. "Surely, we're not that unlucky," Sharon said.

Any doubt, however, soon disappeared; a short time later, Sharon and Vanessa sat on a lobby couch, when Eddie and Bridget walked through, arm in arm.

Twenty-nine

Throughout the week, the UT dorm rooms, classrooms, and Internet sites filled with discussion and commentary on the events taking place inside the Pitonyak courtroom. Students across campus watched the testimony on CourtTV, and then argued about the case. They posted on Hornfans: "The defense is trying to pin as much on Hall as they can," one wrote. "Someone shot into the severed head? Cocaine's one helluva drug," another commented.

On Friday morning, the fourth day of testimony, Lauren and Hailey sat beside their parents. For Lauren, it would be the first time she'd feel as if it were all real, that Jennifer was dead and she wasn't coming home. Up until then, she'd willed herself not to think about what had happened in unit 88, or how it had changed all their lives. In Oklahoma, she'd told few of her classmates about the case, and before she arrived, Lauren dreaded making the trip for the trial. Yet in the courtroom, the youngest Cave sister realized she didn't want the trial to end. It was all she had left of Jennifer to hold on to. Off and on, as she listened to testimony, she thought back to her last conversation with Jennifer, remembering how before hanging up they both said, "I love you."

As Lauren considered the loss of her sister, Hailey looked across at Bridget and Eddie and wondered what they were thinking. What would it be like to have a son who'd committed such a horrific crime? The Pitonyaks sat alone, just the two of them, appearing to have the weight of the world on their shoulders, and Hailey found herself feeling sorry for them. That sympathy brought on yet another wave of guilt. For more than a year, she'd battled regret that she hadn't stayed closer to Jennifer, and now it felt disloyal to have any sympathy for the parents of her killer.

Outside the sun shone in a bright blue, nearly cloudless sky, while inside the courtroom, Colton, in a brown suit, a blue shirt, and a precisely knotted tie, sat placidly beside his lawyers. By five minutes to nine, every seat in the courtroom filled. At the bench, Judge Flowers talked in a low tone to Bishop, Minton, and Bassett. Something had happened the evening before, after they'd left the courtroom, and they were discussing how best to handle it. When Judge Flowers was ready, Bassett stood and called his first witness, an odd choice it would seem: the lead investigator on the case.

On the witness stand for the second time, Detective Mark Gilchrest explained that he'd discovered something inside Jennifer's small, orange, barrel-shaped purse after testifying the day before.

"And what is it?"

Using the projector, Bassett displayed a tattered card for the "Thong Club," a discount card from a lingerie store. What Gilchrest hadn't noticed at first was writing on the back. In pencil, someone had written Laura Hall's name. Why this could be important, no one explained. The two young women were both friends of Pitonyak's, so it didn't seem particularly odd. Seated behind the prosecutors' table, Bill Bishop wasn't concerned; instead he decided to take advantage of having Gilchrest back on the stand. "When you went back to apartment eighty-eight with Detective Walker did you look for a third bullet?" Bishop asked.

"Yes, we did . . . because there were [two bullets recovered but] three shell casings found in the apartment," Gilchrest said.

"Did you ever find the third bullet?"

"No."

That there were three bullets was important to Bishop, something he wanted the jurors to remember. Yet he moved quickly on, hoping not to give it so much attention that he alerted Minton and Bassett. Instead, Bishop changed the subject, asking Gilchrest a question that explained Hall's absence from the courtroom. "Is Laura Hall charged with an offense arising out of this set of circumstances?" Bishop asked.

"Yes," Gilchrest said, looking at the jurors. "Hindering apprehension."

Laura's friend, Ryan Martindill, was on the prosecutors' witness list, but since the defense admitted Pitonyak fired the fatal bullet, Bishop and McFarland hadn't called him to testify. There were, however, points the defense attorneys thought Martindill could make for them, and he was their second witness to take the stand.

"You told me this morning that it was obvious to you that Laura was in love with Colton, and you said, 'I sometimes can't differentiate between love and obsession,'" Bassett said. "Is that correct?"

"Yes," Martindill testified. Bassett wanted to put into evidence more proof of that obsession: Martindill's account of the night Hall had "Colton" tattooed onto her ankle. Charging it was irrelevant, Bishop protested. After argument from both sides, Judge Flowers ruled in favor of the prosecutor.

In Austin, Roy Minton had a long and illustrious reputation. "One of the best," says a lawyer he'd sparred with over the years. "A gentleman and a great attorney."

Stephanie McFarland and Bill Bishop knew enough about their elder opposing counsel to understand that when Minton called Edward Hueske, a gray-haired gun expert from Denton, Texas, to the stand, that the attorney would put on a display of ballistic expertise. Two days earlier, Minton had grilled the prosecutor's gun expert until the man finally agreed with him that a bullet could be in the chamber of the Smith and Wesson .380 after the magazine was pulled out, and that could lead to accidentally firing the gun. With his own expert, the defense attorney wouldn't have to push as hard to get the same result.

In front of the jury, Hueske and Minton displayed the

weapon, pulling out the gun's narrow black magazine, and explaining that the gun could be thought empty, although a bullet remained lodged in the barrel.

"Where is the safety on this gun?" Minton asked.

"There's no safety," Hueske said.

The gun, a type that police officers often carried a decade earlier, he explained, "was suitable for rapid fire in a tactical situation." Hueske labeled the .380 a cheap and poorly designed gun. Minton instructed him to demonstrate how the gun was loaded and emptied. Although the magazine was removed, the gun could still be dangerous.

"It will fire," said Hueske. The prosecutors' expert judged the pressure necessary to pull the gun's trigger as 8.5 to 11.5 pounds. Hueske placed the number lower, between 6.5 and 7 pounds. Then McFarland stood up, and the defense attorney's gains were tempered.

"[The gun's trigger pressure is] within normal range?" she asked on cross-exam.

"Yes," Hueske said.

"Certainly it's not a hair-trigger?"

"No," he agreed.

"State your name for the jury," Minton instructed his fourth witness.

"Colton Aaron Pitonyak," the defendant said to an over-flowing courtroom.

"How old are you?"

"Twenty-four," he said.

On the witness stand, Pitonyak showed no more emotion than he had sitting at the defense table the preceding three days. His voice was hoarse, his face blotched with even more blemishes than at the beginning of the trial, and he reached often for the water glass beside him. Minton would later blame his client's flat affect and thirst on an antidepressant prescribed by jail doctors. Watching the testimony, the DA's investigator, Jim Bergman, scoffed. "That kid wasn't drinking water like that until he got on the witness stand," he whispered. "Medicine my eye. He's drinking to give himself time to think before answering. You've gotta do that, if you're going to lie."

"Is that your momma and daddy?" Minton asked, pointing at the Pitonyaks.

"Yes, sir," Colton politely answered.

Minton took Pitonyak on a journey that must have been painful for his parents to relive, one that began when he was a straight-A honor student, and ended when he became a drug addict and a dealer. He talked about his drunk-driving charge and his time in jail for possession, the sentence he'd finished serving only six weeks before he shot and killed Jennifer Cave.

"Did you realize you had a drinking problem?" Minton asked.

"Yes, sir," Pitonyak answered.

Yet when his parents sent him to La Hacienda for an expensive round of rehab, Pitonyak admitted he hadn't gone there to reap the benefits. "I just told the counselors what they wanted to hear."

Minton called Pitonyak's behavior insincere, and his client didn't disagree with him. "I was ashamed," he said. " . . . I didn't have a desire to quit in the first place."

Colton Pitonyak recounted how he met Jennifer Cave in early spring 2004. "After a while we got to be really good friends," he said.

"Did you ever, either one of you, fall in love with the other?" Minton asked.

Despite his protestations on the night in Justin's apartment, when he'd pleaded with Jennifer to be with him, saying over and over again that he loved her, Colton Pitonyak answered, "No, it wasn't like that. She was my best friend."

If he had loved her, and she didn't return his affection, of course, that could be motive, so Pitonyak had a reason to lie. And the prosecutors still didn't know what Pitonyak's true feelings had been for his victim, so they weren't able to call him on his deceit. Throughout his testimony, Colton repeated each time he was asked, "She was my friend."

"When did you start sleeping with Laura Hall?" Minton asked.

"I think it was late spring 2005," he said.

"Did you realize the girl was in love with you?"

"Yes, sir," he said, then admitting that he'd "taken advantage" of the situation to have sex with her at least once a week. He denied owning a gun, saying the .380 was left at his apartment as collateral from someone who owed him money.

"Why did they owe you money?" Minton asked.

"For drugs," he responded, staring blandly at the audience. He sold drugs, he admitted, but classified it as "a little bit . . . to pay for my party habits."

Even on the witness stand, Pitonyak couldn't help but appear the campus thug, bragging about how he bought drugs for other college students who were "scared of a lot of people" who sold them. Drugs were a lucrative business, he said, yet he didn't have enough money to get his car back after it had been towed. "I think my mother helped me with that."

It was Jennifer's idea to go out that night, he said, but he didn't remember where they went or what they did after they left Jazz, the Cajun restaurant where Colton couldn't remember, but assumed he drank a "Bermuda Triangle," a rum punch concoction so potent the restaurant limited two to a customer. "I know we didn't eat much," he said. "I was taking a bunch of pills that day, too . . . Xanax."

What he didn't mention were the methamphetamines Jason Mack said his good friend Colton abused continually in the months leading up to the killing. Of course, his own attorneys had already mentioned before the jury that meth could make users aggressive.

In his folksy, grandfatherly manner, Roy Minton put both hands on his narrow hips. "Tell me this, why when you were drinking perfectly good whisky, do you take Xanax?"

"You don't have to drink as much to get messed up as quick," his client responded.

After the restaurant, Colton Pitonyak insisted the next thing he remembered was waking up the next morning. When did he realize Jennifer was in the bathtub, dead? "I'm not sure. Everything kind of blurred together," he answered. He believed he saw her when he used the bathroom. He admitted shooting the fatal bullet, saying he must have because no one else was in the apartment that night.

"Did you know this child is dead?" Minton asked, his voice rising like a parent scolding a misbehaving teenager.

"I knew . . . I got scared and panicked," he said, when asked why he didn't call 911.

From that point on, Colton blamed everything that happened on Laura Hall. It was her idea to dismember the body. In fact, she must have done the work, for he certainly couldn't have. He didn't have the stomach for it. "I wouldn't have done that," he said.

"Why cut up the body?" Minton asked. While his client admitted he'd shot the fatal bullet, the defense attorney was attempting to separate Pitonyak from the horrific aftermath. Colton admitted that he and Hall discussed cutting up Jennifer's body and that he wanted to "get rid of it," but again he insisted he wasn't the one who wielded the machete and hacksaw.

" . . . I didn't cut on the body . . ." He tried to, he said, " . . . I couldn't."

Why had he gone to Breed's Hardware with the list? "[Laura] said something wasn't working and that she needed some things," he said.

"Who killed [Jennifer]?" Minton asked.

"I did," Pitonyak said, although again he stressed that he didn't remember anything that happened. Why then did he believe he'd fired the bullet? "Everything points to it." As to why he would have done such a horrendous thing, he didn't have an answer, beyond that he wouldn't and couldn't have done it on purpose.

The escape to Mexico in the green Cadillac, Pitonyak said, was also Laura Hall's doing. He thought they were going to Houston, simply to flee the apartment with the body in the bathtub and give himself time to think.

Once again with a grandfatherly scowl, Minton asked, "Did you ever realize the grief you were causing?"

Remarkably, Pitonyak answered, "I know now."

Apparently, it had taken Pitonyak's arrest, more than a year in jail, and a trial before he understood the vast harm he'd done.

Minton railed at his client, accusing him of having to have known what Hall wanted the masks, gloves, hacksaw, and ammonia for. Yes, Pitonyak admitted. He knew. "Didn't your momma and daddy tell you, if you're ever in trouble, call me first?" Minton asked, as if talking to a child.

"Too many times," Pitonyak answered. Again and again, the defense attorney and his client talked about the booze and the pills, and Colton insisted he remembered nothing of the horror of either the killing or the mutilation of Jennifer's body.

"Did you fire the shot into Jennifer's severed head?"

"No, I did not," Colton insisted.

"Then who did?" Minton asked.

"I can only assume," Pitonyak said.

"Who else was around the body?"

Pitonyak looked at the jury. "Laura Hall," he said.

"Did you knowingly cause the death of Jennifer Cave?" Minton asked.

"No I did not," Pitonyak answered.

The judge called a morning break, and everyone filed out of the courtroom. Sharon left crying. The last question Minton had asked before he'd passed the witness was who had written "J. Ribbit" with Jennifer's cell phone number on his wall. Jennifer wrote it, Colton said. "Ribbit, like a frog," he added.

Frog, of course, was Jennifer's family nickname. "Colton Pitonyak had even stolen that from me," Sharon says. "Something that was between us would now be linked to him and to her murder."

As he left the courtroom to get lunch, Bishop considered the morning's testimony. He knew Pitonyak's flat affect probably wasn't playing well for the jury. They wanted to see the young man show remorse. "That kid didn't even look flustered," says Bishop. Yet he worried about the cross-examination. Most murder defendants don't testify, so it's unusual for a prosecutor to get to question one on the witness stand. And that Pitonyak said he didn't remember could be tricky. Says Bishop: "It's hard to trip someone up if that's all they're going to tell you."

"You testified this morning, basically, that you were a victim of an addiction to drugs and alcohol," Bishop said to Pitonyak. "Is that fair to say?"

At first, Pitonyak hesitated, appearing to think over his response, "Yes, sir."

"Didn't you cultivate a gangster persona?" Bishop asked, his eyes boring into Pitonyak.

"No," Pitonyak said.

Scoffing, Bishop laid out the Internet evidence, first Colton's ILoveMoneyAndHos screen name.

"That was a joke," Pitonyak said, his voice strained.

In the kitchen, Colton hung one poster: "Make way for the bad guy," written under Al Pacino as *Scarface*. When Bishop asked Pitonyak to read quotes off his Facebook.com profile from Al Capone and John Gotti, Colton did as instructed, but then, without being asked, read one more, a Warren Buffett quote: "I always knew I was going to be rich . . ."

"You didn't just use drugs, you sold them, a lot," Bishop said.

Pitonyak agreed that was how he'd made money, while Bishop put up on the screen images APD experts had pulled off the young man's computer, photographs of Xanax and ecstasy tablets, Pitonyak's drug catalog. His sign-on name on the Web site was C-Money.

"Is it fair to say that's the image you were trying to portray yourself, as a gangster?" Bishop asked.

"No, I wasn't," Pitonyak protested, but when Bishop asked for the names of Colton's drug contacts, his suppliers, the scene played out like a bad TV cop show. "I don't have specific names," Pitonyak said. Under questioning, Pitonyak admitted he carried a gun at times, and when Bishop asked who Pitonyak owed money to, again, the young man's answers were evasive, saying simply, "Some guys."

On the witness stand, even the meticulously pressed suit he wore couldn't camouflage what he'd become; Colton Pitonyak acted like a criminal. Bishop rattled off a summary of Pitonyak's life at the time of the killing: Colton owed his drug suppliers money, he'd gotten a D in his summer school class, his car had been towed, and he was on the Internet in the middle of the night looking for a silencer and an assault weapon.

When it came to the night of Jennifer's death, nearly every question Bishop asked was answered by Pitonyak, "I don't know," or "I don't recall."

Again, Bishop trailed back to Colton's Facebook profile, first going through the list of gangster rappers Pitonyak idolized, and then reading off the movies he'd listed as his favorites. In *Goodfellas*, "that movie has a pretty graphic scene of a dismemberment of a human body, doesn't it?" Bishop asked.

"I don't recall specifically, but . . ."

"You don't recall in *Goodfellas* where a combination of a large butcher knife and a machete were used to dismember a body?" Bishop asked, his voice incredulous.

"I don't recall. It has been a while since I have seen that movie," Pitonyak said.

There were dismemberments in the other movies as well, including in *Donnie Brasco*, where "they used a hatchet or a machete and a saw," Bishop said.

"I don't remember specifically, but, yes," Pitonyak admitted.

Then Bishop asked about the Netflix folder police found on Pitonyak's coffee table. The *Sopranos* DVD inside included an episode where a body was taken to a bathtub and the head and hands cut off, eerily similar to the condition of Jennifer's body. "I don't recall that specific scene," Pitonyak said.

"How many times between four-twenty-eight that morning when you were on Sherdog.com and three-eighteen that afternoon when you checked out at Breed's did you go to the bathroom?" Bishop asked. How could Pitonyak say he didn't participate in or even know about the dismemberment when he'd spent the day inside the apartment? There was only one bathroom.

"Quite a few times, I assume," Pitonyak said.

"So it's not really accurate to say you didn't know what Laura Hall was doing?"

"No," Pitonyak admitted. "I knew what was going on."

"In fact, you were either doing it yourself or assisting her in the process . . ."

"By letting it go on . . . but I didn't assist . . ."

"You don't think using the machete on a deceased body is taking part?" Bishop asked.

"I didn't use the machete," Pitonyak said.

It was habit, he said, that made him order his value meal at Burger King that afternoon without onions, not evidence that he wasn't in the drugged fog he'd testified to. When he'd talked to Scott Engle and said, "That bitch is going to get me arrested," Bishop asked if Pitonyak was talking about his good friend Jennifer Cave, who was in pieces in his bathroom?

"I don't specifically remember," Pitonyak said for what seemed like the hundredth time that day.

In the gallery, Sharon, Lauren, Vanessa, and Hailey sobbed. Disgusted by Pitonyak's performance on the witness stand, Vanessa ran from the courtroom, unable to listen anymore, and a moment later, Lauren, Hailey, and Sharon followed.

On the screen, Bishop projected a photograph of Jennifer's severed head, the side of her face covered with gaping cuts. "How did that happen?" he asked, furious.

"I don't know," Pitonyak said.

The prosecutor displayed the photo of the cuts on her chest, and asked the same question. Again, Pitonyak answered, "I don't know."

"Who put her hands in the bag?" Bishop demanded.

"I don't know," Pitonyak said.

"Who put her head in the bag?"

"I don't know."

"How long did it take to cut her head off?" Bishop asked.

"I don't know," Pitonyak replied.

Bishop asked if Pitonyak purchased the hacksaw because the machete wasn't working, and he again insisted that he wasn't the one wielding the weapon.

"But your DNA is on the grip," Bishop pointed out.

"I didn't use the machete," Pitonyak answered, kneading his hands and appearing nervous. "I admit it was my machete, but I didn't use it."

Bill Bishop eyed Colton Pitonyak with total disgust. "I have no further questions, your honor," the prosecutor said.

On redirect, Roy Minton attempted to repair the damage. "The last number of questions that Mr. Bishop asked you were about who had done those things to Jennifer's body. It was either you or it was Laura. Is there any question about that?"

"No there is no question," Pitonyak said. He looked angry, but controlled. "I know I didn't do those things."

Then, Minton asked his client, a young man who contended he was so drugged and drunk that he couldn't remember shooting and killing Jennifer Cave, dragging her body to the bathtub, or the bloody result, "Is it clear in your mind that it was Laura?"

"I can't think of any other options," Pitonyak said.

As if it were a deep confession, something he was

ashamed of, Pitonyak admitted he'd lied to the hardware store owner about the purpose of the hacksaw. Colton, Minton said, had to realize that since he bought the tools, he was as guilty as "if you'd been capable of doing it?"

"Yes, sir," Pitonyak said.

In his self-description, Colton Pitonyak was a young man who wasn't able to do such a ghastly act. He was too weak-stomached. Then, Minton, again, portrayed his client as little more than a youngster, asking about the paintball guns found in his apartment. What had Colton done with them? He'd horsed around like a college kid.

"My friends and I used to have little . . . play games of war with them," Pitonyak said, smiling.

"Here in Austin?" Minton asked.

"Yes, sir."

With that, at 2:30 that Friday afternoon, Colton Pitonyak left the witness stand, while in the background his mother could be heard crying.

A key defense witness wasn't available until Monday, so testimony was about to wrap up for the week, when Sam Bassett called a last witness. Javier Rosales walked into the room. A construction worker, he'd been brought in directly from his job, wearing jeans and a bright yellow T-shirt with a tropical cocktail on the back. Prosecutors had just heard about Rosales the day before, and Detective Fugitt tracked him down and took his statement the previous night. Rosales had worked as a waiter at Baby Acapulco, the same loud, brightly painted Mexican restaurant where Laura Hall waitressed for a period after the killing. As usual, it would soon become evident that Hall hadn't been averse to talking about the killing.

"As soon as we listened to what Rosales would say, we knew we wanted the jury to hear it," says Sam Bassett.

"What did Laura Hall tell you?" Bassett asked.

"That she masterminded the escape, and would have gotten away if she hadn't called her father," the heavyset man said. But then, Rosales said Hall had told him something else, something that didn't jibe with what Colton Pitonyak had just said on the witness stand, something that didn't bolster the defense: "that she *helped* cut up a human body."

As the jury and spectators left the courtroom, McFarland thought that it had been a good day for the prosecution. Pitonyak hadn't been believable on the witness stand, she judged. His story had too many holes, too many conveniently remembered memories versus his insistence that he remembered nothing of such grisly scenes as the cutting up of Jennifer's body. As for Javier, he'd only reinforced the prosecutors' views: that Colton Pitonyak was the one who'd done the major work dismembering the body. McFarland had one more thought: She hoped Laura Hall was watching the trial. She wondered how Hall felt hearing that Pitonyak laid the blame for the dismemberment entirely on her shoulders.

"Pitonyak was on the stand burying Hall, to save his own hide," Bergman concurred. "He'd used Laura Hall for sex, and he was using her again."

Much of the courtroom cleared out, with the exception of a few reporters and the two families, as Judge Flowers took up with the attorneys the most important legal argument of the trial: the defense attorneys' request to give the jury the option of lesser charges against Pitonyak, specifically the additions of manslaughter and negligent homicide.

"Do you have an opinion on that?" Flowers asked the prosecutors.

"My position is that they haven't raised evidence in such a manner as to deserve any consideration," Bishop responded. Colton Pitonyak hadn't gotten on the stand and testified to either shooting Jennifer as she attacked him, in self-defense, or holding the gun and having it accidentally discharge and kill her. Saying he wouldn't have done it on purpose, Bishop argued, wasn't enough.

"I want to know why you think you're entitled to it," Flowers asked Minton.

"We believe the evidence raised issues and we're entitled to it," Minton said. He went through the points they'd raised during the trial, including that Pitonyak said he didn't know the gun was loaded, that the defense expert testified it could easily misfire, and that Pitonyak insisted he and Jennifer were friends and he wouldn't have killed her on purpose.

The gun was so bad, Minton said, that it was more than likely that the shooting had been an accident. "I'm ashamed Smith and Wesson put it out," he added, his voice rising emotionally in the courtroom.

The evidence to support a lesser charge wasn't there, Bishop responded. "The possibility of an accidental discharge doesn't raise the evidence, or it would in every court and every murder."

With the fervor of a preacher pounding home the message of the week's gospel, Roy Minton repeated Colton Pitonyak's version of the events that led up to the murder. The gun had been in the house for only forty-eight hours. He didn't know it was loaded. There was no evidence that showed any altercation, nothing to suggest there'd been a struggle. And the prosecutors had no motive. They'd shown no evidence of any prior violence or even anger between Colton and Jennifer.

Judge Flowers, looking tired, said, "I will read some cases on it."

The weekend was a sad one. Sharon thought often of Jennifer, wondering what she'd seen in Colton, why she continued to be his friend. The trial was expected to conclude the following Monday, and they drove back to Austin and checked in at the Radisson on Sunday afternoon. That evening, Sharon and Jim had dinner with Jack and Tracey Bissett. When Sharon was in the lobby, she noticed Eddie Pitonyak walking toward her. It was obvious that he didn't recognize her at first, and she simply crossed her arms and stood her ground. When he looked up and saw her, he turned and walked away.

At 8:30 the following morning, Judge Flowers was on the bench, and Minton and Bishop again argued that lesser offenses with shorter maximum sentences should be included in the charges against Pitonyak. Doing so would give jurors more options to choose from, increasing the chances of a lighter sentence. It was the ball game for Minton and Bassett. They needed that lesser charge to ensure that the jury, so horrified by the photos, didn't come down hard on their client. To counter Bishop's charge that they hadn't presented sufficient evidence to support a lesser charge, Minton said that was coming. "[The reason] we are putting Dr. Richard Coons on is to discuss the effect of alcohol and Xanax on the brain, to explain how the memory works," Minton told Judge Flowers.

"I don't think it's helpful to the jury for someone to say this is an accident due to alcohol and drug abuse," Bishop countered.

Dr. Richard Coons, a favorite in Texas law enforcement, was an expert witness used by prosecutors and defense attorneys alike. Minton argued that Coons would explain that Pitonyak probably didn't remember that night, by detailing the effects of drugs and alcohol. The judge considered Minton's suggestion, then announced he'd made his decision. The only charge the jurors could consider against Colton Pitonyak was murder. Disappointed, Minton walked back to the defense table, Bassett beside him. They'd fought hard, but they'd lost.

Minton's first witness on the stand that Monday morning was Bridget Pitonyak, there to tell the jury about the night in February 2005 when she and Eddie went out to dinner at Sullivan's steak house with Colton and his group of friends, including Jennifer and Scott. "Anything unpleasant about that experience?" Minton asked.

"No," Bridget said. It had been a cordial evening. Her son liked Jennifer. The implication: He wouldn't have intentionally killed her.

On cross-examination, Bill Bishop asked Bridget to focus on August 17 and 18, 2005, the time of the killing. "Do you recall sending your son several messages?" he asked.

Bridget said she did. Colton had text-messaged that he was going to Houston. She didn't dispute that she might have text-messaged and told him it was driving her crazy "not knowing what's happening."

"Did he tell you what happened in Austin?" Bishop asked.

"No," she said.

"Did he tell you why he went to Mexico?"

Again, Colton's mother insisted, "No."

On the witness stand, Richard Coons was impressive, tall, solidly built, with glasses and graying hair. A forensic psychiatrist, Coons had testified in many of the most sensational cases in Texas history, including a few years earlier in the trial of Celeste Beard, a former country club waitress, for the murder of her multimillionaire husband. Not only was Coons a medical doctor, but he had a degree in law from the University of Texas, and he was more than comfortable in a courtroom.

"Have you done work for the DA's office in Austin over the years?" Minton asked.

"For thirty-two years," Coons said. Answering questions, Coons explained how memory works, how the brain stores it in layers that consist of immediate, short-term, and long-term in the hippocampus, the part of the brain central to memory. Then he discussed the possible effects of alcohol and Xanax on the brain. Large amounts of both combined, Coons said, "and you can't lay down the memory." Using the drugs over a long term and in large amounts had "an additive effect."

Yes, Coons said, the result could be blackouts, whole periods of time that were unaccounted for when no memory existed.

"Take someone twenty-two years of age who is drinking

one fifth to a quart of vodka daily and using Xanax, two, three, four, five of those pills a day. Is it inconsistent that he has forgotten an entire day or an entire night? Can it be blocked so entirely?" Minton asked.

Bill Bishop objected, saying the question had already been asked and answered, but the judge allowed Dr. Coons to answer, "It will impair the memory for all the time you are sufficiently intoxicated."

"During that period of time, you don't have any memory to pull back up?"

"Yes."

The prosecutors asked Coons no questions, and at 9:30 that Monday morning, the defense rested.

After Dr. Coons left the witness stand, Sam Bassett rose to register an objection to be officially entered in the trial transcript. "We object that the charge does not include manslaughter and criminally negligent homicide," Bassett said, preserving the objection for appeal, as the court reporter, Rita Grasshoff, typed his words into the official record.

Judge Flowers ordered a twenty-minute break, and then closing arguments would begin.

Thirty

At 9:50 that Monday morning, court reconvened. The two alternate jurors were dismissed, and Judge Flowers read the charge to the remaining twelve, the law they were to adhere to when deciding Colton Pitonyak's fate. There were aspects that cut both ways. "Voluntary intoxication does not establish a defense to a crime," Flowers read. " . . . the burden of proof rests with the state" and "if you have any reasonable doubt, thereof, you will find the defendant not guilty by your verdict."

"Ladies and gentlemen," Stephanie McFarland said, walking up to the jury, as she began closing arguments. On the screen Bishop projected the Burger King receipt from the day of the killing. "Colton Pitonyak didn't like onions. Colton Pitonyak didn't eat onions. You should believe that not because the defense told you but because it's supported by the evidence, the undisputed evidence that this man," she said, pointing at Pitonyak. "Shortly after buying a hacksaw to carve up his friend, he stopped at Burger King and ordered a meal, and remembered to make sure it didn't have onions . . . You need to rely on the undisputed evidence in this case. The defendant's testimony is full of inconsistencies not supported by the facts."

Quickly McFarland zeroed in on the issues she knew the defense would emphasize, that there'd been no evidence of an argument or a struggle and that the prosecutors hadn't proven Colton Pitonyak had any reason to kill Jennifer Cave.

"The state didn't need to prove motive," she maintained. "Specific intent is formed in an instant."

During voir dire, Roy Minton discussed manslaughter and criminally negligent homicide with the jurors. "[Those options aren't in the charge] because there's no evidence disputing that this act was knowingly and intentionally [committed]," she said. "The law says that if you kill someone with a deadly weapon, then specific intent can be inferred. There is no evidence that this was an accident."

McFarland stood and looked at the jurors, from one face to the next: "Their whole case is 'I don't remember, but I know it couldn't have been intentional.'" Pitonyak, she said, wasn't credible. He would lie to keep from going to prison; he was a drug addict and a dealer. "Don't be fooled by his nice hair cut and nice suit."

The day of the killing, Pitonyak was "losing it," McFarland said, his lifestyle evaporating around him, a thug who owed money for drugs. After he killed Jennifer, she was stabbed in the face and the chest, a bullet shot through her severed neck into her brain, her head and hands cut off. "No decent person would do that, so he blamed Laura Hall," she said. "He is lying, and the DNA evidence proves it.

"You can't find someone guilty of murder for mutilating a body, but it tells you a lot about their intent toward the person," she said. To Colton, "Jennifer was just a body, just a piece of meat . . . He called Jennifer's mother, while [Jennifer's] dead body was in his bathtub, and said, 'Dude, don't bother me' . . . He called Jennifer a bitch to Scott Engle."

Putting the photo from Mexico on the screen, the one of Pitonyak and Hall smiling as if on a holiday, she asked, "Is he panicked, grief-stricken? . . . He knows he's guilty of murder. All you have to do is tell him that you're going to hold him accountable."

When McFarland reclaimed her seat, Sam Bassett took over the courtroom floor. He paused and looked at the jury, thoughtful, with irritation in his voice. "You ought to be angry with Colton. You ought to be disgusted with some of his behavior after Jennifer died," he said. "But don't confuse the way she died with the cause of her death . . . Is there evidence beyond a reasonable doubt to prove that Colton killed his friend Jennifer Cave on purpose, intentionally and knowingly?" There wasn't, he insisted.

As the prosecutors knew he would, Bassett then turned his attention to motive. "The state's not required to prove motive," he said. "But don't you know that if they had any instance or evidence of Colton being mean to Jennifer, threatening Jennifer, doing anything bad to Jennifer, you would have heard about it?"

Then Bassett turned to the subject of Laura Hall, insisting she was responsible for the condition of Jennifer's body and the run to Mexico. "In Laura's words, 'I masterminded the escape,'" he said, quoting Javier Rosales. Colton could have tried to blame Laura for the killing, but he didn't. "Wouldn't that have been more convincing if he's a liar?"

Finally, Bassett pleaded, "[Colton's] telling the truth: 'I can't remember. God I wish I could. I'm sorry my friend is dead. There is no way I could have killed her on purpose.'"

Looking weary, Roy Minton stood before the jurors. He walked to the judge's bench, where he picked up from the ledge the SW .380 gun that was used to kill Jennifer Cave. In his calm, unaffected manner, Minton said, "Let me begin, folks, by talking to you about this gun . . ."

As he had during testimony, Minton called the gun unsafe, poorly designed, an accident waiting to happen. The buck knife with the Pitonyak Machinery Corporation logo on the handle, Minton called "a cheap little old knife that his father buys by the hundreds. PMC. That's his daddy."

Was there, Minton asked, "some speck of motive? Some idea why these two kids were mad at each other? Why he wanted to take this girl's life?"

"Was [Colton] lying when he tells you he is drinking the way he has? . . . I am telling you I don't know what happened. Colton doesn't know what happened," he said, his voice rising. "All of this evidence has indicated that Colton didn't have any feelings for Jennifer. She was his buddy, his pal . . . the drugs were part of their relationship."

Why? he asked, over and over, hitting hard on the absence of a motive.

Again Minton took the stance of an old man scolding unruly children. "I don't mean to criticize the child," he said, referring to Jennifer. "But what business do either of these kids have going out to Sixth Street when she has to be at work the next morning?"

After listing the drugs and alcohol Pitonyak said he'd ingested that fateful night, Minton returned to the main issue: "Intentionally means that he meant to kill her. Knowingly means that he knows what he's doing when he picks up the gun and pulls the trigger . . . There is no way . . . So we have to decide how likely it is that something came up that he decided to murder Jennifer . . . I just don't see it . . . you are dealing with a drunk, drugged up kid . . . he hasn't got a brain, folks."

When it came to the mutilation of Jennifer's corpse, the dismemberment, the cuts to her face and chest, the bullet shot up into her skull, the disgrace of it made Minton furious. "Both of them [Colton and Laura] involved up to their eyelashes, and they're smiling for a picture. I don't defend that conduct at all," he said. Yet, he urged the jurors to think of Colton's actions and his wannabe gangster persona in the context of modern culture. "I hope some of ya'll have got kids that buy posters and put their names on websites and call themselves Dillinger," he said. "Oh this has been a heartbreaker, just a heartbreaker . . . I'm getting too old to try cases where kids get killed," Minton moaned . . . "[But] I do not want to see this boy get convicted of something he's not guilty of."

Finally, Bill Bishop addressed the jury, as in his opening statement, with his hands clasped behind his back. "Mr. Bassett and Mr. Minton want you to ignore the fact that Jennifer Cave was mutilated. Her hands were removed. Her head was removed. Because that is something they can't explain . . ." he said. "I think if we apply stories to the evidence we know, I think we can make sense of it."

The jurors, Bishop said, needed to remember who Colton Pitonyak was in August 2005, when Jennifer died. He was abusing drugs and alcohol, portraying himself in a gangster image. He owed people money, and his good customer, Jennifer Cave, wasn't buying drugs from him anymore. "The mutilation shows you and the flight shows you that he had a guilty conscience. He knew what he had done, he knew he shouldn't have done it, and he was going to get out of there," Bishop said. "They want to blame [Laura Hall] for all that happened, but the evidence doesn't support that . . . Look at the DNA." It was Colton Pitonyak's DNA all over the bathroom and the tools. "There is a green towel with his blood. There are jeans in the washer with his blood. You don't get injured; you don't bleed as the result of [firing] an accidental gunshot . . . You get injured [and bloody] mutilating a body in a bathtub."

If Hall, a slightly built woman, had been able to cut up Jennifer's body without leaving DNA, "she's an absolute genius." Colton Pitonyak, Bishop charged, told the jurors what they wanted to hear, just as he admitted he'd done with the drug counselors at La Hacienda. "He wasn't going to Houston. He took his passport."

Then Bishop played what he saw as his ace in the hole, the piece of evidence he'd subtly driven home to the jurors: that there was a second bullet casing found in the living room. Why was the second casing important? During his testimony, Colton had testified that he'd never shot the gun before that night. If Colton shot at Jennifer only once, unintentionally, there would have been only one casing. But there were two.

That second cartridge was proof, Bishop said, that Colton lied. Could he have fired twice at Jennifer that night, perhaps missing the first time and firing again? "You don't fire accidentally twice!" the prosecutor said. " . . . There is nothing more intentional than pointing a gun and shooting it."

Bishop suggested the jury consider Colton Pitonyak's actions. From the moment he showed up at Nora Sullivan's that morning, Colton worked on setting up an alibi, laying the groundwork to explain away the gunshots. "[Colton had] seen all the movies, *Donnie Brasco*, *Goodfellas*, *Sopranos*," Bishop said. "[H]e [knew] the next step: get rid of the body."

"Unfortunately for Mr. Pitonyak, movies are movies, and life is life," Bishop said. "And [cutting up a body] is a lot harder than he thought."

Roy Minton had espoused a theory that had Jennifer sitting on the bed when Colton picked up the gun and it accidentally went off. Bill Bishop disagreed. He proposed that Jennifer was in the kitchen, "the one room that's been cleaned within an inch of its life."

"You have heard nothing, nothing in this case that leads you to believe anything but that Colton Pitonyak intentionally shot Jennifer Cave."

The jurors left the courtroom single file to deliberate. The judge retired to his chambers shortly after noon. By nature, Stephanie McFarland could be fiery, but Bill Bishop had surprised many in the courtroom. In his closing, his voice had taken on an emotional edge they hadn't heard before. This case had touched him.

Three friends had come to support the Pitonyaks, and they walked from the courtroom with Bridget and Eddie. From the Cave side came Sharon, Jim, Vanessa, Lauren, Hailey, and the rest of their family, including for this final day, Clayton; Whitney, who took time off from medical school to come; and her husband, Shawn. Jennifer's grandmother, Myrtle, was there, along with Jim and Sharon's good friend Harold Shockley, and many of Jennifer's aunts, uncles, and cousins. While they waited, they filed downstairs to a lounge in the victims' assistance office, anxious and apprehensive.

On the way to his office, just across the street from the courthouse, Roy Minton stewed, wondering if the jury "fully understood and appreciated that the shooting could have been an accident." Downstairs in his office, Bill Bishop worried that he'd left something out, some crucial piece of evidence that it was now too late to present. He looked at the brief outline he'd pulled together, one that read: "Memory does not equal intent"; "Mutilation and flight not as they told you because of DNA"; and more. Everything had been covered, but he still felt restless.

"I always worry," he says. "Always."

In his office, Jim Bergman considered the word "motive." It was fine to say jurors didn't need to have a reason for murder, that the prosecutors didn't need to prove Pitonyak had one, but he understood all too well that jurors are only human. In their hearts, he feared, they'd want an answer to the question, "Why?"

Less than an hour after deliberations began, at 1:10, word swept through the crowd congregated in the hallway: The jury had reached a verdict. Soon the families, attorneys, reporters, and observers again packed the courtroom so tight there was hardly room for a breath, when Colton Pitonyak was escorted back in by an armed deputy. The judge entered and ordered everyone in the courtroom to maintain calm when the verdict was read. "You cannot show any emotion," he warned. Then the jury filed in.

As he waited to hear his fate, Colton looked placid, even disinterested. The bailiff brought the verdict to Judge Flowers, who read it and handed it back to be given to the jury foreman. The man rose and read: "On the charge of murder . . . we find Colton Pitonyak guilty."

Showing little emotion, Colton glanced at his parents, and Bridget rested her head on her husband's shoulder, as they both quietly wept.

Not having heard the judge's order, Scott Engle walked in just as the verdict was read, and shouted, "Yes," throw-

ing his arms up in the air, upon hearing the word "guilty."
The judge pounded his gavel and ordered quiet, then asked
that the jury be taken to their room. They were excused
until two o'clock, when the punishment phase of the trial
would begin.

Once the jury cleared the courtroom, a wave of voices
filled the air, crying and cheering. Sharon threw her arms
around Lauren, Vanessa, Hailey, and Clayton, as they all
sobbed. Two sets of families sat across a courtroom from
each other crying, the Pitonyaks out of grief to losing their
son to prison, Jennifer's family out of relief that the man
who murdered her would be punished.

Sentencing was, as Sam Bassett put it, "the ball game." The
two defense attorneys had been arguing for lesser charges
and a lighter sentence since the trial began. Judge Flowers vetoed the lesser charges. Now, the only hope the defense had was to persuade the jury to come in with a lighter
sentence. The options were vast, from probation to life in
prison. "If we got Colton twenty to thirty years, he should
be cheering," says Bassett.

While Minton would argue for a light sentence, Bishop
would press the jurors for the maximum, life. Who would
Bishop put on the witness stand to convince the jury they
needed to come down hard on Pitonyak? At first, the prosecutor had considered putting the officers who arrested
Colton on the drug charge in 2004 on the stand. They'd seen
him at his worst and would be able to explain to the jury who
Pitonyak was at the time of the murder. Instead, as court reconvened, Bishop asked Sharon to get ready. She would be
the prosecutor's one and only witness. Sharon alone would
shoulder the responsibility of sharing the grief caused by
Jennifer's death, the suffering Colton Pitonyak caused when
he raised his gun and fired.

"Jennifer was a middle child," Sharon said, looking at
the jurors, her eyes dark and sunken, and her manner quiet.
When Stephanie McFarland asked her to tell of the toll on

first herself and then the family, Sharon said: "I go to the doctor now. I've never gone to the doctor before. I'm on antidepressants now. Sleep is hard to come by . . . It hurts every single day."

Sharon worried about Vanessa, who was with them the day they found Jennifer's body, and Lauren, who suffered stomach problems since the killing. Clayton was close to his lost sister and missed her deeply. Hailey no longer felt safe in crowds, and Whitney hated sitting in a bathroom. "Jim takes a licking and keeps on kicking," she said, wiping away tears and smiling at him in the gallery. "He's our Bondo, and he holds us all together. He loves us even when we're not very lovable."

In the jury box, two of the women jurors dabbed at their eyes. The murder had torn all their lives apart, Sharon said. It had affected them all. And none of them would ever be the same person again. Jennifer, Sharon said, was the family mediator, the one all the others counted on to run interference. "Jennifer, bless her heart, she was a big old sounding board."

For the past year, Sharon said, she'd gone to a counselor. But it was their pastor, Father David, who "taught me how to live again." She'd been so nervous about the trial, but her pastor's words spurred her on. "He said, 'This is it, kiddo. This is the last thing you can do for Jennifer. The last gift you can give her.'"

Sharon held a tissue to her eyes and sobbed, then shuddered, as if to shake off the grief. Whitney had married the June before, and Sharon said, "It's hard to have what's supposed to be such a happy event and have it tinged with so much sadness. So much loss."

When did Sharon miss her dead daughter? "It's Christmas. It's Easter. It's Thanksgiving, which was her favorite because she loved buttermilk pie. It's hitting a sale at Dillard's. It's the little everyday things, like seeing something and thinking Jennifer would love that."

Roy Minton asked no questions, and as Sharon walked

back to her seat, many had tears collecting in their eyes, both on the jury and in the gallery. When she reached him, Jim stood up, wrapped his arms around her, and hugged her. She sat beside him, her head resting on his shoulder. One of the few who had remained unaffected as she talked was Colton Pitonyak. But Sharon thought she did see something, when she looked at him from the witness stand, a look that said the trial didn't go as he'd planned.

"I think he truly believed he'd be getting in Eddie's Toyota Sequoia and driving home to Arkansas with his parents," she says.

The state rested, and the defense put on their witnesses. The first two were Colton's high school friends: Ben Smith and Louis Petit. They were well-mannered young men, evidence of their strict Catholic schooling. "If you asked anybody, Colton had one of the brightest futures," Smith said. "He was a good guy."

Then how could he be in the courtroom today? How could Colton, "a good guy," be found guilty of such a horrendous crime? "He fell in with the wrong people, and just kind of went out of control," Smith said. "He was constantly drunk or high, but now, since he's had a chance to clean up, it's helped him to get perspective on things. I think he understands how bad everything was."

From the witness stand, Louis Petit recalled how he first met Colton at Catholic High School. "I was new at the school at the time, and he befriended me. He was my best friend," he said. "We did everything together . . . football, worked out, played sports . . . he was almost genius level, driven, ambitious. He had a brilliant future."

Like Smith, Petit talked of the change the drugs brought on, and then about the letters he'd received since the arrest. "He's sober now, clear-minded, able to assess situations better." Sadly, of course, Colton Pitonyak's rehabilitation, if he'd had one, had come too late to save Jennifer Cave's life.

A portly man with large glasses, Johnny Morris, a structural steel salesman and Colton's middle school football coach, got on the stand. "Colton was a good kid. A shining star. He got along with everybody, and was always willing to help. Good natured," Morris said. He'd known Bridget and Eddie for thirteen years. "They're good people."

Roy Minton asked if Morris ever thought he'd be testifying for Colton in a case like this one. "Never," Morris said. Like the others who'd come to support the former scholarship student, Morris knew where the blame lay: " . . . drugs are a problem where society looks the other way. I've seen many young men go this route. Drugs get a hold of them. They're afraid to ask their parents for help. Once it gets you it gets you. Out of control and tragedies like this happen."

Colton's math teacher, Tommy Coy, then took the stand. "Colton made the highest grades in all assignments, all tests, he never had anything lower than a 98. Academically, he was always at the top of his class," he said. "He was always very respectful . . . Colton was the last young man I would have anticipated something like this happening to."

As Colton's father then took the stand, he appeared nervous, his hand shaking slightly with the papers he held. And he looked angry, his dark brows arched. The son of generations of farmers, in his dark suit he appeared as he was in life, a successful business owner.

With Sam Bassett, Eddie put before the jury two photos of Colton, one at age twelve or thirteen, his soft, dark hair long across his forehead, a smile on his face, an appealing adolescent with bright eyes. The second photo showed Eddie, Colton, and his brother, Dustin, on a family fishing trip, the wholesome freshness of the outdoors surrounding them. Then Bassett suggested Eddie read a statement he prepared.

"First I'd like to tell Mrs. Cave that my family and I are very sorry for the loss of your daughter Jennifer," he read. He paused and looked up at Sharon, then quickly back down at the paper before him. He recounted the two times he'd met Jennifer, including the dinner at Sullivan's. Eddie read the statement, glancing up, appearing nervous. "Colton was very defensive to Jennifer about us."

To show the jurors that Colton wasn't as he'd been portrayed in the courtroom, a would-be gangster, Eddie said his younger son didn't like to hunt and would rather be home playing his guitar or out with his friends. "He just wasn't interested in guns and hunting."

Colton was in the top ten in scholarships when he graduated from Catholic High. He'd had so many opportunities, but he'd chosen UT, and the Pitonyaks were glad. "Colton was honored to be accepted into the program," Eddie said. He talked about Texas, over and over, in positive terms, how good UT's reputation was, how happy he and Bridget were that Colton chose the McCombs Business School. Perhaps Eddie Pitonyak felt out of place coming from Arkansas. Perhaps he thought praising the university would please the jury.

Then Colton's father again addressed Sharon. "As previously mentioned to Mrs. Cave, we're all truly sorry for *the accident* [emphasis added] with Jennifer's death," Pitonyak said. Perhaps he didn't realize that the jury had discarded the accident theory, labeling the killing murder, or perhaps he meant to reintroduce it, to assert it once again. Even after the verdict, Eddie Pitonyak insisted his son wasn't guilty.

"There's nothing any of us can do to bring [Jennifer] back," he said, dismissing any notion that coming down hard on Colton could alleviate her family's pain.

For the jury, Eddie described seeing Colton for the first time at the jail, separated by a glass wall, Colton so encumbered by chains he couldn't "even scratch his nose." Colton had already spent seventeen months in jail, his father pointed out, a hardship for their entire family. Bridget longed to put her arms around her son, and had asked her husband what police would do if she ran up to him in the courtroom and hugged him. Eddie said, "I told her they would take their billy clubs out and beat her silly or worse. Bridget said, 'It might be worth it.'"

"We're not a rich family," Eddie said, maintaining they couldn't put up the million-dollar bond to get Colton out of jail. "[T]his was a terrible experience for both families. There were TV crews parked outside our house and everyone in the world had heard about this . . . Colton and his family will suffer from this tragedy for years to come . . . it affects both families . . . Colton will have to deal with this for the rest of his life."

Once the defense attorneys passed the witness, Bill Bishop asked about Eddie Pitonyak's conversation with Sharon the day she'd come to Austin looking for Jennifer. "Do you remember telling her that you were upset that she'd contacted your sister[-in-law] in Arkansas?" Bishop asked.

"If I'd known what was going on at the time, I would have handled it differently," Eddie conceded.

"Do you remember telling Mr. Sedwick that you and your wife thought it was all Jennifer's fault, that she was part of the problem?" Bishop prodded.

A blank look on his face, Pitonyak shook his head, hesitated just a moment, and then said, "No."

Eddie didn't pat his wife on the shoulder or make any physical move toward her when they passed as she walked to the witness stand. Roy Minton introduced Bridget again to the jury, and then asked her to read the letter she'd prepared, saying everyone would understand if she became overcome with emotion and needed to stop.

From the start, Bridget's eyes filled with tears, and pain twisted her voice. "First, Sharon, I'm so sorry for all your family is going through," Bridget said. She said she'd met Jennifer only once, but she was lovely. And "she's the only girl Colton ever, ever mentioned when he was down here. He always talked about Jennifer being his friend, something they'd done together or laughed about. I never heard any other girl's name. He was very fond of her.

"For the past seventeen months, I've listened as my son has been portrayed as a monster," she said. "Nothing could be further from the truth . . . because of his problems with alcohol and drugs, I wouldn't have been surprised about a call about his death, and had on some level prepared myself for it. But I never imagined this could happen. It's not in his character to hurt anybody . . . especially a friend. Especially someone he loved deeply."

On the stand, Bridget was likable, warm, smiling at the jury, as she talked. The mother talked of her pride in the old Colton, the bright, precocious child, and behind the defense table, for the first time in the entire trial, Colton Pitonyak cried. His face flushed, and he sobbed as his mother talked about his good qualities, how he'd helped others, and poured himself into everything he did, from swimming competitions to studies. He'd always had a lot of female friends.

"He was always very protective of his female friends. He called home a few years ago, extremely upset that a friend had been raped," she read. "Colton couldn't understand how someone could hurt a woman like that. He was sad and angry."

Colton had sat stone-faced through Sharon Cave's emotional testimony, but having his mother on the stand had finally gotten through to him, perhaps driving home for the first time that it had all truly happened. He was no longer playing the tough guy, the wannabe gangster. The jury had named him a murderer.

Bridget, however, like Eddie, disagreed. "It is beyond my comprehension," she said, "that Colton would ever intentionally harm someone, especially a woman."

In his letters home, Colton, she said, was always trying to comfort them. "When Eddie and I spoke with him last Thursday night by phone, his concern was for our state of mind, not his," Bridget said, as her barely controlled demeanor broke and she began sobbing, her face a bookend of grief to the way Sharon had appeared on the witness stand when talking about Jennifer.

"I believe with everything . . ." Bridget began, but she

was overcome with emotion, stopping and covering her mouth with her hand. "I believe with everything I am that Colton could not and would not harm his best friend Jennifer. He's not a cold-hearted murderer. He's not."

Colton, she said, had suffered. The last year and a half, he'd been in "anguish and pain for the loss of his friend. Undoubtedly he'll spend the rest of his life with this pain.

"We love him so much and he's such a good man," Bridget said. Looking at her son in the courtroom, her eyes welling with tears, she said, "I love you, Colton."

After Bridget finished, the defense rested, and Bishop asked to call a rebuttal witness. There was a matter in Eddie's testimony he wanted to contradict. Jim, already sworn earlier in the trial, took the stand, and Bishop asked about the telephone conversation with Eddie. "On the phone, I said, 'We're just looking for Jennifer. We need some help,'" Jim recounted. "'If you can help, because your son was the last person she was seen with.' And Eddie said, 'I don't have any idea where they are. I don't know what you're talking about. And as a matter of fact, my wife tells me that when she met Jennifer down there, that she thinks Jennifer is really the whole problem on this deal.' And that was the end of the conversation."

Between the testimonies of Colton's parents, Eddie calling the killing an accident and Bridget saying she couldn't believe their son killed Jennifer on purpose, Jim's words only drove home that the Pitonyaks, despite all they'd been through with Colton, still had no idea what the drugs had done to him. They didn't understand the man he'd become or what the new Colton, fueled by meth, was capable of.

Of the four attorneys, perhaps Roy Minton was the only one not worried about his final argument before the jury that would decide Pitonyak's destiny. Minton didn't believe what he had to say at the very end would change minds. "The overwhelming amount of decision making is done by jurors a little at a time throughout the trial," he said. "Those jurors had been making up their minds from voir dire on."

Sam Bassett, meanwhile, hoped jurors would show "a little compassion."

As she had during the guilt and innocence phase, McFarland was the first to address the jurors. She explained the law, that the jurors could assess a punishment anywhere from probation to life in prison. She told them that she expected life. "What we have here is the most heinous of murders," McFarland said. Colton's parents had asked for leniency, but were they entitled to consideration? "Jennifer is not only dead, but what they did to her . . . that is the most cruel thing I can think of. The defendant didn't show any leniency to Jennifer, and the state asks you not to show any leniency toward him."

"I think you have the hardest job," Minton said to the jurors. "Particularly when you are dealing with young people."

Colton, he said, was not a hardened criminal with a long rap sheet. Instead, he was a "youngster who'd led an incredibly great life," the defense attorney said. Before the drugs, Colton had discipline, charm, thoughtfulness, and until he got to UT, he had never been in trouble. In fact, Colton Pitonyak had lived an admirable life, one that should have led to a stellar future.

Again, Minton talked about Colton as if he were still a young boy. The defendant was the age of Minton's grandchildren. "You never quit worrying about them . . . It's a constant pain," the elder defense attorney confided, his voice low. "Put yourself in the place of Eddie and Bridget, with a youngster who had done so well. He came down here to this school and went to hell in a hand basket."

Society's biggest problem was drugs, Minton said, and it was "devastating our young people." Minton shook his head, and sighed. "How the drugs seem to get a hold of a youngster. That is inconceivable . . . Compare the conduct of the Colton who came to Austin in 2001, with the world ahead of him."

Turning to the jurors, he advised them to watch their children carefully. If their grades drop, "jerk them out like a rocket shot," he advised, and then send them for counseling and treatment. "I wish that I could have told Eddie that. I wish I could have told Bridget that." But then, Minton said, he, too, had made mistakes as a parent. "And who in the world would know better than I?"

What the aging defense attorney didn't acknowledge was that the Pitonyaks had done just that. Could they have done more? Perhaps. But they'd sent Colton to rehab and brought him home to attempt to turn him around. It hadn't worked. Colton hadn't wanted to change.

"Rehabilitation is what we're supposed to be doing here," Minton said. He'd seen young people sentenced to prison who spent their lives behind bars. "I don't want to see Colton in the penitentiary . . . What are we thinking about but revenge if we are talking about sending a youngster to the penitentiary for a life term?"

As he continued, Minton again argued that Colton hadn't cut up Jennifer's body; the blame for that rested with Laura Hall. Colton, he admitted, would be going to prison. But for how long?

"You are going to give Colton more than five years," he said. Then Minton made a suggestion: "Twenty years. I didn't say ten and I didn't say five . . . this young man is salvageable . . . this boy is not hopeless."

"I disagree with something specific Mr. Minton said, when he said there's not one scintilla of evidence Colton Pitonyak has a mean streak . . . the evidence in the trial is before you. I don't think you could have any more evidence of someone having a mean streak," Bill Bishop said. He talked of how Pitonyak was arrested for the drunk-driving charge, and he was sent to counseling. After the possession charge, he went to rehab. Both charges were plea-bargained down. "He got off easy. Now this attorney is standing before you asking you to let him off easy?

"If you let him off easy, it's on the twelve of you that he's out there again," Bishop said. He agreed with Minton that there was a chance Colton could come out of prison a better person. But there was another possibility. "There's a chance he could do this again . . . He had every opportunity in the world to rehabilitate, and he sat there and told you he had no interest in that."

Colton's mother had been highly emotional on the stand, touching, overcome with pain. "It's very hard to look at Bridget Pitonyak and tell her that her son needs to go to prison for life, but that, ladies and gentlemen, is not your grief to feel, because you are not the reason she is here."

"He did this," Bishop said, staring at the defendant. "Colton Pitonyak. If there is grief to be felt it is not on your shoulders. It is on his."

Much had been put before the jury to show them that they weren't judging an underprivileged young man, one who'd had to scrape to survive. "This is not a person who didn't know better," Bishop said. "This is not a person who didn't have every opportunity to succeed. And he threw that back in the faces of those who gave it to him.

" . . . the depravity involved . . . does not deserve leniency . . . there could be no other sentence than life in prison."

At 4:30 P.M., the jurors again left to deliberate Colton Pitonyak's fate.

Afterward, one, Alan Stuber, would say that while they'd agreed on Pitonyak's guilt with the first ballot, when it came to punishment, they were vastly further apart. They'd all been affected by the case. The night the autopsy photos were shown, few had been able to sleep. "It was hard to go through that experience and not even be able to talk about it," Stuber said, referring to the judge's order not to discuss the case with anyone until the trial ended. While their hearts went out to Jennifer's family, Stuber and others on the jury felt for the Pitonyaks as well. Some wanted the sentence to be life, others fifty years, and some ten or fifteen years. For a while, Stuber feared they'd deadlock, unable to reach a unanimous agreement. The wait would again not be long, however. At 5:55, the word came down. The jury had reached a decision.

Minutes later, the jurors reentered the courtroom. The Pitonyaks huddled together, as Sharon and Jim held hands. The entire courtroom felt on edge, as the jury foreperson rose to read the decision. Colton Pitonyak was sentenced to fifty-five years in the Texas prison system.

Bridget and Eddie Pitonyak sobbed, as Colton rose to make a statement. The brilliant student, the kid with the bright future, uttered his final words before disappearing into the jail to await the van that would take him to prison.

"I just want to apologize to everyone here," he said.

The courtroom remained silent. Judge Flowers dismissed the jurors, and Sam Bassett remembered feeling "like I was at a funeral."

Colton was handcuffed and taken from the courtroom, as his father tried to comfort his sobbing mother. On the opposite side of the courtroom, Jim made a fist and raised it into the air, and Jennifer's entire family cried as well. Bill Bishop's face flushed, and he, too, cried. He hugged Jim, then Sharon, then the rest of the family. Fifty-five years was a formidable sentence. Pitonyak wouldn't be eligible for parole for nearly thirty years.

Outside the courtroom, the media waited. Eddie and Bridget left quickly, without giving a statement. But Vanessa stopped to talk to reporters. "Colton got what he deserves," she said. "Jennifer was one of the best people you could ever meet. She cared for the world."

It was over. The nightmare had ended. Or had it? Laura Hall was still free, and Bishop now had Pitonyak's version of Wednesday, August 17, 2005, the day Jennifer died. In Colton's recitation of the events, Hall played the major role in not only the flight to Mexico but the gruesome desecration. Javier Rosales said Hall admitted helping to cut up the body.

"We're looking at filing additional charges against Laura Hall," Bishop told reporters. "We now believe she played a bigger part in the case."

Thirty-one

That spring, following Colton Pitonyak's conviction, Sharon Cave tried to pick up the shreds of her life. It was hard. She'd found no closure from Colton Pitonyak's conviction. "I have this vision of Jennifer," she said, her face contorted in grief. "In it, Jennifer is angry. She's furious, saying, 'Momma, it wasn't supposed to be like this. Not that day. That day I was trying so hard. That day I was turning my life around. That day, Momma, I was making you proud."

Determined to use her family's tragedy to help others, Sharon mounted a campaign. She met with her state representative, Juan Garcia, and asked him to sponsor two bills. Called the Jennifer Cave Act, the proposals would elevate the mutilation of a corpse when done for the purpose of covering up a crime to a second-degree felony. The second bill was a gift to jurors across the state who sat through terrible testimony about heinous crimes, a bill to provide state-sponsored, after-trial juror counseling.

Throughout Pitonyak's trial, Sharon noted the stricken looks on the faces of the jurors charged with hearing the evidence. One woman cried much of the day the autopsy photos were shown, while others wiped away tears. "It wasn't right," Sharon said. Despite the distressing testimony jurors were often forced to sit through, Texas, along with forty-eight other states, didn't offer posttrial counseling. Sharon wanted that changed. "We expose them to this horror and then send them home and tell them they can't even talk about it with their wives and husbands until the end of the trial," she said. "Then the trial ends, and we tell them to go on with their lives, without any help to cope with all they've seen."

On July 12, 2007, in the red granite Texas capitol building topped with a statue of the goddess of liberty, less than two miles from the site of Jennifer's murder, Texas governor Rick Perry signed both bills into law. Sharon had her victory, but the laws wouldn't affect the charges pending against Laura Hall.

Yet Hall's situation had changed.

While Sharon Cave lobbied the legislature, Bishop upped the stakes in the Hall case. Instead of one, she faced two third-degree felonies: hindering apprehension and, now, tampering with evidence, principally the dismemberment of Jennifer Cave's corpse. Colton Pitonyak's testimony had convinced Bishop that Hall had more to do with the murder than whisking the killer away to Mexico.

Interest in the case hadn't died in the media. Many wondered: Could Laura Hall be the one behind the gruesome crime scene? On Monday, July 2, 2007, the headline for an article by Steven Kreytak in the *Austin American Statesman* asked: "Is She 'Good Girl' or Killer's Helper?" It was a question people all over Austin were asking.

In Kreytak's article, Hall's father defended his daughter, saying, "She'd always been a good girl until she ran into Colton." Pitonyak, he said, had been physically and psychologically abusive, burning Laura's arm and carving his initials into her hand. During her five months with Pitonyak, Loren maintained, his daughter suffered like a battered wife.

Certainly Laura Hall had a positive side. She was a determined student. While Pitonyak waited for his trial in jail, Hall finished UT, earning her degree in government. And, Loren said, his daughter had suffered. Even with her diploma, she was nearly unemployable, let go from jobs she took under the name Ashley Hall, when those she worked for realized she was in fact *that* Laura Hall, the one whose photo had been all over the front page. An attorney, Bill White, hired her because her résumé stood out among the pile on his desk, and when he met her she seemed excited about the position. Then he discovered her true identity and fired her, not wanting a staff member who faced a felony indictment in a courtroom where he practiced.

As the summer wore on, there were pretrial hearings: one to consider a motion to bar Laura's two conflicting statements from her trial. Hall's court-appointed attorney, Tom Weber, mounted a series of arguments, but after Judge Flowers watched a video in which Hall agreed to waive her rights, the judge ruled both statements were admissible.

Through it all, Weber's client appeared to be enjoying the media frenzy.

At the courthouse one day, Laura showed up with her parents Garboesque, hiding her head in a wildly colored silk scarf and much of her face behind large sunglasses. Yet when the *Statesman*'s camera caught her, Hall was grinning. Once she toyed with the cadre of reporters outside the courtroom, carrying a book with its title prominently displayed: Maureen Dowd's *Are Men Necessary?*

Later, Laura would say the title had a message, "from a 'what have you done for me lately' standpoint, I'd say, you know, try to get me sent to prison, destroy my reputation and probably my career, force me out of my city, and cost me my Cadillac . . . definitely a commentary on Colton."

Despite Hall's bravado in front of the camera, Andrea Jiles had the impression that her old high school friend was finally grasping the severity of her situation. "I could tell Laura was beginning to understand that she was in deep trouble," says Jiles. "For the first time, I think, she knew this could end badly for her."

Behind the scenes, Weber worked on Hall's defense, hoping to find some way to mitigate the damning evidence of the crime scene photos. With court-supplied funds, he hired a psychologist to assess Hall. After examining her, the therapist warned Weber not to put him on the stand: What the psychologist had to say about the health of Laura Hall's psyche wouldn't help her.

Although he was well-respected in Austin, Weber hadn't been Laura's choice from the beginning. That he was being paid by the court, not privately by her parents, rankled her. In late July, Weber and Hall's attorney/client relationship deteriorated further. Bishop offered Hall a deal: Plead guilty to either of the felonies and accept a six-year sentence. Weber advised that they negotiate, to try to get the sentence down to four or five years, and then take it. Hall refused. Despite everything, she still dreamed of law school, and a felony on her record would prevent that forever.

Less than a month before her trial, in early August, Loren Hall hired a new lawyer for his daughter: well-known Austin defense attorney Joe James Sawyer, who'd represented one of the alleged killers in the city's infamous Yogurt Shop Murders, the bloody slaying of four girls in an I Can't Believe It's Yogurt! shop in 1991. Not a wealthy man, Laura's father was reluctant to supply the money, but by then he had a plan to recoup it. Fashioning himself a writer, Loren planned to sell a book on the Pitonyak case, one he'd tentatively titled *Cocaine, Murder, and Mutilation: A Parent's Perspective*. In it, he'd argue, among other things, his daughter's innocence. "We have a story the publishers should be willing to pay for," he'd later say, his eyes glistening with excitement. "We have a story to tell."

As the trial approached, despite a gag order imposed by Judge Flowers, Loren mounted a very public campaign. On television news interviews, he courted public opinion, repeating his contention that his daughter wasn't a criminal but a victim, saying that she'd been physically and emotionally abused by Pitonyak. Asked by one television reporter why Laura returned to Pitonyak's apartment on August 17, 2005, after she'd left and could have called police, Loren cried out: "She was afraid for her life!"

"The only thing Miss Hall is guilty of is being silly enough to love a self-indulgent sociopath," Sawyer, Hall's new attorney, told another reporter. When it came to the evidence against her, he classified it as coming from Pitonyak and being untrustworthy. "I guess if you're in the habit of believing killers and sociopaths, you might believe that this case has some weight and merit."

As August drew to a close, Bill Bishop reviewed the evidence Detectives Gilchrest and Fugitt had amassed against Hall. What did they have? The self-proclaimed Mouth of the South, Laura had bragged to many about her part in the carnage in the apartment and Pitonyak's escape attempt. Had anyone repeated her words to police? It wasn't assured. In the more than a year during which he prepared the murder case against Pitonyak, no one told Bishop that Colton was in love with Jennifer. No one recounted the evening Pitonyak came at her with a knife. Would anyone step forward to testify against Laura Hall?

The opening day of Laura Hall's trial looming, Sharon Cave had no qualms about what she wanted. "I want Laura Hall to get everything she deserves," Sharon said. "Everything."

Thirty-two

The moon shone a tarnished red-gold over Austin just before sunrise on Tuesday, August 28, 2007, Laura Hall's twenty-fourth birthday and the first morning of testimony in her trial. The color came from a celestial event, a lunar eclipse. The day before, a panel of eighty jurors had filled the courtroom. One quarter had to be disqualified because they'd read press reports and already formed an opinion about Hall's guilt or innocence. In the end, the jury consisted of six women and six men.

In the courtroom, many of those who'd been at the Pitonyak trial congregated again. Missing were Pitonyak and his parents. Colton, who was already appealing his conviction, would not testify at Hall's trial. This time Laura's parents, Loren and Carol Hall, occupied the front bench on the courtroom's left side, flanked by Laura's grandmother and her husband, and Carol's sisters. Directly in front of them, Laura, dressed in a severe black suit, heels, and an ivory blouse, her hair now a walnut brown, sat between her attorneys: Joe James Sawyer, a dapper raconteur, whose expensively cut suit had a white handkerchief precisely folded in the right breast pocket; and Antonio Wehnes, a balding, somewhat portly man, who would ask no questions but monitored testimony.

Something was new about Stephanie McFarland, who sat beside Bill Bishop at the prosecutor's table. Roundly pregnant with a daughter, she smiled a bit more freely and, with an additional seven months of experience in the courtroom, seemed more at ease. After McFarland read out loud the two felony indictments against Hall—hindering apprehension and tampering with evidence—Bishop rose to begin opening statements.

Sharon and Jim appeared weary, and Hall, poised with her ballpoint pen over a yellow legal pad, sized up Bishop with contempt as he laid out the case, leading jurors through the events that preceded and followed the murder. That was important, he explained, because Jennifer's murder "leads us to the charges against Laura Hall." He described again that fateful night, another Tuesday in August, two years earlier, when Jennifer went out to dinner with Colton Pitonyak. She died in the early morning hours, and two days later, Jim Sedwick walked into Pitonyak's bathroom.

There would be evidence that proved Hall was Pitonyak's willing partner in the murder's bloody cover-up and his attempted escape, Bishop said. Then he detailed bits of that evidence, including the border crossing videotape that clearly showed Laura driving the man she loved into Mexico. What would the jury base their decision on? In addition to the physical evidence, Bishop said he would present "statements made by Laura Hall."

After Bishop's brief opening, Sawyer stood and looked sternly at the jury. "The devil is in the details," he said. The evidence would be in the dates and the times, he proposed, alerting the jurors to pay close attention to minor details.

Ironically, he then reconstructed the crime the way prosecutors had to convict Pitonyak, theorizing that Jennifer was killed as she pulled away from Colton, cleaning up her life and ridding herself of him. But Sawyer proposed something else, something new: that Pitonyak killed Jennifer because he coveted the experience of taking a human life. Colton Pitonyak, Sawyer said, fantasized about murder. Bloodthirsty, Pitonyak lusted over not only the killing but desecrating a body. Why did this exclude Sawyer's client from the dismemberment? Pitonyak was too greedy to share either experience with Hall, the lawyer hissed. "There was a beast inside Colton Pitonyak, and no one had ever seen his face," he said. "The beast who wanted to see what it was like to kill."

Charming but diabolical, Pitonyak victimized two women, Sawyer said: one, Jennifer; the other, Laura Hall. Rather than a Ma Barker, the young woman at the defense table was frightened and abused, a girl in love who unquestioningly believed when Pitonyak claimed Jennifer's death had been an accident. "She was as much a pawn in the hands of Colton Pitonyak as Jennifer Cave," said Sawyer, his voice rising. Laura Hall's "not guilty except of loving someone too much, and making stupid, foolish mistakes."

From that point on, that first day of trial laid out a trail of events. Jennifer Gass, another of the friends, recounted seeing Jennifer and Colton on Sixth Street that night, and Jennifer's warning to Melissa Kuhl: "Colton is crazy." Ryan Martindill and Star Salzman told how Hall stayed at their apartment, and Michael Rodriguez recounted his last conversations with Jennifer before her death. At times it was difficult to see Hall as the victim Sawyer described, as when Martindill testified about the night she had "Colton" tattooed on her ankle.

When Martindill said Hall appeared traumatized by Colton's arrest, Sawyer had him repeat that on cross-examination. Laura Hall was a woman suffering, the defense attorney wanted the jurors to understand.

Sadly, Jim and Sharon took the stand and detailed for one last time to a jury the events of the terrible day they'd found Jennifer's violated corpse. Sawyer asked them no questions, but he had one for Scott Engle. "Did Jennifer relate to you that [Colton] once threatened her with a knife?" he asked.

"Yes," Scott said. "She did."

It was the first glimmer in the courtroom at either trial of Pitonyak's true character, and that he hadn't snapped that night but had a history of violence. Sawyer wanted that episode before the jurors because it fit the picture he'd paint of Pitonyak, a threatening man who abused women.

Still, it was Nora Sullivan's time on the stand that proved

the focal point of the day. After she testified to her early morning visit from Pitonyak, in which he tried to cover for the noise of the gunshot by making up a gunfight with drug dealers, McFarland asked Sullivan to recount a conversation she'd had with Laura Hall, one in which Hall described her role in the aftermath of the killing.

Blustering, Sawyer rose to his feet, objecting, and the jury was removed from the room. The prosecutors weren't playing fair, he maintained. Under the judge's orders, they were required to inform him of incriminating statements made by his client.

Bishop protested. The judge's order included only statements to law enforcement personnel, he said. The argument built, both men standing before the judge, insisting the law was on their side.

What admission elicited such fervor?

Sawyer read out loud from McFarland's notes: Hall told Sullivan that on the Wednesday following the killing, Hall lost patience with Pitonyak. Instead of using the hacksaw to dismember Jennifer's body, he sat in the living room drinking beer and watching television. Sullivan had the impression that Hall took over and finished the job.

Judge Flowers looked at both attorneys, appearing uncertain, and then put off his decision until later. He wanted time to consider his ruling. Hall's words to Sullivan were incriminating, and the stakes were high.

The afternoon filled with police officers and crime scene specialists, all testifying as they had at Pitonyak's trial about their roles on the crime scene and in the investigation. Sharon and Vanessa left the courtroom before the twelve jurors looked up at the screen on the courtroom wall at photos of Jennifer's desecrated body in Pitonyak's bathtub, and the horror was again driven home. Then jurors heard that Laura Hall was a probable contributor to DNA found on a blue shop towel purchased at the hardware store, the gun and its six-bullet magazine, and flip-flops found in the bathroom.

With the DNA expert on the stand, Sawyer asked for more time to review his notes, and the trial ended for the day. As she left the courthouse, Sharon fumed over an encounter with the woman on trial. Leah Smith, one of the counselors in the DA's victims' assistance office, blocked the door to keep others out briefly that morning while Sharon and Vanessa used the woman's restroom, a common practice to protect victims and their families in high-profile cases. Carol Hall walked up to the restroom door with Laura, and Smith asked them to wait. Her mother agreed, but Laura stormed past Smith into the restroom. Vanessa stood guard outside the door to the stall her mother used, as Hall chided: "There's no law that says we can't use a public bathroom."

At that moment, Laura Hall looked far from Sawyer's depiction of a young woman easily controlled or victimized.

More DNA testimony began day two of the trial. On cross-exam, Sawyer went through the long list of items processed by the lab, pointing out that most tested positive not for Laura Hall's DNA, but rather for Jennifer's and Colton's. Had investigators checked Jennifer's nail clippings for blood? he asked. No, the DNA expert admitted. They didn't. Sawyer looked mystified.

Compared with Minton and Bassett, Sawyer was a different breed of lawyer, more the showman, and more openly aggressive. When the bullet found inside Jennifer's head was put before the jurors by Dr. Peacock, Sawyer tried to defuse the damaging information by demonstrating in a nonchalant manner for jurors how the gun was shot into the severed neck. Still, one of the women turned away while Peacock held up the X-ray of Jennifer's skull with the bullet inside. The X-ray showed the head unattached to the body, seeming to float in space, a disturbing image. On another X-ray, one of Jennifer's severed hands looked like a glove without an arm, except for the ghostly white outline of bones.

At Colton Pitonyak's trial, autopsy photos were displayed on the courtroom screen. This time, Dr. Peacock held them up to show jurors as she talked of the knife wounds across Jennifer's face, throat, and chest. "The flesh appears waxy," she said, pointing at the deep cuts. That there was no hemorrhage, no blood, meant, Peacock explained, that they were postmortem, after death, most likely between four and twenty-four hours after the killing.

Throughout the grisly testimony, Laura Hall sat nearly motionless, her face without emotion, as if it meant little or nothing to her. She adopted a lawyerly pose, writing in her yellow legal pad, as jurors stared at her with questioning eyes. When Dr. Peacock talked of the difficulty of decapitating a corpse, one male juror looked at Laura Hall and gulped.

During cross-examination, Sawyer took up the wound to Jennifer's hand, the only cut on the corpse that showed signs of hemorrhage, albeit slight. That wound, Dr. Peacock said, was different from the others. It took place before all blood pressure was lost, making it peri-mortem, either just before or after death. Sawyer described it as a defensive wound, one that could have happened when Jennifer grabbed Pitonyak's knife. Dr. Peacock agreed that was possible, but she failed to give the defense attorney what he wanted. Sawyer floated a theory that the wound to the hand meant all the wounds covering Jennifer's face, throat, and chest happened soon after her death, before Laura arrived on the scene.

"I can't say that," Dr. Peacock said.

Yet it would be the afternoon witnesses that would deal the worst blows to the defense. One after another they took the stand and talked of Hall's love of Colton or what she'd told them about her own actions in the Orange Tree bathroom.

Deputy U.S. Marshal Joseph Smith recounted how an agitated Hall paced the border crossing office waiting for her father in the early-morning hours following Colton's arrest. She talked without being asked questions, sometimes as if to herself. Smith said she ranted about her love of Pitonyak and quoted Hall as warning at one point that she'd "kill anybody who hurt Colton."

What Smith insisted he didn't see were any injuries on Hall, any signs that Colton Pitonyak abused her. The only injury Hall complained of that morning was that Mexican police had been rough with her during the arrest. She said they'd "tried to give her a compound fracture of her right arm." But when Smith inspected Hall's arm, he saw nothing.

During cross-exam, Sawyer asked Smith to look at two dates: the first on the entrance of the green Cadillac into Mexico and the second the date on the warrant for Pitonyak's arrest. "There is no question that at the time the car crossed into Mexico, there was no signed warrant for Colton Pitonyak's arrest?" Sawyer asked.

"No question," Smith agreed.

On the stand, Said Aziz looked guarded. He clearly didn't want to be there, as he read from his statement to police the many things Hall told him on the day after Colton's arrest, including the first phone call when she said, "I have been all up in this shit since like two hours after the shit started."

When he asked her why she'd protect someone who'd murdered a girl much like herself, Laura professed her love for Pitonyak and said, "That's just how I roll."

When he asked how they'd gotten to Mexico, Hall said, "We just hauled in my Caddy." As they'd talked, Said grew angry. He liked Jennifer, but Hall voiced no concern that her boyfriend had just killed a girl. Instead, Hall bragged that she'd do anything to protect Pitonyak. In front of the jury, Aziz put Laura Hall's plan: that she'd stay out of trouble by telling police she thought they were on a vacation.

Aziz said he warned her several times to cooperate with the police but had the impression Hall wasn't listening. Only after he pointed out that he thought she was crazy for helping Pitonyak and that "everyone else would be talking to police," did Hall change her attitude. After detectives Gilchrest and Fugitt were at her parents' RV park questioning her, Hall told Aziz a completely different story: that she didn't know about Jennifer's killing when she and Colton left for Mexico.

"Were you lying before or now?" Aziz asked.

"Before," Hall answered.

When he took over, Sawyer tried to defuse the damaging testimony. During cross-exam, Aziz agreed with Sawyer that Laura was a "pretty nice girl," yet his agreement sounded halfhearted. And Laura's old friend said something else: Hall never appeared afraid of Pitonyak, and she had a long history of telling lies. "I don't know that I ever knew her to be very truthful," Aziz said.

That was only the beginning of a bad afternoon for the defense.

Soon, Nora Sullivan got back on the stand. Backed with a favorable ruling on the admissibility of her testimony, she recounted a conversation with Hall about the afternoon following Jennifer's killing. Pitonyak watched TV, drinking, and Hall was miffed at him for not carrying through with the dismemberment. Sullivan had the impression that a frustrated Hall did the work herself.

Sawyer stood behind the defense table, his face flushed, angry. "Ms. Sullivan, you have lied to this jury from the start about your relationship with Colton Pitonyak, [haven't] you?" Sawyer stormed.

"That's incorrect," Sullivan said.

Sawyer argued over and over, suggesting that, like Hall, Sullivan was enamored of Pitonyak. That wasn't true, Sullivan insisted. Yet she hadn't called police after his early-morning visit and didn't come forward even after the crime scene tape went up around Pitonyak's apartment.

"You said nothing?" he said.

"That's true," Sullivan agreed. She also hadn't told prosecutors about Hall's statements, not until the week before the trial. Sawyer found that odd. Sullivan's explanation was a simple one: "No one asked me about Laura Hall before that."

On the witness stand, Henriette Langenbach looked like the neighborhood grandmother. She told in detail her conversations with her cellmate in the Travis County jail. Laura couldn't understand "the fuss" being made over the murder. Colton, after all, was brilliant, a scholarship student. He mattered. Jennifer? "She was nothing. She was nobody. Just a fucking waitress ho," Langenbach quoted Hall as saying.

Hall loved Colton, and her main concern was finding a way to free them both. She was angry with her father, calling him "that fucking bastard," because he'd called police. Laura wanted him to hire a new attorney, someone "to help her concoct a credible story to get her and Colton out of the mess they were in."

In the gallery, Loren Hall sat stoic. One could wonder how many times his daughter, his only child, had screamed at him. At the defense table, Laura, too, showed no emotion. In fact, throughout the trial, she remained focused on the testimony and appeared calm, as if someone else, not she, were on trial. "The Ice Princess," a few members of the media congregating outside in the courthouse hallway dubbed her. Her face unnaturally pale, she appeared bloodless and cold, her eyes vacant.

There was something else the elder woman said Laura told her: "that the six days she spent with Mr. Pitonyak in Mexico were the happiest of her life." Along with destroying evidence, Hall told Langenbach another reason to mutilate the body: "How many grandmothers can tell their grandchildren that they cut up a human body?"

From under her dark hair parted in the middle and falling over her eyes, Hall glanced up at the jurors, and half of them stared back at her as if she were an alien.

"Everyone in jail knows about jailhouse snitches, don't they?" Sawyer charged, detailing how information could be traded for favors, including lighter sentences.

"But I didn't get anything," Langenbach answered. Yes, she had a criminal record, but her case had already been disposed of when she first spoke to police about Hall. And Langenbach had never asked either the police or prosecutors for any favors in return for her testimony. She wanted nothing. "It was just the right thing to do," she said.

Langenbach's offenses involved fraud and deception, Sawyer said, and she'd swindled or deceived.

"Yes," she admitted. "Yes, sir."

"You are good at deceiving people?" he accused.

"If you say so," she answered.

Yet, if Langenbach lied, how did she know so many details? And why was her testimony eerily similar to that of others? After the woman left the stand, Javier Rosales testified, repeating his words from the Pitonyak trial, that Laura Hall said she "masterminded the escape and helped cut up the body."

"We would have gotten away with it if I hadn't called my father," Rosales said Hall had told him. "He turned us in."

To Langenbach, Hall had said Jennifer was a nobody. Rosales said his coworker told him, "It was a victimless crime."

In the gallery, Jennifer's mother and grandmother cried.

Detective David Fugitt appeared nervous as he took the stand as the final witness of the day. He had reason to be. Gilchrest was supposed to be the one on the stand, but his father was in surgery, and that duty had fallen on Fugitt just hours earlier. He knew the case, but Gilchrest was the one who'd prepared for trial.

With Fugitt, McFarland went over the cell phone calls and messages Colton and Laura made the morning of Jennifer's death. Sawyer used the detective's testimony to pound home what he characterized as a glaring mistake by police: their failure to obtain records documenting what towers Hall's cell phone calls bounced off on the day the body was dismembered. Those records could have confirmed where she was during important times.

The problem was that until Pitonyak's trial, Hall wasn't a suspect in the dismemberment. Her location on that day didn't become an issue until she was under investigation for tampering. By that time, more than a year after the murder, Fugitt said the cell phone companies had long since destroyed all the tower records.

Sounding infuriated at APD, Sawyer charged, "Did you ever so much as just try to get cell phone information on those calls?"

The jury left for the afternoon with the charge that APD hadn't done its job hanging in the air. The following morning, Lauren, Hailey, and Whitney joined Myrtle, Sharon, and Jim in the gallery. When court reconvened, Sawyer again attacked Fugitt about the lack of tower records. Only this time, the detective came prepared, holding up a textbook from a course he'd taken on cell phone records in which it said companies retained tower activity records for one month.

"Is it still your answer to this jury that cell phone information is only kept for thirty days?" Sawyer stormed.

"Yes," Fugitt said.

Quickly, Sawyer changed the subject, asking, "How many jailhouse snitches contacted APD on this case?"

"Two I'm aware of," Fugitt said, but Sawyer attacked again, saying he didn't want Fugitt's recollection, but the exact number.

"What about Virginia Hill?" the defense attorney asked.

Looking perplexed, Fugitt said he'd never heard of Hill. "There are only two statements in the case book," he said, pointing at the two thick loose-leaf binders on the shelf before him, the notebooks where Gilchrest had tracked the investigation and evidence.

Hill was a fellow inmate of Hall's, and raising her name but not explaining any more left an unanswered question before the jury. If Sawyer hoped to put APD on trial, claiming they'd botched the investigation and unfairly charged his client, Gilchrest's absence played into his hands. Fugitt, however, refused to cooperate.

Rather than losing his patience, he simply stood his ground. "To the best of my knowledge, there are only two statements," he said.

With Fugitt, Sawyer constructed a chart, showing the times of phone calls between Jennifer, Colton, and Laura that day before the murder. He implied this would be important later, but didn't explain how. The defense attorney pulled out Colton Pitonyak's Facebook profile, asking David Fugitt to read the movies listed as his favorites: *Goodfellas*, *Donnie Brasco*, *Scarface*, and more.

"*Goodfellas* has one of the most graphic dismemberment scenes in the movies, doesn't it?" he asked Fugitt.

Fugitt said he had heard that but didn't know, and Sawyer went on, detailing scenes in the other movies and in a *Sopranos* DVD found in a Netflix envelope on Pitonyak's coffee table, including an episode in which Tony Soprano dismembered a body in a bathtub.

"Did you determine what course Colton Pitonyak took that summer, his last course at the University of Texas?" Sawyer asked.

The course was entitled The Human Body.

"As a detective, do you see a pattern developing that is going to culminate in violence?" Sawyer asked.

Bishop objected.

When she again had the witness, McFarland asked Fugitt to read from Hall's Facebook page, including her favorite movies, many the same as Pitonyak's, and her favorite quote from horror writer Peter Straub: "You're part music and part blood, part thinker and part killer. And if you can find all of that within you and control it, then you deserve to be set apart."

What was written on Facebook next to Hall's summer plans on the day Jennifer was murdered? "I should really be a more horrific person. It's in the works."

Sawyer went on the defensive. "Laura Hall isn't guilty of killing anyone, is she? She didn't kill Jennifer Cave?" Sawyer demanded.

"We don't believe so. No," Fugitt said

The questioning of the detective ended, and Bishop stood and said, "The State of Texas rests."

Joe James Sawyer had presented many issues during his emotional arguing before the jury, among them that Laura

Hall was an abused woman manipulated by Colton Pitonyak and that something in the timeline of the telephone
calls would prove she couldn't have participated in butch-
ering Jennifer Cave's dead body. But when he took over
the courtroom, his first two witnesses were recalled state
witnesses.

First Sawyer brought back the AT&T employee who testified earlier about Pitonyak's cell tower activity as he fled
Texas. Yes, the manager said, he'd made up the chart prosecutors presented, one showing the locations of the towers.
When Sawyer asked when the chart was constructed, the
manager said just weeks before the trial.

Did that mean that Fugitt misled the jury, that phone companies stored information indefinitely and that it could be
accessed at any time? Sawyer's line of questioning seemed
to suggest that. Still, the information on Colton Pitonyak's
cell phones had been requested even before his arrest, and
kept at APD for evidence. What about Hall's?

"Do you know how long the information is stored as re-
gards to cell towers?" Bishop asked on cross.

The man frowned. He wasn't sure.

"It isn't kept forever?" Bishop asked.

"No," he said.

In his second appearance as a witness at Hall's trial, Keith
Walker, who'd recently earned his sergeant's stripes, was
asked by Sawyer about a subpoena that had been referred to
during Fugitt's testimony, a subpoena issued within a week
of Jennifer's killing for Laura Hall's phone records. In the
document, Gilchrest requested not only her call records but
accompanying tower activity. When the information from
the cell phone company arrived, however, the tower information wasn't included.

"Isn't this an enforceable subpoena?" Sawyer asked.
"Why didn't you follow through?"

Walker said he didn't know, but added that many of the
companies are uncooperative.

With Walker, Sawyer again emphasized that the warrant

for Pitonyak's arrest hadn't been signed yet when Hall drove him out of the United States and into Mexico.

Then, to the surprise of many in the courtroom, after Walker's testimony, Sawyer rested. Other than the two re-called prosecution witnesses, the defense attorney presented no one to bolster his client's case. Laura Hall did not take the stand in her own defense.

Still, as the attorneys and the judge prepared for closing arguments, Sawyer would prove victorious in an important way; he successfully argued to include lesser, misdemeanor offenses as options for the jury on each of the two charges against Hall. Bill Bishop appeared disappointed. For Sharon, it was a grave setback. "I want a felony on her record, so she can never be a lawyer," Sharon said. "I want what she did to follow her for the rest of her life."

After a short break, closing statements began, with McFar-land taking the lead.

Laura Hall loved Colton Pitonyak, she said. But hers was a dangerous love. "This dark obsession led Laura Hall to a place none of us can imagine. Colton Pitonyak led Laura Hall down the road to hell, but he went down it with her and exposed both their inner beasts."

"What did Laura Hall tell Deputy U.S. Marshal Smith?" McFarland asked. "That she loved Colton Pitonyak so much she would kill for him."

Hall's love for Pitonyak was tattooed onto her body, and she defended him whenever she could. At the same time, "she refused to acknowledge the humanity of Jennifer Cave," calling her names and labeling her murder a "victim-less crime."

How did jurors know what she'd done, that Hall under-stood Pitonyak had committed a murder and helped him anyway as he first tried to destroy evidence, and then spirit-ing him off to Mexico? Hall's DNA was in the bathroom. She had to have been in the condo after Pitonyak returned from the hardware store, McFarland pointed out, because

Laura's DNA was also on a blue shop towel Colton purchased that day. Sawyer's suggestion that his client wasn't at the Orange Tree while Pitonyak cut up the body didn't hold up in the face of the evidence.

When it came to Hall's motive, McFarland pegged it as her love for Pitonyak. "She wanted to solidify that relationship," the prosecutor said. "She wanted him indebted to her . . . this obsession quenched her beast."

"I'm going to talk to you first about the law," Sawyer said. "You are a jury, not vigilantes, and you have to follow the law as best you can."

Their decisions were to be logical, not based on passion or emotion, he said. Then he asked them to keep in mind when they considered the hindering charge that the warrant had not yet been issued for Pitonyak's arrest when Laura drove him into Mexico. While the dismemberment was horrific, Sawyer suggested it didn't constitute tampering with evidence. Why? "Dr. Peacock didn't tell you that she wasn't able to do a complete autopsy on the body because of the dismemberment," he said. "The evidence was still there . . . Dr. Peacock could still examine it. It was used as evidence."

"Laura Hall has no burden at all. She is cloaked in innocence," he said, reminding them that defendants are presumed innocent unless proven guilty.

Arguing again that Hall wasn't involved in the dismemberment, he insisted that if she had been, she would have made Pitonyak dispose of the bags holding the head and hands. "[Pitonyak] couldn't let Laura know that he'd dismembered the body. He ran out of time," Sawyer said. "He knew damn well that if he asked her for help to dispose of the body, she would have refused . . . the state is wrong!

" . . . If my daughter had made these choices, I'd be down on my knees just like her dad," the attorney said, gesturing to Loren, who began sobbing, loudly enough so the courtroom could hear him. While her father cried, Laura didn't blink, instead staring blankly at her attorney, as if involved in some macabre show of emotional fortitude.

Colton was again put on trial as Sawyer asked: "What did Laura Hall and Jennifer Cave have in common? Both were drawn to this man. He murdered for no reason. He is the center of his universe and no one else exists." Colton Pitonyak was a man who primed himself for murder and fantasized about cutting up a human body. "If Laura Hall had been with Colton that night, she might be dead," Sawyer speculated.

The defense attorney attacked those who said Laura confided in them that she'd helped Colton cut up Jennifer's body: Nora Sullivan, Henriette Langenbach, Javier Rosales. All lied, he said.

At the end, Sawyer's voice quieted. Laura Hall became enmeshed in this tragedy out of love. "I've never loved anyone that much. I've never loved anyone that way," he said. Then he pleaded with the jurors to stand their ground if they believed the state hadn't proved their case. "In the end, I'm confident you'll say not guilty."

"I don't envy you your job. It's hard. It's especially hard when you're dealing with a word-master, someone who is going to twist what you see, twist what you read and try to make it seem something that it's not," Bishop began.

Sawyer jumped to his feet. "Pardon me, Mr. Bishop," he called out. Turning to Judge Flowers, he said, "If he's talking about me, I object. That's outside the scope of an acceptable final argument."

Looking amused at the banter between the attorneys, Judge Flowers dismissed Sawyer's objection, and Bishop forged ahead, detailing what jurors knew to be true, including that Hall gassed up the car and washed it for the flight to Mexico. It didn't matter that the warrant wasn't yet signed, the prosecutor maintained. If jurors let Hall off because of that, they were setting a precedent for "an efficient hindering apprehension . . . if you procrastinate you might be guilty . . . That's not the law."

As to the tampering charge, it wasn't necessary for them to succeed in hiding the evidence, they simply had to try. "If you intend, then you are guilty . . . I know that you know that."

If jurors doubted that Hall tampered with evidence, Bishop suggested they look at two photos in evidence, and he held them up before the jury: Jennifer's high school graduation picture, and one of the gruesome photos of her dismembered body on the autopsy table. "The manner in which she was found, that's the offense," he said.

And then there were the admissions the woman who called herself "the Mouth of the South" had made to so many, including telling Said Aziz, "I have been all up in this shit since like two hours after the shit started."

"'All up in this' does not mean that you don't know there was a body in the bathtub," Bishop said. The other witnesses backed up Aziz, and none of them had anything to gain from their testimony. In all their accounts, there were common threads, that Hall loved Colton, that she'd do anything for him.

"That's how I roll," she'd said. She was proud of her role in the murder. "She wanted to be a Bonnie to his Clyde, but for that to work he had to be out on the streets to continue the spree."

The jurors left the courtroom at 2:53 on Thursday, the third day of the trial, and the waiting began. The hours clicked by slowly. Members of the media speculated on what time a verdict would come in, but the guesses of one after another didn't materialize. Dinner hour passed, and the jurors sent out for a pizza, working on hammering out a verdict.

Shortly after, at 7 P.M., the interested parties returned to the courtroom. The jury had a question. It wanted to review testimony: the answers of the expert who placed Laura Hall's DNA in the bathroom.

When ordered to by the judge, with the jury again in their seats, Rita Grasshoff, the court reporter, read the DNA testimony to the jury directly from the trial transcript. According to the forensic expert, the odds were 1 in 43 Caucasians that it was Laura Hall's DNA on the blue shop towel. When it came to the flip-flop found next to the bathtub, the odds were higher: 1 in 402 for Caucasians.

The jury left to continue their deliberations, and as soon as they were gone, Laura Hall grinned, made a fist, and said, "Yes. Oh, yes."

If the jurors were looking at the DNA, did that mean they didn't believe the witnesses? Laura appeared to believe that it did. Jennifer's family worried that Hall was right, that jurors might find her either not guilty or guilty of only the lesser charges, both with maximum sentences of one year. Two misdemeanors would allow Hall to become a lawyer, to go on with her life as if she'd played no part in the horror of Jennifer's murder.

The jury left for their homes that evening at 10:30, and the Cave family, the Hall family, and the crush of media reporting on the case left as well. At nine the next morning, they were back, and the jury again deliberated. As the day wore on, the worrying started. Was the jury hung? Would they reach a decision?

Finally, at 4:40 that afternoon, Billy Pannell, the bailiff, escorted the twelve jurors back into the packed courtroom. They'd reached a verdict. As the foreman read the decision, Lauren and Jim sat on either side of Sharon, and they all held hands. Whatever it was, they would have to live with it. To reclaim their lives, they had to move ahead, they had to put Jennifer's murder and the pain of the past two years behind them.

"On the felony charge of hindering apprehension, we find the defendant not guilty," the foreman read, and Sharon and Jim both grimaced. Sharon hung her head, and put her arm around Lauren to comfort her. As they had all feared, the jurors had found Laura guilty not on the felony hindering apprehension charge but on the misdemeanor. Sawyer's argument that Pitonyak's warrant had not yet been signed at the time Hall spirited him across the border had won.

Behind the defense table, Laura Hall grinned, but it would prove premature.

"On the felony charge of tampering with evidence," the man continued. "We find the defendant guilty."

Sharon's frown turned into a soft smile. Her eyes closed, and she seemed to be praying, thanking God. Jim, wrapped his arm tighter around her, and Lauren looked at her mother, their eyes meeting. Hailey, not understanding what had happened, fumed, believing the jurors had decided against them. Jim would later explain to his younger daughter that Laura Hall would pay for what she had done to Jennifer, for her role in their suffering.

In the end, the jurors decided that while Colton Pitonyak may have led Laura Hall down a path that descended into the depths of hell, she walked with him willingly.

The jury filed out. They'd return the following Tuesday, after the Labor Day weekend, to decide what punishment Hall should receive. Bishop rose and addressed Judge Flowers. "We ask that Ms. Hall be taken into custody," he said.

"Denied," Flowers said.

Meanwhile, Laura Hall remained emotionless. If there were any indication that she understood what had just happened, it was only that as she stood for the judge to leave, she appeared just slightly unsteady.

The court adjourned, and a short time later, Jim, Sharon, Laura, Myrtle, Hailey, and Whitney all left the courtroom, believing that justice would be served the following Tuesday.

A short time later, Loren Hall sat alone outside the courthouse on a black wrought-iron bench, his eyes wide and disbelieving. He shuddered slightly, holding back tears. "I don't disagree with what the jurors said," he whispered. "I'm only sorry for all Laura's been through."

At five minutes to nine the following Tuesday morning, Laura wasn't in the courtroom. Her parents stood in the hallway waiting for her, and a murmur went through the audience. Could she be on the run, reliving the flight into Mexico with Colton Pitonyak? When she finally arrived, she had her new boyfriend in tow, a young man who resembled Pitonyak, his dark hair buzzed short; he slouched in his seat with a scruffy five o'clock shadow. As she had every day of her trial, Laura looked like the lawyer she now could never be, her hair resolutely anchored into a severe bun with a heavy silver clasp.

The first witness called by the state was Doug Conley, a nattily dressed taxi driver who'd picked up Laura on August 6 of the previous year, to take her from her West Campus apartment to her job at Baby Acapulco. In the cab, Laura mentioned that she was facing a felony, as if to explain why she was working as a waitress. When Conley asked what it was about, Laura said it had something to do with her boyfriend who was facing a murder charge.

"Who did he kill?" Conley asked.

"Some bitch," Hall snapped. A full year after Jennifer's death, Laura Hall still had no remorse, no understanding that a young woman had lost her life and that Jennifer's family had suffered.

When Bishop asked if Conley could pick Hall out in the courtroom, he pointed directly at her.

"Do you have a tape recording of this conversation?" Sawyer asked on cross-exam.

"No," Conley said. With that, the state rested.

On the witness stand, Loren cried. His daughter, he said, was a gifted athlete and a determined young woman. "Has she ever been convicted of a felony, prior to this?" Sawyer asked.

"No," Hall answered.

He talked of Laura's prowess as a swimmer and on the soccer field. She'd played trombone in high school and been on the debate team her freshman year in high school. The year she was the captain of the team, she took them all the way to a national competition. "That's where she excelled," Loren said. "She wanted to be a lawyer."

Like Bridget and Eddie Pitonyak with Colton, the Halls had given Laura advantages. In high school, Laura had gone to a camp at the University of Michigan and spent a month at Dartmouth, honing her debating skills.

"Even after [her arrest], she went back and got her UT degree," Hall said, crying.

Seated at the defense table, a glassy-eyed Laura dabbed away faint tears, her first in front of the jury.

Loren listed the law firms Laura had worked for. What he failed to mention was that at all but the first she'd been hired under the name Ashley. When the firms discovered she was Laura Hall, she was fired.

To demonstrate his daughter's fortitude, Loren Hall recounted how she struggled with math. To graduate from UT, she needed to pass a math class. Her final semester, she had a 24 average until she hired a tutor. Working hard, Laura brought her average up to 84 and graduated.

"That's determination," he said. "We were really proud of her."

Colton changed Laura, her father said. After meeting Pitonyak, Laura talked of women in derogatory terms, calling them bitches, strippers, and the like.

"Has she talked that way ever since?" Sawyer asked.

"It's taken a while," Loren said. " . . . But she's trying to build herself back up."

Laura was on medication, her father said, although he didn't say what kind or for what reason. "Give her a chance," he pleaded. "She's on her way to recovery. I'm asking for probation. I know she'll prove herself worthy."

In the gallery, Sharon Cave seethed, wanting to get on the witness stand to beg jurors to come down hard on Laura. Sharon wanted to tell jurors how her life and the lives of everyone who loved Jennifer had been torn apart by both the murder and the atrocity of what Colton and Laura had done to Jennifer's lifeless body. Their actions had cheated them of even being able to see Jennifer, of one last opportunity to say good-bye. Laura Hall didn't kill

Jennifer Cave, but she'd dealt everyone who'd loved her a devastating blow.

Sharon, however, wouldn't get that opportunity. Not long before, in Judge Flowers's court, a drug case against the girlfriend of a convicted murderer was reversed because the murder victim's family gave emotional testimony during sentencing. The appeals court ruled that since the girl wasn't charged with the murder, the testimony of the victim's family was improper. "We didn't ever want to have to retry Laura Hall," Bishop said. "We didn't want to take any chances."

After Laura's father, Sawyer called a surprise witness, Colton's good friend Jason Mack, wearing baggy jeans and T-shirt, his arms covered by tattoos. He explained how he'd stayed with Colton in the months before Jennifer's murder. The Colton he described on the stand was edgy from drugs and itching to kill. High, Pitonyak hadn't slept in days when he killed Jennifer. His Xanax prescription had run out, and he was wired, even the smallest things annoying him. The week before, Mack said he was at Colton's when Hall came over. In a foul mood, Colton kicked her out. Laura sat outside in the courtyard, crying, as Colton pulled the gun out of a drawer. "She's driving me fucking crazy. I ought to just kill the bitch," he said, referring to Laura.

Mack talked Pitonyak into putting the gun away, and then he took Laura to a friend's house, where he cautioned her to stay away from Colton Pitonyak. "He's too fucked up. It's too dangerous."

Left unsaid was what everyone in the courtroom knew: Laura Hall hadn't stayed away. She idolized Colton, and no one could have convinced her to leave him. Instead, when he needed a ride to pick up his car, he knew Laura would take him, and she did.

Stephanie McFarland began closing in the punishment phase by explaining the law to the jurors, their options on both charges from probation to prison time, one year for the misdemeanor and up to ten years for the felony conviction in tampering with evidence.

"You are the representatives of the community, and the state wants you to send a message," she said, asking for the maximum penalty.

"If a life can be salvaged, isn't that better than not?" Sawyer countered. "The idea of redemption is central to many of us. Forgiveness is a concept that for many of us is a core value."

Bill Bishop wrapped up the arguments, speaking for Sharon, who hadn't been allowed to speak for herself: "Jennifer Cave can never graduate from UT. She'll never work at a law firm," Bishop said. Laura Hall "caused her mother to have to endure a funeral with a closed casket . . . I never thought anything could be worse than burying a child, but it is worse to bury a child and have to have a closed casket."

Again, the jurors filed from Judge Flowers's courtroom, and the waiting began. Six hours later word spread and the courtroom filled. Laura Hall stood between her attorneys as Judge Flowers read the jury's decision: one year on the misdemeanor hindering charge and five years on the felony tampering with evidence conviction.

Hall didn't cry, nor did her parents. But she appeared shaken, and when the judge asked her if she had anything she wanted to say, in a shaky voice she said, "No, Your Honor."

Eight jurors left the courtroom, but four remained to hear Sharon Cave's allocution, her post-trial opportunity to personally address Hall. "Laura, I want you to know that this would never have been a victimless crime," Sharon said. "Unlike you, people loved Jennifer. Unlike you, Jennifer had a beautiful soul and heart. Unlike you, Jennifer will be missed. . .

"I hope Jennifer haunts you every day of your life, because what you and Colton did was horrific," she said. Laura sat at the defense table, ashen white, glaring at Sharon, while she continued. "If there is a hell, I hope you burn in it."

When Sharon returned to her seat, Jim held her while she cried. By then, two deputies surrounded Laura. Sawyer's cocounsel, Wehnes, handed Loren his daughter's purse, and then Laura's hands were handcuffed behind her. All the while the woman the press had dubbed "the Ice Princess" stood proud, head up, never bowing, even as the deputies urged her toward the side door, where she'd be taken to the Travis County jail.

Author's Footnote

There was something I'd wondered for a long time, a nagging thought that refused to leave as I watched Sharon and her two surviving daughters cope with their grief, but at the same time worry more about those around them than they appeared to about themselves. I saw Jennifer in them, the girl who, despite everything, never gave up on Colton Pitonyak. Even after he'd threatened her with a knife, she saw him as a friend, one she brought a home-cooked dinner on a foil-covered plate. "Do you think we teach our daughters to care too much about others?" I asked. "In the process, do we mislead them into thinking they can fix people?"

"Maybe," Sharon said, wiping away a tear. "Maybe that's true."

In Austin, little Madyson was growing up. Jennifer's surrogate daughter was a first grader, a pretty little girl with sad eyes, so much older than her scant years. "Want to see my sister?" she asked me the first time we met. "I'll show her to you."

She took my hand and guided me upstairs to Scott's bedroom, and he popped a DVD into the television. Moments later the video from the funeral filled the television screen, one of Karissa Reine's photos of Jennifer, taken just a few months before her death. On the screen, Jennifer grinned coyly at us, lighting up the room, her red hair cascading down her freckled shoulders and her blue eyes sensual and content. On the dresser beside us, Scott had propped up the painting his friend had done before Jennifer's death, the now prophetic painting of just her torso. Before it he had a plaque that read: "Heaven."

"My sister comes and plays with me," Madyson told me. "We play dolls in my room. And at night, she tells me stories in my bed."

I looked at Scott, and he smiled. "Yeah," he said. "Madyson talks to Jennifer. A lot. She says Jennifer visits her when she's alone in her room."

So many still felt Jennifer in their lives, her joy and her sadness. Some remarked that they believed she watched over them, working in their lives.

After more than twenty years of writing about unexpected and all too often violent deaths, I'd often talked to family and friends left behind who recounted smelling their dead loved ones' perfume, feeling their touch, sensing that they were standing beside them, even hearing their voices or seeing their fleeting images. Unfinished business, they told me. Their loved ones returned to them, they said, visited one last time, perhaps to say good-bye.

Over the years, I'd had some strange occurrences, including unlikely coincidences. None prepared me for what happened in Austin one sunny Saturday morning. I was nearing the end of my research and wanted to canvass the apartment complex Laura Hall lived in at the time of Jennifer's death, to see if anyone who lived near her remembered her. I got a late start and then forgot something and had to return to the hotel to retrieve it. An hour later than planned, I pulled up in front of the sprawling brown brick complex on Oltorf, south of downtown. I was disappointed to see that it was fenced and gated, when I noticed an open exit gate. I made a U-turn and pulled into the parking lot.

Driving around, I saw scattered families, a few men, and two or three women, coming and going, but talked to no one, searching for the right apartment. Then I changed my mind. Before I sought out Laura's neighbors, I decided I'd talk to a few people at random, to ask about the apartments in general, get a sense of who lived there. As I made my decision, I noticed a young woman with long brown hair putting a cooler into her trunk. I parked behind her, got out of the car, and walked up, introducing myself.

"I'm Kathryn Casey," I said, holding out my hand. "I'm working on a book on the Colton Pitonyak case, and Laura Hall once lived in this apartment complex. May I ask you a few questions?"

The stranger took two steps away and began shaking. I backed up a few steps, fearing I'd unintentionally frightened her. She folded her arms across her chest as if to get warm, although it was in the mid-eighties that day.

"You're Kathryn Casey?" she asked.

"Yes, I'm an author, and I'm—"

"I know who you are," she cut in. "I'm Nicole Ford."

Nicole was Jennifer's friend, and I'd been trying to reach her for a year, without success. Now, in a metropolitan area of more than a million, I stumbled upon her in an apartment building parking lot. Making it even odder, it wasn't her apartment complex. A friend lived there, and Nicole had walked outside only moments before I saw her.

"Jennifer brought you here," Nicole said, absolute certainty in her voice. "She wants me to talk to you."

The sun beating down on us, we stood next to her car, and she talked. What she told me that day would change the way I saw Jennifer. I'd talked to many people who knew Jennifer, but only Nicole understood how Jennifer felt about the drugs she was taking, especially the methamphetamines, because Nicole had been there with her. "The drugs were eating away at our lives," Nicole said. "Jennifer called meth a demon, said that it was chasing us, and that if one of us couldn't get away from it, the other one had to promise to go on with her life.

"I never thought it would end this way," said the young woman. After Jennifer's death, Nicole had at first gone on a drug binge, then, with the help of her family, she kicked her habit. She was going back to school, doing the things Jennifer had so wanted. "Jennifer was determined to kick the drugs and make something of her life. I thought she would leave me behind," Nicole said. "Instead, I had to go on without her."

Nicole and I talked once more after that day, and I e-mailed her a photograph of Jennifer. She had none and wanted something to remember her by.

Jennifer Cave. Colton Pitonyak. Laura Hall. Three young lives, three bright students, three devastated families. So much had been lost: Jennifer was dead. Colton and Laura were both sentenced to years in prison. Perhaps we'd never know precisely what happened in Colton Pitonyak's apartment that night. But, after more than a year of research, I felt I understood. So many pieces had come together that the puzzle took shape.

Colton had a knife the last night he and Jennifer went out, the one he used to cut the girl's wristband off at the Treasure Island bar on Sixth Street. He was high and drunk, as he'd been for days, and strung out like he was a week earlier when he threatened to get his gun and shoot Laura.

Why did Jennifer go into unit 88 that night? Why, when she'd told so many she feared Colton? I don't believe she did so willingly. In my theory, Jennifer agreed to see Colton because she worried about him. He was upset about the test, the car, his life. She drove her car to be in control. She simply hadn't counted, however, on Colton being armed with a weapon. High and drunk, he used the knife to force her inside his apartment.

One statement in Laura Hall's strange second statement to police that rang true was when she said Colton killed Jennifer because she didn't want to be around him anymore. I believe this was the night Jennifer Cave finally gave up on Colton Pitonyak. When the girl he loved told him their relationship was over, the angry, bitter Colton, the one who picked fights on Sixth Street and broke a drug customer's nose, emerged. Perhaps Colton demanded money, claiming Jennifer owed him for all the drugs he'd given her during their friendship. Perhaps he refused to allow her to leave him alone, to face the reality of what he'd become, a drug-dealing heavy.

Two pieces of evidence, one supplied by Henriette Langenbach and the other by Dr. Peacock, the medical examiner, answer the question of what happened in Jennifer Cave's final moments. Laura told Langenbach that Colton and Jennifer argued, and that they were fighting when the gun went off. The medical examiner's testimony backs that up. Two wounds to Jennifer's body were peri-mortem, occurring near the time of death. One was a defensive wound, a cut in the palm of Jennifer's hand, as if she'd tried to grab Pitonyak's knife. The other, a bruise, could have been the result of a fall or a blow to the head.

Was the shooting an accident? A week earlier, on a meth binge, Pitonyak threatened to kill Laura Hall. If Jason Mack hadn't been there, he might have murdered her. The night of Jennifer's death, Pitonyak was angry over his lost cell phone, and then, perhaps, over what he saw as Jennifer's desertion. Again, he reached for a gun. This time, Colton pulled the trigger.

Laura's defense attorney, Sawyer, was right when he said Colton Pitonyak was itching to kill. Murder was the last step in his transformation into the gangsters he idolized.

Hours later Laura Hall entered unit 88, and from that point on, all became chaos. Hall's account to Henriette Langenbach fit so much of the evidence, perhaps it's as close as Hall or Pitonyak will ever come to disclosing the madness that followed Jennifer's murder. His DNA all over the bathroom indicates he did most of the work dismembering Jennifer's body, but Hall's DNA was there as well, including on that blue shop towel that proves she was there after he'd purchased the hacksaw.

After Pitonyak's trial, when Sharon and I first spent time together outside the courtroom, she still seemed consumed by grief. His conviction had given her little peace. Despite the guilty verdict, she found no comfort, and Sharon envisioned

Jennifer, too, in turmoil, unable to accept death. "I think she's still saying, 'It wasn't supposed to happen, Momma. Not that day. Not when I was turning my life around.'"

In the seven months that followed, there were good times and bad. That summer, Jim gave Sharon a beautiful engagement ring. They made plans for the future. But the pain wasn't behind them. Passing the Jennifer Cave Act helped, but it wasn't enough.

At Laura's trial, Sharon and I sat together waiting for the verdict to come in. "I've been thinking about something," she said. "I keep thinking I'd like to go back to the late nineties and just stay there."

"Why?" I asked.

"It was hard then. I was a single mom with four kiddos to take care of, but it was good. It was just the kids and I, and we were happy. They were young, before the hard times came," she said. "I love Jim, but this isn't about him. I just want . . ."

Sharon stopped, but she didn't have to finish the sentence. I understood. She wanted her family back, before she learned how real evil is in the world. She wanted Vanessa, Lauren, and Clayton before life spread them from Oklahoma, to Dallas, to Sinton, and Jennifer before the nightmare that put her in her grave.

"I finally put up her headstone," Sharon said. "Jim and the girls insisted. It was hard, but I picked out one that's very simple, just Jennifer's name and dates, and a little frog in the corner." A smile edged across Sharon's face, not of happiness but of loss. Sharon and Jim also planted a bush upon the grave, an esperanza that blooms with beautiful orange trumpet-shaped flowers. *Esperanza* is Spanish for "hope."

After Laura's trial ended, we talked again. She and Jim were back in Corpus. She'd spent the day after they returned in bed, hugging their little dog, Lulu Belle. "She's so sweet and warmhearted. Jim and I think she has Jennifer's sweet spirit. Her kind heart," Sharon said. At times, Sharon felt they all carried Jennifer with them. "She's made us better people. I know she's made me more tolerant of others, taught me patience. But she's so missed. That's why we look for her in hummingbirds and a little dog."

Despite all she'd endured, Sharon wondered if more pain waited in her future. An invitation to a wedding had arrived, and the bride was one of Jennifer's friends. Sharon cried while reading it. "How many weddings, graduations, babies will come, and I'll have to think, that'll never happen to Jennifer?" she asked. "We'll never see that splash of red hair walk into a room. It just kills me that I'll never have a redheaded, blue-eyed grandbaby."

The pain had never eased. Two years after Jennifer's murder, time hadn't healed. Perhaps it never would. But Sharon and Jim were both determined Colton Pitonyak's bullet wouldn't end their lives as it did Jennifer's. Somehow they had to find the strength to put the horror of Jennifer's death behind them. "I tell the kids, now we all have to really live. We need to enjoy our lives, relish them, not waste a single day," Sharon said. "You see, we have to live for Jennifer, too."

Acknowledgments

I'd like to express my appreciation to:

Manuscript readers: Terry Bachman, Peter Black, Mary Pat Bleier, Maureen Casey, Claire Cassidy, Carol Ginger, Mary Kay Zanoni, Lisa Hughes, and Yvonne Morrison

My long-time agent, Philip Spitzer, and his assistant, Lukas Ortiz

My editor at Avon, Sarah Durand

Sergeant Robert Mourot and Sergeant J. B. Stephens of the Little Rock Police Department

For Internet research, Varsha Naik and M. Shelby McDonald, Esq.

Austin American Statesman reporter Steven Kreytak

Jim Loosen and his magic computer at JAL in Seattle for his able assistance tracking sources and documents

My aunt Elaine Larson and her good friend Rosemary Mosca for their brilliant ideas

As always, a special thank you goes out to all of my family and friends. Your support means the world!